THE AMATEUR AND THE
PROFESSIONAL

THE AMATEUR
AND THE
PROFESSIONAL

Antiquarians, Historians and Archaeologists in Victorian England, 1838–1886

PHILIPPA LEVINE

The Flinders University of South Australia

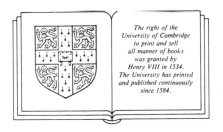

The right of the
University of Cambridge
to print and sell
all manner of books
was granted by
Henry VIII in 1534.
The University has printed
and published continuously
since 1584.

CAMBRIDGE UNIVERSITY PRESS

Cambridge

London   New York   New Rochelle

Melbourne   Sydney

Published by the Press Syndicate of the University of Cambridge
The Pitt Building, Trumpington Street, Cambridge CB2 1RP
32 East 57th Street, New York, NY 10022, USA
10 Stamford Road, Oakleigh, Melbourne 3166, Australia

First published 1986

Printed in Great Britain at the University Press, Cambridge

British Library cataloguing in publication data

Levine, Philippa
The amateur and the professional: antiquarians,
historians and archaeologists in Victorian
England, 1838–1886.
1. Great Britain—History—1837–1901—
Historiography
I. Title
942′.072   DA550
ISBN 0 521 30635 3

Library of Congress Cataloging-in-Publication Data

Levine, Philippa.
The amateur and the professional antiquarians,
historians, and archaeologists in Victorian England,
1838–1886.
Originally presented as the author's doctoral thesis.
Bibliography: p.
1. Antiquarians—Great Britain—History—19th
century.   2. Historians—Great Britain—History—
19th century.   3. Archaeologists—Great Britain—
History—19th Century. 4. Great Britain—Cultural
policy. I. Title.
DA1.L48 1986   941.081   85-19492
ISBN 0 521 30635 3

SE

To my mother and father

Time which antiquates Antiquities, and hath an art to make dust of all things, hath yet spared these minor Monuments

Thomas Browne, *Hydriotaphia*

Contents

Acknowledgements

No work of this kind is an entirely individual exercise, and like all authors I have a strong sense of indebtedness to the many people on whose support and expertise I have called over the past few years. Asa Briggs and John Burrow have given unstintingly of their time, and their help and encouragement has been legion. Angus MacIntyre's insights were invaluable in helping me restructure a rather shambling doctoral thesis. The enthusiasm and energy of the archivists in the various local archaeological societies I visited served to convince me of the value of this work in moments of doubt; other librarians and archivists too were generous with their time and advice. Ruth Vyse at the Bodleian Library Oxford and the librarians of Jesus College Oxford and the Society of Antiquaries of London were all patient with the questions of a beginner. John Cantwell at the new Public Record Office in Kew and Elizabeth Hallam Smith at the Chancery Lane office were enthusiastic about the project and vastly knowledgeable. Louisa Sadler's calm efficiency in the face of technical problems ensured the final appearance of the manuscript. Finally, I should like to thank King's College Cambridge without whose initial financial generosity this project could never have come to fruition.

PHILIPPA LEVINE

University of East Anglia
May 1985

Abbreviations

The following abbreviations have been used in the notes:

Archaeologia Cantiana	*Arch. Cant.*
Archaeological Journal	*Arch. Jnl.*
Bodleian Library, Oxford	Bodl.
Bristol & Gloucestershire Archaeological Society	B & G. AS
British Archaeological Association	BAA
British Library Additional Manuscript	B.L. Add. MS.
Bulletin of the Institute of Historical Research	*BIHR*
Camden Society	Camd. Soc.
Architectural, Archaeological & Historic Society of the County, City and Neighbourhood of Chester	AAHCh.
Collections	*Collns.*
Correspondence	Corresp.
Deputy Keeper of the Public Records	DK
Historic Society of Lancashire & Cheshire	HSLC
Jesus College, Oxford	J. Coll. Oxon
Journal	*Jnl.*
London & Middlesex Archaeological Society	LAMAS
Magazine	*Mag.*
Master of the Rolls	MR
Proceedings	*Proc.*
Public Record Office, PRO Collection	PRO
Royal Historical Society	RHS
Society of Antiquaries of London	Soc. Ant.
Somerset Archaeological & Natural History Society	Som. ANH
Surrey Archaeological Society	SAS
Surtees Society	Surt. Soc.
Transactions	*Trans.*
University Archives	Univ. Arch.
University College London Library	UCL Lib.
Wiltshire Archaeological & Natural History Society	Wilts. ANH

1

~~~~~~

Introduction

Professor Brown with level baritone
Discoursed into the dusk.
             Five thousand years
He guided us through scientific spaces
Of excavated History; till his lone
Roads of research grew blurred; and in our
                        ears
Time was the rumoured tongue of vanished
                       races
And Thought a chartless Age of Ice and
            Stone.
      (Siegfried Sassoon, *Early Chronology*)

I

Paradox lay at the heart of Victorian culture and nowhere was it more apparent than in their simultaneous adulation of their own age and their reverent fascination for the past. The coalescence of past, present and future, so common in Victorian writings, lends peculiar significance to the intellectual developments taking place in historical scholarship during the course of the nineteenth century. Historical studies ranked alongside those of the sciences as the dominant intellectual resources which shaped Victorian culture, providing the means to justify, to deplore, to praise or to abuse, to determine the means and portents of the changes affecting the structures of society so profoundly in this period.

Historical studies in this period were a motley combination of antiquarian and specifically archaeological interests alongside more orthodox document-oriented scholarship. The relationship between history and the text, and between archaeology and the artifact represents the theoretical culmination of the intellectual developments in this field in this period, a change with important institutional corollaries. This increasingly closely defined and methodologically more rigorous approach earned the subjects a newly respectable institutional status towards the close of the century. It is the interplay between the acquisition of specific and appropriate epistemologies

1

and the institutional developments around which they cluster which forms the basis for a social history of ideas, an exploration of the three historical communities of antiquarianism, archaeology and history, and of the divisions between them which by the close of the century had crystallised so clearly.

In the 1840s in particular, organisations devoted to historical pursuits began to determine, as much through strength of numbers as intellectual endeavour, the course of historical activities and scholarship.[1] The success of the early printing clubs of the 1830s gave the impetus for the foundation of both local societies and of new national bodies designed to promote an interest in the past. Before long some of that individual initiative had passed into the hands of the state and in the 1850s government began to undertake a whole host of historical projects from the long-awaited erection of a central record office to the publication of items too specialised and costly either for the more usual commercial consideration or for the printing clubs with their limited funds. Soon after, history won academic recognition with the creation of university history courses particularly at the ancient universities and the slow expansion of both the professorial and the tutorial ranks. The reforms of Oxford and Cambridge ushered in by Liberal governments in the 1850s and 1870s alongside the foundation of new civic universities created a new niche for historians, as did government's acceptance of the responsibilities of at least some areas of record administration. Here, in the new Public Record Office in Fetter Lane, were to be found history's first truly professional class. It is the civil servants responsible for the classification of national records and much of their calendaring who may lay claim to the title of the earliest of professional historians.[2] They were followed, of course, by the university professionals, those who taught, lectured and researched the subject in a specifically academic context.[3]

These institutional changes stand out as central to the socially-based questions addressed in this work, and the precedence thus accorded them has exercised a profound influence on the materials used. The rejection of a textual approach for one stressing organisational development arose because of the many important institutional changes occurring throughout this period. 1838 saw the passing of the act establishing the need, if not the funding, for a general record office as well as the foundation of one of the most successful and tenacious of the new printing clubs, the Camden Society. 1886, when this episode somewhat artificially ends, was the year in which the *English Historical Review*, the first voice of the new professionals, appeared. In the fifty or so intervening years, individual and state enterprise had ensured that antiquarian, historical and archaeological pursuits remained interests of national proportion and substance. The minute books of local societies, the papers of

[1] Joseph Ben-David in his *The Scientist's Rôle in Society. A Comparative Study* (New Jersey, 1971) maintains that science was similarly determined and at roughly the same time (p. 170).
[2] See Chapter 5.   [3] See Chapter 6.,

Record Office administrators and of self-taught archaeologists, and the early records of university history have thus variously provided the raw materials around which this work has been structured. It is the relation of the individual to the community and of the community to the institutions created by it which forms its substance.

The absence of two celebrated figures of nineteenth-century historiography – Thomas Carlyle and Lord Macaulay – deserves comment. Strictly, neither come within the definitions which these historical communities would have laid down for themselves, but were more accurately part of an older tradition of essayists and reviewers. Though both are remembered as authors of great and influential historical works, neither was ever part of the wider historical community but found their associates and friends rather in literary and political circles of a more general kind. In absenting themselves from communion with like-minded men, and in their deliberate distancing from historical institutions, they themselves dictate their exclusion from detailed mention in the following chapters.

II

The relationship between science and history in Victorian culture has ramifications far wider than a simple similarity in their organisational growth. New and challenging conceptions of time initiated by scientific and technological innovation profoundly affected the Victorian historical perspective. The radical alteration in perceptions of time and speed induced not only by the introduction of faster travel and communication, but also by an increasingly quantitative approach to work and leisure governed far more by clocks and public time, forced Victorian intellectuals to reconsider accepted notions of continuity and change. In such a context, history was to acquire powerful human appeal as the intellectual mechanism whereby time could be measured and evaluated. The transition from myth to history was an uncomfortable and often painful process which involved very centrally the questioning of assumptions about universality and permanence.[4] New conceptions of time began to prompt, albeit gradually, questions relating to the idea of relativity and of truth as a function of human history rather than an unchanging and simple value.

Historical continuity is both the inductive guarantee that respect for precedent builds more lastingly than abstract theories, and also the content of the myth by which that respect is sanctioned and inspired. At its most emphatic, the myth presents the national history and identity as the continuous self-renewal and development of a spirit.[5]

[4] M. I. Finley, 'Myth, Memory and History', *History And Theory* IV (1964–5) 3, pp. 281–302.
[5] J.W. Burrow, '"The Village Community" and the Uses of History in Late Nineteenth-Century England', in *Historical Perspectives. Studies in English Thought and Society* ed. N. McKendrick (London, 1974), 255–84 (p. 267).

This was the Victorian dilemma; history throughout the century was the standard-bearer of an ultimately fixed universe governed by good Providence, but the seeds of doubt sown in the first instance by science were further questioned by the direction of the new historical disciplines. Most significantly, the archaeological discoveries which challenged received theories of the age of the earth, and the new higher criticism which sought to distinguish myth from inspiration and looked for historical verification of the life of Jesus, bespoke the collapse of this fixed and timeless code. At the same time the Victorian fascination with the past was peculiarly preoccupied with posterity. The urge to preserve and to pass on a heritage legitimised by the contemporary motivated the development of the Victorian historical consciousness. The belief and faith in progress which this implied fostered a strongly teleological approach to history, such that it became, ironically, the gospel of heritage, nullifying the less palatable conceptions newly prompted by its study.[6] It could thus justify simultaneously both an obeisance to the past and an invocation of the future. Ideals were not submerged but redefined. For the proclamation of the triumph of English progress, wedded to the imperialist ambitions of a strong commercial and naval nation, the focal point of that ideal was shifted from the vision of ancient Greece as the ultimate pinnacle of human perfection to the rougher-hewn powers represented by a Gothic and Teutonic inheritance. Teutonism provided a Christian alternative and ideal.[7]

National ideals were thus prominent. The three historical communities all shared a strong sense of national duty and of national pride, revelling in the bygone feats of their country. Interestingly, it was not this nationalism which eroded the strength of the provincial cultures which had created so strong an institutional framework around the county archaeological societies. They were diminished in stature rather by the centralisation concomitant upon professionalisation, and indeed shared with the *afficionados* of the metropolis and the universities a firm belief in the innate superiority of their own island kingdom.

Tradition and change were thus both justified within a single historical perspective in which the security of class interests suggested by the shared religious and political opinions so characteristic of the historical communities at this juncture helped articulate a consensual image and intellectual conception around which they could cluster. It was this coalescence of community and class that prompted perception of their common experience as binding and correct, as possessed of an authority and a code of practice largely unspoken but nonetheless powerful. History proved a consistently popular pursuit precisely because of its seeming ability to provide a framework for justified beliefs; the action of selective memory governed the historical topics

---

[6] H. Meyerhoff, *Time In Literature* (Berkeley/Los Angeles, 1955) p. 97.   [7] See Chapter 4.

most appropriate to the institutions and ideals dominant in Victorian England.[8]

The emphasis in historical and antiquarian work thus focused primarily upon a recreation of the English past, although the new archaeology did not follow quite the same path. The pioneers of excavation were principally active in the Middle East, uncovering sites familiar to their fellow countrymen primarily through the Bible. Despite clamours for a greater concentration on national antiquities, indigenous archaeology found far less public approbation. The activities of barrow diggers and Roman numismatists tended to attract less attention than the exotic and sensational finds unearthed in Mesopotamia. These latter discoveries could be accounted for within the traditional time-span, and their consequent authentication of Biblical narrative necessarily lent them weight and favour.

It was the archaeological work closer to home which was challenging the fundamentals of time and of religious belief. Discoveries in the south of England and in France suggested the need to extend backwards ideas about the age of the earth.[9] Thus, like the new history, archaeology was simultaneously a subject which presaged far-reaching intellectual changes and yet supported the ideology of progress so vital to the maintenance of Victorian values.

Crucial to an understanding of the following chapters is a strong denial of any 'presentist' perspective. Neither the professionals – the historians and the archaeologists – nor the antiquarian community acquire their latter-day interest or importance from a desire to trace the development through them of our modern forms of study. To see in the historical studies of the nineteenth century no more than the nascent germs of our own thinking would be a collective egoism of massive proportion. The task of the historian can never be to pronounce arbitrary judgments on the relative merits of past scholarship. Our function is to understand the nature and context of that scholarship and the circumstances under which changes in it come about. This work seeks to illuminate neglected corners of Victorian culture, valuable in extending our understanding of a complex and confused world. The historical disciplines clearly exerted a fascination over Victorian England and it is that rather than a desire to unfold, Whig-like, the origins and appearance of present and doubtless transient forms of historical scholarship, which informs the subject of this study. The simultaneity of the threat posed by new and relative conceptions of time and of the confidence afforded England by expansive reference to the past and to progress suggests the central rôle which history played in the Victorian consciousness, a rôle which must be explored not just through textual but through individual, collective and institutional manifestations.

[8] See, for example, P. B. M. Blaas, *Continuity and Anachronism: Parliamentary and Constitutional Developments in Whig Historiography and in the Anti-Whig Reaction between 1890 and 1930* (The Hague, 1978) and Roy Strong, *And When Did You Last See Your Father?: The Victorian Painter and British History* (London, 1978).   [9] See Chapter 4.

This work has thus concentrated first on an analysis of the social location of many historical practitioners – their education, their employment, their religion – and second on the organisations and institutions in which they gathered. It was within this framework that the widening gap between amateur and professional in the historical field was realised. The emergence of new professions was a characteristic trend in nineteenth-century Western societies; as well as the creation of new types of employment largely spawned by the needs of a market economy, many of the older professions began to create the élite conditions we now associate with professional standing. Attempts to limit entry to these avenues of employment through more stringent training and qualification provided both a sense of community and of status for those within. The class symbolism of such developments did not leave Victorian intellectuals untouched, and the particularly public rôle played by history in promoting national and Christian pride guaranteed that those engaged in such pursuits were prey to this quest for public prestige and recognition. Intellectual developments cannot thus be considered except within the wider context of social and political structures and it is therefore necessary to attempt to determine the change in status over time of each of the individual historical communities within the spectrum of developing professionalisation.

The structural changes of intellectual institutions are nonetheless only of interest to the historian of ideas insofar as they throw light upon the status and state of knowledge in society and this study is thus concerned at base with the interplay between intellectual debate and the institutions created by it for its own survival. The significance of these institutions leads inescapably back to the immeasurably important phenomenon of professionalisation and the marginalisation of specific groups and interests consequent upon it.

The starting point of this work, then, is the enduring appeal of history in its many manifestations throughout the Victorian period. It explores the new institutional bases of the discipline alongside the ideology of its debates and, in doing so, seeks to examine the impact of professionalisation on the re-defining of the intellectual boundaries which were so successfully to distinguish the academic and the dilettante, the metropolitan and the provincial, the professional and the amateur from this time on. Its importance lies not merely in the alternative proposals it offers for redefining and categorising early professionalisation, but at a different level, in its attempts to seek new and empirical ground for the history of ideas; if the marriage of ideas and institutions seems now more convincing, and an additional basis for intellectual history secured, then this study will have proved itself worthwhile.

2

∞∞

Community and consensus

> . . . must they live unsung
> Because deaf ears flap round them?
> (W. S. Landor, To Layard, Discoverer of Nineveh)

I

Antiquarian, historical and archaeological studies of the past attracted a body of enthusiastic and committed devotees throughout the nineteenth century who, whether able to involve themselves full-time or only in their leisure hours in these pursuits, formed a highly motivated self-taught élite on familiar and friendly terms with one another and sharing a common body of knowledge.[1] Historical interests in the broadest sense maintained a steady popularity amongst the literate classes of nineteenth-century England, with their propensity for involvement in the activities of both local and national organisations committed to these subjects.

The social dimension of intellectual pursuits has in recent years received attention, in particular from historians of science who have argued that the public value of a subject and the social status of its proponents have often served to influence its achievements.[2] In the case of history, the seeming homogeneity of its practitioners, both in their social standing and in their views of the subject, suggest that intellectual considerations cannot be divorced from an investigation of social position. Who, then, were the men who sustained the many historical and archaeological societies of the period, who exploited the newly systematised records of past government, who published campanologies and

---

[1] Robert H. Kargon developed this notion of the 'devotee' in his book *Science in Victorian Manchester: Enterprise and Expertise* (Baltimore, 1977) pp. 32–5. He saw them as 'savants' representing the transitional stage between gentlemen of leisure and professional scientists. See too Morrell & Thackray (1981) and Roy Porter (1978) cited below.

[2] J. Ben-David, *The Scientist's Rôle in Society. A Comparative Study* (New Jersey, 1971); Kargon, *op. cit.*; J. Morrell & A. Thackray, *Gentlemen of Science. The Early Years of the British Association for the Advancement of Science* (Oxford, 1981); Roy Porter, 'Gentlemen and Geology: the emergence of a scientific career, 1660–1920', *Historical Journal* 21 (1978) iv, pp. 809–36; S. Shapin & A. Thackray, 'Prosopography as a Research Tool in History of Science: The British Scientific Community 1700–1900', *History of Science* XLII (1974) pp. 1–28.

county histories, chronologies and collections, accounts of barrow digging, of medieval costume and of church architecture? Countless were tempted to exhume the treasures hidden between the covers of their local parish register, buried deep in the nearby tumulus or turned up by the spade of the rail builders. Amongst them there are indubitably those who stand out by virtue of their commitment to and participation in historical studies, those whom Alan Macfarlane has dubbed 'the historically visible minority'.[3] Their lives, at least, open up to the historian some idea of both the social and intellectual factors which brought them involvement in historical studies. Although such categories are of necessity an artificial construct, there are six broad areas in which nineteenth-century antiquarians, archaeologists and historians tended to concentrate their energies.[4]

The easiest to resurrect are, of course, those publishing in these fields.[5] There were also those who derived their livelihood from the subject in some way, such as the record and archive administrators, and those employed in related work in museum departments. At a later date, posts in history and archaeology began to proliferate in universities and equivalent institutions. There were also those who were active in archaeological and historical societies; often with multiple membership of such bodies and there were the many collectors – of books, manuscripts, antiquities, coins and the like. Those who fulfil the conditions of at least one of these categories – and there were many whose activities spanned them all – form the basis for an investigation into the link between their social background and their historical activities; 'to inquire after these individuals [. . .] and to understand how friendship, intellectual ambition, curiosity, career and competition' rendered them the foremost proponents of their chosen fields both at that time and for posterity.[6] It is Macfarlane's contention that 'the methods of studying small, delimited, sets of people or other objects is of fundamental interest to many disciplines', and not least to the historian seeking the relationship between a discipline and its social environment.[7]

Richard Altick's early study of the class basis of nineteenth-century British writers establishes a series of common characteristics shared by most writers. Overwhelmingly male and middle class, they were largely university educated – particularly at Oxford and Cambridge which, until quite late in the century, continued to dominate English élite education – and often boasted a

[3] Alan Macfarlane, *Reconstructing Historical Communities* (Cambridge, 1977) p. 130.
[4] Other commentators have used similar constructions to define their inquiries – Shapin & Thackray, *loc. cit.* p. 12; Francis Galton, *English Men of Science: their Nature and Nurture* (London, 1874) pp. 2–3.
[5] Ancient History is specifically omitted as bearing more relation to the traditional classical studies of the day. Ancient and modern historians espoused distinctly different attitudes to the text – see Chapter 6.   [6] Morrell & Thackray, *op. cit.* p. xxii.   [7] A. Macfarlane, *op. cit.* p. 24.

professional standing as well.[8] The English historical, antiquarian and archaeological communities thus quantified revealed a similar bias. The active élite was almost all male.[9] A high proportion were graduates of the universities of Oxford and Cambridge, more with Oxford than with Cambridge degrees. Together, these graduates account for 44% (88) of the total sample of 201. They were, of course, all Anglican, as were most of those who did not boast a university education; Dissenters, Catholics and other non-Anglicans form a very small proportion of the total. Of those whose religion is known, 62% (124) were Church of England and there were a further 28% (57) of whose religious beliefs no evidence could be found. Many took holy orders, though not all were practising clerics; 16% (32) of the sample were attached full-time to livings;[10] 8.5% were connected with the legal profession and a surprisingly high 7% (14) were in commerce or trade ranging hierarchically from bankers to publishers and stationers, a miller, a grocer and a wine merchant. There were also a few Members of Parliament – 6% (12) of the total. Thus as in Altick's far larger and therefore more statistically reliable sample, the dominance of the professional sector of the middle class – architects, artists, organists, surgeons, military officers and engineers – is indisputable. A small number earned their livelihood from their historical pursuits, and there were a few whose private incomes allowed them to devote themselves more or less full-time to their studies without urgent need for remuneration. For the majority of the enthusiasts, however, these were the occupations of their leisure hours.[11]

The sample also establishes the central rôle of the institutions in which these men met and conversed with one another – 40% (80) of the total were Fellows of the Society of Antiquaries of London, although from the 1880s on the proportion drops substantially. A similar number were known to have been

[8] R. D. Altick, 'The Social Origins, Education, Occupation of 1100 British Writers, 1800–1935', *Bulletin of the New York Public Library* 66 (1962) vi, 389–404.

[9] Those few women who were active in these fields are highly individual and interesting women, and include the founder of the Egypt Exploration Fund, a government State Papers editor and the justly renowned Harriet Martineau. By virtue of their minority status they warrant little mention hereafter. Additionally, there were women members in many of the local archaeological societies. In general, they suffered an inferior status, were rarely permitted a vote on the society's council and frequently paid a smaller membership fee in consequence.

[10] The large number of Oxford and Cambridge graduates may help to explain the high incidence of ordination. Fellowships at Oxbridge colleges were only tenable in tandem with holy orders until 1882. Francis Galton's survey of 1874 showed seven out of every ten of his sample to be members of the established church (p. 126).

[11] Again, Galton's conclusions are similar. In his sample, one-third had been Oxbridge educated, one-third at the Scots, Irish or London universities, and one-third had received no university education at all (p. 236). His findings regarding their professions also roughly correspond: of the 107 who answered his questionnaire, he found 11 lawyers, 6 clerics, 6 teachers, 7 bankers, 21 merchants, 15 manufacturers, 9 noblemen and private gentlemen and a single architect. Not surprisingly, his sample showed more medical practitioners: 9 compared with the historical communities' 2 (p. 22).

active in various of the county, printing or specialist societies of the period (43%: 87) and their number shows little diminution over time.[12] The picture is similar to that in nineteenth-century scientific communities. As well as Galton's survey of 1874, the recent work of Morrell and Thackray shows most of their 'gentlemen of science' to be university educated, active in a number of scientific societies, and in practice if not avowedly in principle, jealous of their Anglican supremacy. 'No Jews, Roman Catholics, Methodists, Congregationalists, Baptists [. . .] were to be found among their number.'[13] Roy Porter too found a similar association between intellectual dominance and social acceptability among nineteenth-century geologists.[14] The scientific and historical communities were for the most part distinct, but clearly drew on the same professional and respectable segment of Victorian English society for their participants and in the context of the 'cultural pluralism' that marks this period their similarities seem appropriate.[15] (See Appendix I.)

The three historical fields were further cemented by the gradual creation of an intellectual genealogy or 'intellectual aristocracy'.[16] Francis Palgrave, first Deputy Keeper of the Public Records, married the daughter of Dawson Turner, an East Anglian antiquary. Turner himself was a banking partner of another Norfolk antiquary Hudson Gurney. Palgrave's successor at the Public Record Office, Thomas Duffus Hardy, was a nephew by marriage of Samuel Lysons, Fellow of the Society of Antiquaries and author of *The Romans in Gloucestershire* (1860) and various other antiquarian publications. James Orchard Halliwell, Shakespearean scholar and founder of numerous antiquarian societies, married – albeit without her father's consent – Henrietta, daughter of the eccentric Sir Thomas Phillipps whose vast collection of books and manuscripts was legendary and whose private printing press was responsible for a substantial proportion of nineteenth-century editions of early manuscripts. One of the daughters of historian E. A. Freeman married archaeologist Arthur Evans, excavator of Minoan civilisation on Crete and son of Sir John Evans. Edward Bond, founder of the Palaeographic Society and both Keeper of Manuscripts and Principal Librarian at the British Museum married the eldest daughter of the Rev R. H. Barham, author of the satirical *Ingoldsby Legends*.

This genealogical connection is traceable not only in patterns of marriage but between generations. Thomas Duffus Hardy's younger brother William succeeded him as Deputy Keeper at the Public Record Office. John Gough Nichols inherited not just a profitable printing business but a taste for

[12] See Chapter 3 pp. 65–6 for details of post-1880 society membership figures.
[13] Morrell & Thackray, *op. cit.* p. 26.   [14] R. S. Porter, *loc. cit.* p. 817.
[15] I. Inkster, 'Aspects of the history of science and science culture in Britain, 1780–1850 and beyond', in *Metropolis and Province. Science in British Culture, 1780–1850*, ed. I. Inkster & J. Morrell (London, 1983) pp. 11–54 (p. 25).
[16] Noel Annan, 'The Intellectual Aristocracy', in *Studies in Social History. A Tribute to G. M. Trevelyan*, ed. J. H. Plumb (London, 1955) pp. 234–87.

antiquarian pursuits from his father John Bowyer. The same may be said of James Raine, founder and first secretary of the Surtees Society. His son James was subsequently the Society's secretary for a period of forty years. W.H. Ainsworth, the historical novelist, became a lifelong friend of James Crossley, the Manchester lawyer who founded the Chetham Society, during the period when the young Ainsworth was articled to Crossley's father. The architectural antiquary Matthew Holbeche Bloxam, was an articled clerk in Rugby attached to the firm owned by the father of George Harris, the first man to suggest the establishment of a Historical Manuscripts Commission. Thus their commitment to historical pursuits was strengthened by a close sense of social belonging; not only were these men on the whole, successful, professional and securely middle-class members of the Victorian establishment, but they reinforced their connections in more intimate ways through marriage and family ties.[17]

In the case of the scientific community in England, participation in science was often a form of economic and social upward mobility.[18] For those of antiquarian, archaeological or historical tastes, their social position was already likely to be secure; what divided them was the manner in which they approached their work and the subjects they chose within the field. Four major strands of work and interest are distinguishable, often overlapping in both personnel and method, but definable as separate communities of interest.[19] In his study of nineteenth-century French historians, Charles-Olivier Carbonell has maintained that social class and occupation were the major determinants affecting the type of history which Frenchmen chose to pursue. Thus clerics indulged a taste for hagiography and other ecclesiastical material while the nobility collected family heirlooms and compiled family memoirs.[20] Other than that pride in the locality which sustained many a county archaeological society, the English evidence bears little resemblance to Carbonell's French model. The different spheres of interest all attracted men of similar background; historians, antiquarians and archaeologists alike read for degrees at the ancient universities, earned their living in the professions and worshipped in Anglican congregations meanwhile pursuing all manner of studies. Beyond the obvious conflation of clerical antiquarianism with ecclesiological enthusiasm, the appetites of the English communities were omnivorous.

The largest of these groups was the antiquarian, whose work spanned

---

[17] Galton also explored the importance of what he called 'pedigree', tracing the family connections of a number of families of repute – Playfair, Darwin, Latrobe, Wedgwood and nine others, pp. 40–73. Annan also takes up this theme in his work, *loc. cit.*

[18] See T. W. Heyck, *The Transformation of Intellectual Life in Victorian England* (London, 1982) pp. 60; 88; Shapin & Thackray, *loc. cit.* p. 7; Inkster, *loc. cit.* p. 39.

[19] Ben-David talks specifically of 'communities specialised by fields' in his *The Scientist's Rôle in Society, op. cit.* p. 4.

[20] C. O. Carbonell, *Histoire et historiens. Une mutation idéologique des historiens français, 1865–85* (Toulouse, 1976) pp. 215; 219; 230–2; 236–40.

excavation and collection, who compiled local histories and topographies and who formed the spearhead of the ecclesiological movement.

The science of the real antiquary is not of a narrow and limited character. To him, every relic which he picks up or secures, is pregnant with instruction, as bearing upon the history or the social life or habits of some past age [. . .] [He is] a man of large and liberal mind.[21]

The historians formed a separate community. Many of them held university posts or examined in the new schools of history established at Oxford and Cambridge in the latter half of the the century. Their published work ranged from the Anglo-Saxon researches of J. M. Kemble and Benjamin Thorpe to the eighteenth-century histories penned by Philip Henry, fifth Earl of Stanhope. Others such as Paul Willert concentrated on European topics or, like Sidney Owen, on colonial history.[22] Archaeologists formed a third obvious group, concerned almost exclusively with non-documentary sources and increasingly with pre-literate periods and societies. Most were active in excavation, both in Britain and further afield, and it was thus that 'the dig' became, by the end of the century, the distinctive hallmark of archaeological activity. The fourth group consisted of those employed, primarily by government, in museums, libraries and repositories, in work on manuscripts, antiquities and books. They comprise those who staffed the new Public Record Office and Historical Manuscripts Commission, those entrusted with the custody of the books, manuscripts and antiquities of the British Museum and various men employed in institutions such as Lambeth Palace Library, the Bodleian at Oxford and provincial museums and private libraries.[23]

This artificial structuring of intellectual interest and pursuit is far from perfect. The overlap between these four supposed communities is, not surprisingly, considerable. Many of the record employees, in particular, were also enthusiastic antiquarians. Joseph Hunter, known primarily as the historian of South Yorkshire was a Keeper of the Queen's Remembrancer's records; Henry Ellis, principal librarian at the British Museum from 1827 was a secretary of the Society of Antiquaries, and edited manuscripts for a number of printing clubs in the 1830s and 40s. Equally, John Howard Marsden, first Disney Professor of Archaeology at Cambridge, was an active member of the Essex Archaeological Society from the time of its inception in December 1852. These overlaps are hardly anomalies in an age in which specialisation in a professional context was as yet in its infancy. However, the men themselves were both aware of and often jealous of the distinctions between their

---

[21] Charles Roach Smith, *Retrospections* (London, 1883–91) I. 231, quoting an after-dinner speech by Sir John Simeon in Newport, Isle of Wight, *c.* 1859.

[22] Paul F. Willert, *The Reign of Lewis XI* (London, 1873); Sidney J. Owen, *India on the Eve of the British Conquest* (London, 1872).

[23] The archive and museum employees do not feature as a separate group for discussion in this chapter; see Chapter 5 for an analysis of their importance.

communities, differences almost more sharply defined by their similarities and overlapping preoccupations.

II

Throughout the century, though less so in later years, the antiquaries numbered the largest of these groups. The enormous range of their interests, in which they took great pride, accounted to some extent for their large numbers for they could thus absorb more participants from the fringes of historical study than could the more narrowly defined networks of history and archaeology proper.[24] Alfred Dunkin, the Kent printer who both edited and subsequently printed the report of the first full meeting of the British Archaeological Association in 1844 spoke there of this antiquarian characteristic of flexibility.

The true antiquary does not confine his researches to one single branch of archaeology; but in a comprehensive view surveys every fact; and aims to bring in every object to serve the great end and purpose of a knowledge of man and his habits and customs in past ages.[25]

Many antiquarians did specialise in a favourite field, but this rarely prohibited them from a remarkable degree of activity in other related areas. Charles Roach Smith became the leading authority on Roman London, monitoring the finds of building works on sites in the City of London from his chemist's establishment near the Bank of England. He was also a keen numismatist, one of the founders of the British Archaeological Association and author of a number of multi-volume works such as the seven-volume compilation *Collectanea Antiqua* as well as being 'a student of viticulture and Shakespeare'.[26]

John Yonge Akerman was primarily a numismatist, founder of the Numismatic Society and with many publications on that subject to his name. He was also a keen excavator, sometime secretary of the Society of Antiquaries, a subscriber to many of the new printing and archaeological societies and a Camden Society editor. He also published in 1853 his *Legends of Old London* and between 1852 and 1855 his *Remains of Pagan Saxondom*. Specialisation was thus a relative term in a community where a broad approach and a wide range of interests was still encouraged and expected. It was not uncommon, however, for antiquarians to concentrate their attentions on one locality, producing perhaps topographical, architectural or biographical material relating to a specific area, generally that in which they lived. William Thompson Watkin published works on Roman Lancashire and Cheshire in the 1880s; John Gage

---

[24] The term 'network' derives from use by sociologists and anthropologists as much as from historians in their discussions of community.

[25] Charles Roach Smith, *op. cit.* i. 12, A. J. Dunkin in *Report of the Proceedings of the British Archaeological Association*, 1844.

[26] Brian Hobley, 'Charles Roach Smith (1807–90): Pioneer Rescue Archaeologist', *The London Archaeologist* 2 (1975) xiii, 328–33 (p. 328).

Rokewode wrote the 'history and antiquities' of various Suffolk parishes and the Rev Charles Henry Hartshorne made Northamptonshire history his main interest.

The energy of Thomas Crofton Croker, author of *The Fairy Legends and Traditions of the South of Ireland* (1825) has been admiringly described by Richard Dorson. He

edited collections of Irish historical and popular songs [. . .] wrote a pantomime based on one of his fairy legends and two novelettes, edited journals, memoirs and plays, assisted in the founding of the Camden and Percy societies, and the British Archaeological Association, was elected a Fellow of the Society of Antiquaries, collected a private museum of Irish ethnographical specimens – all while holding a government clerkship.[27]

Nor does this fully describe the breadth of Croker's antiquarian zeal. His diary frequently mentions the two or three meetings of learned societies he would attend in one evening. 'Thursday February 26, 1852. At 4 Percy [Society] Meeting [. . .] Not over till 1/2 past 5. Off at 7 to Numismatic [. . .] Mr Williams read nice paper on Chinese coins [. . .] Antiquaries 8.'[28] Croker was not an unusually vigorous example of the nineteenth-century antiquarian. His contemporary Thomas Wright, whom Dorson describes as 'perfectly typif[y-ing] the early Victorian antiquary-scholar', was another such zealot.[29] During and after a Cambridge education, he produced innumerable editions for printing societies and for the Rolls Series, was either secretary or treasurer of a number of historical societies, and produced a local history of Essex besides other publications on, for instance, Shropshire and on Elizabethan England. He was one of the founders of the British Archaeological Association, collaborated on works with the French medieval scholar Francisque Michel, and continued to publish copiously in every decade from the 1830s through to the 1870s when he died. Albert Way, who after a clash with Wright had founded the Archaeological Institute in 1843, was another similarly diligent antiquary.[30] Another Cambridge graduate, he too was associated with many societies both as an editor and as a member. He was a far less prolific writer, but the *Athenaeum* at his death described him as 'indefatigable [. . .] there is scarcely a subject of historical enquiry [. . .] or one of archaeological investigation to which his attention had not been drawn.'[31]

A common enthusiasm amongst such men was that of collecting. The new interest and care which records began to receive in this period had obvious ramifications for the sale, in particular, of early manuscripts and printed materials. The deliberate attempt by the tiny and exclusive Roxburghe Club in

[27] R. M. Dorson, *The British Folklorists: A History* (London, 1968) p. 51.
[28] Soc. Ant. MS. 751. Diary of Thomas Crofton Croker, 1852.
[29] R. M. Dorson, *op. cit.* p. 62.   [30] See Chapter 3, pp 48; 69.
[31] Soc. Ant. MS 700. Notebook and miscellaneous papers concerning the Way family and their possessions. Clipping from the *Athenaeum*, n.d. Albert Way died in 1874.

1812 to create rare and luxurious editions was greeted with disapproval amongst the antiquarian community at large. The printing clubs which began operating in the 1830s were their response to this whim of the wealthy. Nonetheless most antiquarians were keen to develop their own collections of both artifacts and documents. The exhibits which were so common a feature of their societies' meetings testify to the importance of this aspect of antiquarianism. Many amassed fine collections which were posthumously bequeathed to an appropriate institution; Charles Roach Smith's excellent collection of London antiquities, for instance, went to the British Museum in 1855. There were, however, those with whom appropriation became an obsession, notably Thomas Layton and the notorious Sir Thomas Phillipps. Layton was a London merchant whose collection included '11,000 books, 3,000 prints and maps, 3,000 coins, tokens and medals, 9,000 pottery and glass vessels and tiles and 2,600 [assorted] antiquities'.[32] His efforts, however, pale beside those of the cantankerous and tyrannical Phillipps whose collection Munby has estimated at some 60,000 manuscripts and 50,000 printed books and pamphlets, the cost of which had been between £200,000 and £250,000.[33] Mary Ann Everett Green, whose six-volume *Lives of the Princesses of England* owed much to research in Phillipps' private collection, wrote thus to him:

I often think of you, and I wonder how far the encroaching tide of literature has worked its way since we left [. . .] That poor unfortunate drawing room. It ought to have elastic walls to meet all the demands made upon it![34]

Both Phillipps and Layton were motivated more by the size of their collections than on ensuring the quality of their purchases. Careless as to the exact nature of their collections, both libraries revealed enormous duplication when examined after the deaths of their owners.[35] Phillipps in particular was also responsible for diverting important national material from public ownership and for inflating prices by his determination to dominate the market.[36]

Phillipps and Layton may represent the collector run amok, but few antiquaries were not eager to extend their libraries, a desire suggestive as much of economic confidence as of a thirst for antiquarian knowledge. Sale catalogues indicate the large and valuable nature of many of these collections. John Bruce's collection, auctioned in April 1870 and comprising 1,910 lots, yielded £1,139. 11s. 6d. The 1,552 lots which made up Henry Ellis's collection sold in 1869, brought in £1,286. 13s. These were collections of average size;

[32] D. Whipp & L. Blackmore, 'Thomas Layton, FSA (1819–1911): "A misguided Antiquary"', *The London Archaeologist* 3 (1977) iv, 90–6 (p. 90).
[33] A. N. L. Munby, *Phillipps Studies* (Cambridge, 1951–60) iv, 166–7. Munby stresses that catalogue error and confusion may well render these figures inaccurate.
[34] Bodl. MS. Phillipps–Robinson d. 160, ff. 96–7. Mary Ann Everett Green to Phillipps, 28 February 1854.
[35] Whipp & Blackmore, *loc. cit.* p. 92; Munby, *op. cit.* iv, 86–7.   [36] Munby, iv, 35; 169.

Francis Palgrave's books and manuscripts, auctioned in May 1862 and fetching £1,134. 6s. 6d, amounted to 2,647 lots. The Southwark solicitor, G. R. Corner, whose 1,026 lots of books and manuscripts were put up for auction in 1864, went for a modest £360. 17s.[37]

The libraries of antiquaries exhibit too a striking degree of uniformity. In addition to collections of the volumes issued by the printing societies which almost always graced their shelves, county histories both contemporary and by earlier topographers were an invariable element in the antiquarian library. The standard histories of past centuries – Hume and Smollett, Clarendon (without fail), Gibbon, Strype, Rymer – were seldom missing and, of course, the works of their antiquarian friends and colleagues figured prominently. Writing to Joseph Hunter, W. Swifte confessed his 'pleasure in possessing what is not owned by the million, it may be a manuscript of which no copy is known to exist [. . .] It is a pleasure some bookworms and I for one enjoy.'[38]

It was common for members of the antiquarian community to combine their historical activities with other intellectual interests. Sir Philip de Malpas Grey-Egerton was a Conservative M.P., and edited for the Camden and Chetham societies as well as publishing various topographical works. He was primarily, however, an acclaimed palaeontologist and natural historian. Dawson Turner coupled his antiquarian pursuits with those of botany, publishing papers on both subjects. The Worcestershire solicitor Jabez Allies wrote on folklore and on his county's antiquities, and in 1838 also published a book *On The Causes of Planetary Motion*. In his memoir of Beriah Botfield, M.P. and active antiquary, his friend and colleague Thomas Pettigrew stresses that Botfield had been a member not just of many printing clubs and archaeological societies but also of a number of scientific societies.[39] Antiquaries were apt to regard natural history and human history as similar evidences of the activities of Divine Providence.[40] The notebook of antiquary James Yates, with its broad compass of subjects, is a typical example of the concerns of the nineteenth-century English antiquarian. The notebook discusses Phoenician inscriptions, the use of the terms *acanthus, acanthion* &c., in the ancient classics, preserved leaves and branches, a Roman sepulchre in Norfolk, bronze celts in military use and the stone wedges of Java.[41] The antiquarian empire was circumscribed only by the

[37] British Museum Catalogue of English Book Sales: Bruce, S–C. 960(4) 27 April 1870; Ellis, S–C.S. 619(3) 19 July 1869; Palgrave, S–C.S. 513(3) 12 May 1862; Corner, S–C.Sg. 116(10) 30 March 1864. John Bruce was one of the founders of the Camden Society and although a lawyer by training devoted all his time to his antiquarian interests, more particularly in an organisational capacity.
[38] B. L. Add. MS. 24875, f. 410. Corresp. Joseph Hunter XII, 4 August 1858.
[39] T. J. Pettigrew, *Memoir of Beriah Botfield Esq., M.P.* (London, 1863) pp. 4–5.
[40] Stephen Bann's recent work offers some invigorating comments on the yoking together of the two disciplines in his *The Clothing of Clio. A Study of the Representation of History in Nineteenth-Century Britain and France* (Cambridge, 1984) pp. 16: 24.
[41] UCL. Lib. MS. Ad. 71. Notebook of James Yates (1789–1871).

necessity of dealing with the objects and events of the past, be they early chronicles or ancient British antiquities.

The determination and single mindedness with which these men pursued the interests of their leisure hours was remarkably intense. Their publishing output, often of editions requiring minute scrutiny and a good deal of comparative work, was prodigious and their efforts on behalf of the archaeological and historical societies were unstinting. William Baker, an antiquarian and natural historian, described the spartan organisation of his leisure hours.

I get up before five o'clock, and read Ancient History till six, my time to go to work; at breakfast time I read the Spectator for a quarter of an hour; after dinner I have three-quarters of an hour, which I employ in reading Blair's Lectures; after work I read Ancient History from eight till nine o'clock; from nine till half-past ten or eleven, I study Euclid, and on Sundays before and after dinner, I practice drawing.[42]

The antiquarian community had been by long tradition, the legitimate prey of literary fun, if not derision. Before Scott's Jonathan Oldbuck, Pope had poked fun at the eighteenth-century antiquary Thomas Hearne in appropriately Chaucerian parody:

> Of sober face, with learned dust besprent [. . .]
> On parchment scraps y-fed [. . .]
> To future ages may thy dulness last
> As thou preserv'st the dulness of the past.[43]

The growing popularity of such interests in Victorian England did little to temper the vulgar view of the antiquarian as a man so transported by past delights as to be almost wholly unaware of, or at least indifferent to the age in which he lived. The famous passage in Dickens' *Pickwick Papers* in which Mr Pickwick excitedly ascribes great antiquity to a stone bearing the legend 'Bil Stumps his mark', and the various theories he postulates is a fairly typical example.[44] Both Thomas Hughes and Thomas Hardy wrote around this theme of the other-worldly antiquary. Hughes, who is said to have based his character on John Yonge Akerman, has him admitting that 'for the last thirty years [I] have read little else but the Bible and books two hundred years old and upwards'.[45] Thomas Hardy's short story, *A Tryst at an Ancient Earthwork*, is about an antiquary, based upon Edward Cunnington of the Wiltshire Archaeological and Natural History Society, digging secretly at night to prove the mistakes of other authorities to his own satisfaction. 'He, to whom neither weather, darkness nor difficulty seems to have any relation or significance, so

[42] John Bowen, *A Brief Memoir of the Life and Character of William Baker, FGS* (Taunton, 1854) p. 24.   [43] Alexander Pope, *The Dunciad* (London, 1924) iii, ll 185–90.
[44] Charles Dickens, *Pickwick Papers* (Harmondsworth, 1982) pp. 216–17; 228. With thanks to Douglas Bolingbroke for the reference.
[45] Thomas Hughes, *The Scouring of the White Horse: or the Long Vacation Ramble of a London Clerk* (Cambridge, 1859) p. 68.

entirely is his soul wrapt up in his own deep intentions' is in fact reminiscent of many true antiquarians.[46] Thomas Wright, in a letter to the Liverpool collector Joseph Mayer, described the hardships he was willing to undergo in the pursuit of knowledge.

I went to Hull in the earlier part of the month [. . .] and I took the opportunity in spite of the deep snow and intensive frost to [. . .] explore the country where the flint weapons came. I was so resolved not to be daunted, that in more than one instance I walked nearly up to my middle in snow – but I have found an Anglo-Saxon cemetery, totally unknown before, and a Roman villa, and several other things. Above all, I have perfectly satisfied myself [. . .] of the authenticity of the flint weapons.[47]

Thomas Hughes' story *The Scouring of the White Horse* which follows the amorous adventures of a rather forlorn London clerk on vacation in Berkshire tells amusingly of the clerk's disappointment when his new-found antiquarian friend takes him to view the local castle.

I had half expected to see an old stone building with a moat and round towers and battlements and a great flag flying [. . .] I own I was a good deal disappointed [. . .] there is a great flat space [. . .] a bank of earth [. . .] then [. . .] a great broad deep ditch [. . .] and there isn't even a single stone, much less a tower, to be seen.[48]

William Beamont of Warrington, himself the author of numerous local histories, describes a similar but true incident.

Standing near a hedge yesterday my friend Mr Gibson desired me to cast my eyes over that field and say if I saw anything. It was a grass field tolerably uniform and covered with pretty much the same vesture in every part but one [. . .] I was unable [. . .] to perceive anything remarkable. "What", said he, "do you not perceive the Roman road?" "Where?" was my innocent enquiry [. . .] "There", said he, pointing to a brown streak of grass [. . .] "That is the Roman road which has escaped the destruction which has obliterated it in all other parts of the field."[49]

Allowing for fictional licence, these tales whether factual or imagined, sympathetic or parodic, confirm the strength of commitment which characterised the antiquarians. Thomas Pettigrew, a successful and wealthy surgeon, gave up his thriving practice at the age of sixty-three to devote his remaining years wholly to antiquarianism. Even before then, however, he had

[46] Thomas Hardy, 'A Tryst at an Ancient Earthwork' (1885), in *Collected Short Stories* (London, 1928) p. 872.

[47] B. L. Add. MS. 33346, f.39. Thomas Wright to Joseph Mayer, 7 March 1855.

[48] Thomas Hughes, *op. cit.* pp. 58–9.

[49] Warrington Central Reference Library MS. 297. Diaries of William Beamont, 2 August 1844. Portrayals of the antiquarian stereotype differed little from accounts of 'men of learning' in earlier ages. Adam Warner in Bulwer Lytton's *Last of the Barons* is a similar characterisation to those offered by Hughes and Hardy. Even J. R. Green, describing Edmund Rich in his *Short History of the English People*, cannot resist. Talking of the 'barefoot friar' who became Archbishop of Canterbury, Green conjures up a familiar picture. 'To see him in the little room which he hired [. . .] ascetic in his devotion, falling asleep in lecture time [. . .] a chivalrous love of knowledge, that let his pupils pay what they would' (p. 131).

served the community with energy. A member of many scientific and antiquarian societies, he had sat on the first councils of the Historical Society of Science and the Percy Society, was Treasurer and Vice-President of the British Archaeological Association and even edited its journal. His enormous publishing output included fifty-four antiquarian books and papers, another seven on Egyptology and twenty-one on medical and surgical subjects.[50]

This degree of immersion inevitably consolidated the social aspects of the community's function. Most men active in antiquarian circles knew each other personally, or at least through correspondence, rather than simply by repute. Many met at the regular gatherings of the various societies, which brought together 'into personal intercourse large numbers, of congenial tastes and studies, for mutual benefit'.[51] The same men were also likely to meet at the dinners and soirées which were so much a part of the antiquarian scene at this time. Croker records 'a large party, consisting chiefly of members of the Society of Antiquaries and other scientific associations', who dined with Lord and Lady Londesborough on Saturday 24 April 1852. Amongst the guests were J. Y. Akerman, Thomas Wright, James Halliwell, J. R. Planché and the Scandinavian archaeologist, Worsaae. Dinner was followed by the exhibition of a collection of antiquities, presumably the property of Lord Londesborough. Such occasions, if not always so grand, were commonplace. 'Dined at the Pettigrews, meeting Stapleton, Halliwell, Wright' – all antiquarians – notes Joseph Hunter in his diary for 1844.[52] And these examples serve to indicate the social stratum in which antiquarianism found its chief proponents.

The nineteenth century was pre-eminently an age of letter-writing and in this, the antiquarians were no exception. Local historians up and down the country consulted one another, borrowed books and manuscripts and shared their findings with fellow enthusiasts. Men such as James Crossley and Joseph Hunter seem to have numbered virtually all the well known antiquarians of the day among their correspondents. They reported variously on the fortunes of local societies, the success of their own and others' work, requested sundry nuggets of information and invited each other to dinners and meetings. The Honorary Librarian of the Parker Society, writing to Joseph Hunter from Cheltenham, soliciting advice on a volume of manuscript poetry, explained why he was approaching the Sheffield Presbyterian. 'My friend Mr Bruce of the Camden Society, as well as Mr Montgomery advise me to show you the volume.'[53] In short, it was a world small enough for all but the most obscure to know one another, to trust one another with their books, manuscripts and

---

[50] W. R. Dawson, *Memoir of T. J. Pettigrew* (New York, 1931) pp. 130–6.
[51] Charles Roach Smith, *op. cit.* III. pp. 90–1. See too Chapter 3.
[52] Soc. Ant. MS. 751. 24 April 1852.
[53] B.L. Add. MS. 24875, f. 316, 12 August 1845. Corresp. Joseph Hunter XII.

artifacts, and perhaps most importantly, to share the knowledge they valued so highly.[54] Barbara Ronchetti's case study of Warwickshire antiquaries in the first half of the century also found these social contacts to be an important factor in ensuring the continued vigour of antiquarian society.[55]

In an age which valued individual possession and endeavour so highly, the antiquarians displayed a remarkable faith in the importance of collective work. More than a simple acceptance of the shared intentions and objectives, most antiquaries expressed a desire to work towards those aims together: exclusive specialisation – one of the forces which was to mould professional history as the century wore on – and individual competition were rare in antiquarian circles. Many of the county societies saw their major function as being the collective organisations in which successful local history could come to fruition. John Britton, towards the end of a lifetime of antiquarian experience, maintained that a good county history had 'never yet been written by one person; nor is it likely that it ever will'.[56] The notion of a local, or even a national endeavour with its strong and morally unifying tones was greatly tempting to those who saw themselves as rescuing the nation's past glories from oblivion. Nor was it an entirely fantastic proposition: the social homogeneity of the antiquarian network served to ease the passage of that sense of camaraderie and shared purpose which so typified the relations between those working in antiquarian fields.

Whenever I fall upon a scrap of West Riding Genealogy, I think of the Historian of South Yorkshire; and . . . I never scruple to send you such trifles.

A friend of mine has given me a Pedigree [. . .] which I beg leave to inclose [. . .] As the family was of Shropshire and the Pedigree runs far back it struck me that it might interest your friend Mr Hartshorne as well as yourself. Requesting you will be pleased to return the pedigree when quite done with.[57]

They were as diligent and careful in their researches for the work of others as they were for themselves. 'I beg to thank you very sincerely for your kind response to my intrusion [. . .] you have taken the trouble to consult the original

[54] Requests such as that from Thomas Hugo to the Dean of Wells in 1862 (B.L. Add. MS. 30298, f. 23, 8 April 1862) for the loan of the Cathedral's pre-Reformation registers were not uncommon. It is the smallness of this world that makes possible, of course, the prosopographical analysis contained in this chapter.

[55] Barbara Ronchetti, *Antiquarian and Archaeological Scholarship in Warwickshire, 1800–60* (unpublished M.A. thesis, University of Birmingham, 1952) p. 22. She also sees the antiquarian network as primarily middle class. She maintains (p. 107) that the writing of county history died out after 1850 – a surprising assertion in the light not just of the many local societies founded after that date including the local record societies of the 1890s, but also the work of men such as R. S. Ferguson, John Glyde and the Rev William Hunt, all compiling county histories long after that date.   [56] John Britton, *The Autobiography of John Britton* (1850) p. 457.

[57] B.L. Add. MS. 24864, f. 95, 3 April 1874. Corresp. Hunter II; Bodl. MS. Phillipps–Robinson d. 137 f. 14. Jabez Allies to Phillipps, 7 July 1846.

Record, this is far more than I desired and I beg to say that I am truly grateful.'[58] Such harmony was not, of course, invariable. There were major divisions and discords within the community as when the rivalries of Thomas Wright and Albert Way split the new British Archaeological Association into two separate but parallel organisations, each with its own journal and annual congress.

One man who, in his lonely obsessions fed upon strife, was Sir Thomas Phillipps. His violent hatred of Catholicism was matched by his loathing for his son-in-law, James Orchard Halliwell. Phillipps constantly taunted Halliwell with his alleged theft of manuscripts from the library at his Cambridge college, an accusation never proven at law. He withdrew his support for the Cambridge Camden Society which he regarded as tainted with Puseyism, and from the London and Middlesex Archaeological Society because Thomas Hugo had, said Phillipps, declared a wish to see the monasteries restored.[59] Phillipps obviously represents an extreme case, but there were other instances. Eliza Strickland described the plight of the unfortunate Frederick Devon of the Record Office in a letter to Phillipps.

Is it peace between you and him? For some of your great Archaeologists have jilted the poor fellow so desperately, and there are so many feuds, that we peaceable sisters of the historic craft are obliged to mind our p's and q's before we mention Stephens to Gage Rokewode, Hunter to Sir Haris, Bruce to some half dozen and especially Barney Corner to Halliwell. I believe Sir Frederic Madden and Sir Henry Ellis hold themselves apart from all, but all join in defying and tormenting poor Mr F. Devon, why, I cannot think – for he appears very good-natured.[60]

John Cordy Jeaffreson, whose gossip-filled recollections are amusing if not wholly reliable, makes much of the long enmity between Francis Palgrave and Duffus Hardy, successive Deputy Keepers of the Public Records. Jeaffreson maintains that Palgrave's elevation to the post actually exacerbated this antagonism to the point of fisticuffs.[61] Some discord arose too from social snobbery. Charles Roach Smith, writing in old age, remembered his early relations with the Society of Antiquaries. His candidature for fellowship was jeopardised when a letter was sent 'which Sir Henry Ellis, the acting secretary, deemed worth consideration. The writer had stated, not that I was not a fit and proper person to be elected; but that I was in business.'[62] Hunter's correspondent William D'Oyly Bayley obviously knew of others who had suffered similarly. Following a brief genealogical sketch of his ancestry, he ended his

[58] B.L. Add. MS. 24866, f. 45. Richard Brooke, FSA, to Hunter, 15 June [1848]. Corresp. Hunter III.   [59] Munby, *op. cit.* 37; Bodl. MS. Phillipps–Robinson d. 186, ff. 210–17.
[60] Bodl. MS. Phillipps–Robinson c.476, ff. 255–6. Eliza Strickland to Phillipps, 31 October [1841].
[61] John Cordy Jeaffreson, *A Book Of Recollections* (London, 1894) II, 80–1. See John Cantwell's recent work, 'The 1838 Public Record Office Act and its aftermath: a new perspective', *Journal of the Society of Archivists* 7 (1984) 5, 277–85 for a detailed discussion of their differences.
[62] Charles Roach Smith, *op. cit.* I. 115–16.

request for a testimonial from Hunter by admitting, 'I mention these facts as I have heard the Society of Antiquaries is rather scrupulous as to whom it admits, and often enquires whence they originate.'[63]

Roach Smith also remembered the treatment meted out to the young Thomas Wright. 'He was never encouraged; and his contributions were accepted more as a credit and honour to the Society.'[64] Wright was one of the few 'career' antiquaries not blessed with a private income. He was ever eager to find a regular source of money to ease his nagging economic uncertainty. His letters to the wealthy Joseph Mayer are full of allusions to his want of a salary. 'Your banker's draught for £25 has arrived [. . .] I feel quite ashamed at having asked you for it, but I really could hardly help it.'[65] Asked to edit a manuscript for the Rolls Series, he confided to Mayer that, the text being a difficult one, 'it is only the high pay given by the government which would enable one to undergo the labour [and] expense'.[66] He was constantly seeking regular employment; when a permanent exhibition of Celtic and Anglo-Saxon antiquities in Manchester seemed a likelihood, he was furious that J. M. Kemble who 'tells people he is a very great man' was approached over him about getting it established.[67] Fifteen years later, he was anxiously assuring Mayer of his wish to become librarian of Liverpool's Free Library. 'I will devote myself to its service [. . .] with the greatest zeal [. . .] I would gladly take some regular employment which would bring a moderate salary without the same anxiety and uncertainty.'[68] Wright's economic and thus social ambivalence may well have contributed in large measure to his cold reception from the well-heeled and socially assured establishment of the Society of Antiquaries. His position was an unusual one, however. James Crossley, as President of the Chetham Society, frequently received apologies from his editors explaining that it was the encroachment of their non-antiquarian professional duties which prevented speedy completion of their editorial tasks.[69] George Oliver, historian of Exeter and one of the handful of Catholics integrated into the English antiquarian scene, excused himself from attendance at the centenary dinner of the Society of Antiquaries in 1851. 'Tho' I am an ardent lover of Antiquity, I am but a poor Ignoramus. And besides, my professional Duties in Easter Week must keep me a Prisoner at home.'[70]

The pressures of work and time thus combined to keep antiquarianism a largely amateur sport. It was amateur in that specific antiquarian employments did not exist so most of its proponents were necessarily engaged in

---

[63] B.L. Add. MS. 24864, f. 49, 3 February 1846. Corresp. Hunter II.
[64] Roach Smith, *op. cit.* I. 80–1.   [65] B.L. Add. MS. 33346, f. 108, 9 January 1857.
[66] B.L. Add. MS. 33347, f. 82, 4 July 1863.
[67] B.L. Add. MS. 33346, f. 118, 29 January 1857.
[68] B.L. Add. MS. 33347, f. 218, 30 October 1872.
[69] *e.g.* Manchester Central Library. Crossley Papers, VIII. vii. 1853. Letters from William Beamont and J. L. Curtis.   [70] Soc. Ant. MS. 833, f. 124, 11 April 1851.

unrelated full-time employments, and in that no officially sanctioned training aimed at producing antiquarians was ever a serious consideration. Thus R. S. Ferguson, an active Carlisle antiquary, was an examiner in civil law at the University of Cambridge, and H. T. Ellacombe, campanologist and local historian, had begun his adult career as an engineer studying under Brunel before being ordained and working as a Derbyshire rector for thirty-five years. As a result, the standard of work could vary very considerably, as indeed did judgments of it, there being no final arbiter by which it could be evaluated. That was the case in all areas of antiquarian study; whereas neither Thomas Layton nor Thomas Phillipps successfully or systematically catalogued their giant collections, that of the more scholarly Roach Smith was at least chronologically ordered. No single methodology lent coherence to antiquarian work.

A further consequence of the largely amateur nature of antiquarianism was that many enthusiasts began work with much energy but little concrete knowledge of their subject. John Britton described his own myopic entry into the field and although he is speaking of 1798, little had changed in the intervening fifty years.

Mr Wheble, my friend and patron [. . .] advanced me a few pounds, urged, almost goaded me to commence [. . .] Conscious however, of my own deficiencies – of my ignorance of topography, antiquities, and literary composition – I hesitated [. . .] for I knew not how and where to begin. It is true, I had read some volumes on topography and archaeology, but found them dull and uninviting [. . .] I read, and read again, in the hopes of obtaining information, and of finding a key, or clue to the science of topography. But alas! I became rather bewildered than enlightened, and was more repelled, than seduced to prosecute the subject.[71]

The difficulties confronted in seeking entry into the antiquarian world were thus those arising from the individualistic nature of the pursuit, despite its faith in the efficacy of collective organisation.

III

Historians in nineteenth-century England formed a separate and distinct group, less socially cohesive perhaps than the antiquarian camp. They were almost all university educated, and many held university posts though not necessarily in history. Their work was based on written sources, was primarily concerned with political history, and overwhelmingly with the history of England. It ranged from J. R. Green's *Short History of the English People* and Stubbs' *Select Charters* to the more obscure works of the Unitarian John Langton Sanford and the high church Rev. William Nassau Molesworth, whose work the *Dictionary of National Biography* has described as 'rather annals than history'.

[71] John Britton, *op. cit.* 135.

As an academic discipline, history was in its infancy in this period; men such as Macaulay and Carlyle, whose works dominated the popular market in history, had a closer affinity to the *belle-lettrist* tradition. It was rather men such as Henry Hallam, Philip Henry Stanhope (Viscount Mahon) and the Catholic John Lingard who were regarded by their contemporaries specifically as historians rather than polemicists or popularisers. Indeed, in an obituary, the point was made of Hallam that he 'had little ambition to be [. . .] popular. His works are far more for the student than the idle reader.'[72] Nonetheless, his work and reputation earned him one of George IV's gold medals for historical eminence in 1830.

John Lingard was likewise concerned far more with the qualities of accuracy and integrity than with sales. On discovering that the latest volume of Macaulay's *History* was being held back until fulsome reviews had prepared an eager public, he was justly indignant and wrote somewhat tongue-in-cheek to his banker. 'What! – review a book before it has made its appearance? Why, I think that even managers of banks might take a lesson in jesuitry from book publishers.'[73] These men, writing a generation earlier than the most famed of the new English historians, were those who witnessed the tentative arrival of academic history in the ancient universities, but it was their successors in the main who reaped the institutional benefits of this expansion of the university curriculum.[74]

Many of the most acclaimed historians of this favoured later generation were men who had been through Oxford together, some returning there as examiners and professors of history in adulthood. The 'Oxford school' of history which grew up around William Stubbs, John Richard Green and Edward Freeman, was one of the most influential intellectual strands in history at this juncture, and a group with strong social links too. Doris Goldstein makes the point that this group regarded themselves as 'custodians of the new scholarly standard'.[75] Stubbs and Green were both clerics, albeit very different in their approaches; Stubbs rose to the ranks of the bishopric whilst Green devoted the few years his health permitted to a poor East London parish. Freeman wrote full-time, and in old age finally received the accolade of a Regius Professorship of History at Oxford succeeding his close friend Stubbs in 1884. Another group of historians congregated around the relevant chairs at Cambridge, although principally in the period when Creighton, Acton and Maitland were active. It was, however, under the earlier leadership of Sir John Seeley in the 1860s that

[72] Bodl. MS. Eng. lett. e. 123. Obituary of Henry Hallam, 24 January 1859 – probably from *The Times*.   [73] M. Haile & E. Bonney, *Life and Letters of Lingard* (London, n.d.) p. 342.
[74] Macaulay, however, had been offered and had declined the Regius Professorship of Modern History at Cambridge. See Chapter 6.
[75] Doris S. Goldstein, 'The Professionalisation of History in Britain in the Late Nineteenth and Early Twentieth Centuries', *Storia della Storiografia* 1983, 3, pp. 3–26 (p. 14).

the Cambridge Historical Tripos began to emerge as a serious course of advanced study.

On the fringes of Cambridge life was also John Mitchell Kemble who with Benjamin Thorpe had effectively transformed Anglo-Saxon studies in England. Kemble, a Trinity undergraduate, studied philology under Jacob Grimm in Germany, and Thorpe trained in Copenhagen where he had come under the influence of the philologist Rasmus Christian Rask; between them, they produced from the 1830s on, a wealth of influential material – Kemble's *Codex Diplomaticus* (1839–48) and Thorpe's *History of England under the Saxon Kings* (1845). Both tried to work full-time at their researches, accepting minor employments when poverty struck. Kemble turned his hand to private teaching and to the post of examiner of stage plays, while Thorpe accepted – although not always with happy results – commissions for editing under the Master of the Rolls.[76] Independent of the ancient universities were such eminent figures as seventeenth-century specialist Samuel Rawson Gardiner, military historian Edward Creasy and Tudor specialist John Sherren Brewer, all of whom held teaching posts at the new London colleges.

There were also some well known but isolated figures – J. A. Froude, Thomas Buckle whose *History of Civilisation* trod new and provocative ground, and the Irishman William Lecky whose early work in the history of ideas won him sufficient reputation for the Oxford Regius Professorship of Modern History to be offered him in 1892. He was showered with honorary degrees and was one of the first twelve recipients of the prestigious Order of Merit, conferred on him in 1902.

In common with the antiquarian community, the historians were for the most part passionately committed to their work even when burdened with other professional duties. The development of teaching posts in history began to release new opportunities for full-time involvement in historical work although precisely because of its newness some of those who held such posts could hardly be deemed historians proper: the novelist Charles Kingsley, the positivist Edward Beesly, the polemicist Goldwin Smith.[77] Amongst the committed historians, however, their publishing output was often as prolific as that of their antiquarian counterparts. Their histories followed the common pattern of nineteenth-century publications, both fictional and non-fictional, in being largely multi-volumed, appearing over a period of years and often interspersed with other more minor studies. In 1865, E. A. Freeman was working simultaneously on four separate projects.

Time slips away wonderfully when one is making four histories, besides Revilements [reviews] and such trifles. First, there is Federal Government, vol ii, for which I read a

---

[76] See Chapter 5, p. 116.   [77] See Chapter 6.

certain portion of High Dutch daily [. . .] Secondly, a History of England for young folks [. . .] Thirdly, a History of Greece [. . .] Fourthly [. . .] a distinct History of the Norman Conquest.[78]

This disparate range of topics suggests, rather misleadingly, a total lack of specialisation. Rather like the antiquarians, most historians did nurture a specialist topic – Freeman's was the Norman Conquest – but saw that as no necessary hindrance to dabbling elsewhere. John Seeley's anonymous *Ecce Homo* was, like Froude's *Nemesis of Faith*, an excursion outside the historical field. J. E. Thorold Rogers, the pioneer economic historian, published a book on Aristotle alongside his definitive *History of Agriculture and Prices in England*. Montagu Burrows, the naval officer turned history professor, published works as diverse as *The Worthies of All Souls*, *Wiclif's Place in History* and *The Cinque Ports*. Nonetheless, there were many whose claim to posterity rested on their success in breaking ground in a single field: Stubbs in constitutional history, Gardiner in seventeenth-century English history, Seeley in British foreign policy and Maitland in legal history.

The institutional developments from which the historians derived their *raison d'être* were far less coherent a unity than the societies which formed the social and intellectual habitats of the antiquarians. Even so, the network of social contacts among historians suggests a sense of a close-knit fraternity dedicated to particular ends. Stubbs, Freeman and Green, in particular, maintained a lifelong correspondence in which they discussed not only the progress of their own researches but inevitably their estimations of their fellow workers. Clearly, historical circles were small enough for everyone to know everyone else. Freeman, writing to the geologist Boyd Dawkins who was an intimate friend of the Oxford historians, describes a 'light merry party' that he and his friends William Stubbs and the anthropologist E. B. Tylor had enjoyed.[79] Green, in his turn, wrote to Freeman about plans to establish a serious historical journal in 1867, which he had discussed with the young historians William Hunt and James Bryce.[80] When asked to edit a series of historical biographies for Macmillan, Green's choice of authors was significant. In his invitation to Freeman to write the life of Caesar, he lists his preferences. 'If Bryce will do Charles the Great, and Church Dante and Goldwin Smith President Lincoln, and you Caesar, the rest of the series would take the right sort of tone.'[81]

Stubbs, when vicar of Navestock and a still little-known figure, was convinced that there was a camp from which he, as an unproven historian, was excluded. He wrote to Freeman about the new Rolls Series: 'I fear it would be of

[78] W. R. W. Stephens, *Life and Letters of E. A. Freeman* (1895) p. 334. Freeman to Dean Hook, 23 December 1865.

[79] J. Coll. Oxon. MS. 192, f. 25, 26 March 1868. Letters of E. A. Freeman to William Boyd Dawkins.

[80] J. Coll. Oxon. MS. 199, ff. 303–5, 28 January 1867. Corresp. J. R. Green.

[81] J. Coll. Oxon. MS. 200, ff. 18–20, n.d. Corresp. J. R. Green.

little use to propose [. . .] editing [. . .] as the whole thing is so evidently in the hands of a clique.'[82] He was largely correct in his assessment, but it was a clique to which he was himself to belong in time. Moreover, acceptance into that circle brought with it the advantages of collective commitment. Collaboration was common and historians spoke freely to one another of their works and ideas with scant fear of plagiarism. C. W. Boase and G. W. Kitchin, both Oxford historians, collaborated on an English edition of Ranke's *History of England*. Stubbs and A. W. Haddan together produced the first volume of *Councils and Ecclesiastical Documents* in 1869 and fifteen years later Stubbs was planning a companion volume to the *Select Charters* in which he would cover the period to the reign of Elizabeth, and George Prothero, President of the Royal Historical Society, the period from that date to 1688.[83] Green and Boyd Dawkins had planned in their youth a joint historical and geological gazeteer of Somerset which, despite the encouragement of A. P. Stanley, never came to fruition.[84] Boyd Dawkins also regularly helped Freeman who always insisted on a thorough physical acquaintance with the area about which he was writing. When engaged on his *Norman Conquest*, Freeman spent much time wandering around the area of Battle and Hastings, or Senlac as he always called it.

Do tell me, in your character of geologist to Norman Conquest, enough to enable me to draw a picture of Porlock as it stood in 1052. *Where* did Harold land? By the present weir or pier? Or could he then get up to the present town?[85]

They were also candid about one another's work, freely criticising and praising. Green's comments on the *Select Charters* led its author to remark, 'I am glad that you like [it] [. . .] As to your pert criticism on it [. . .] you know our ideas are at variance fundamentally.'[86] Green's *Short History of the English People* published in 1874 was a major bone of contention between the three men. Freeman wrote of it when it was still in preparation, 'to my notions you have largely sacrificed the real stuff to your power of brilliant *talkee-talkee*'.[87] And Stubbs, commiserating with Green over an uncomplimentary review of what the three of them affectionately dubbed 'Little Book' said,

I wish that our views were [. . .] more in unison, so that I might feel more "solidarity" with the Little Book than I do – but if you will tread on my toes about Charles I and Laud, you cannot expect me to trust your views of George III implicitly.[88]

Such criticisms, though seriously meant and soberly accepted, were made in a comradely spirit.

For those outside the boundaries of the community however, disagreements

[82] Bodl. MS. Eng. misc. e. 148, ff. 58–9, 1 March [1860]. Stubbs to Freeman.
[83] W. H. Hutton, *Letters of William Stubbs, Bishop of Oxford, 1825–1901* (London, 1904) p. 358.
[84] J. Coll. Oxon. MS. 198, ff. 68–71, 18 October 1861. Green to Dawkins.
[85] J. Coll. Oxon. MS. 192, f. 15, 14 July 1867. Freeman to Dawkins.
[86] J. Coll. Oxon. MS. no number, 15 March 1870.
[87] J. Coll. Oxon. MS. 201, ff. 231–7, 21 September 1873. Freeman to Green.
[88] J. Coll. Oxon. MS. no number, 16 December [1875?].

were not tempered by mutual respect. The most reviled man in nineteenth-century historical circles was, without doubt, the unfortunate James Anthony Froude whose works on Tudor England are perhaps regarded more highly today than they were by his contemporaries, and certainly with more tolerance.[89] The luckless Froude, whose moral fable *The Nemesis of Faith* had been publicly burnt by the outraged establishment of Exeter College Oxford, was pilloried unmercifully by the Oxford historians. Green reported his gossip gleefully.

Frank Palgrave has just been down at Hatfield [. . .] and has brought back some charming "Notes on Froude." In the library are ten presses full of the Burghley papers, whereof two are shown to the "casual visitor" by the housekeeper. Anthony looked a little into the two, but never discovered the existence of the other eight![90]

Stubbs mused on the prospect of Froude as Goldwin Smith's successor in the Regius Professorship: 'it would be painful to have Froude'.[91] Froude was hardly considered an historian at all. Freeman compared him unfavourably to Gardiner whose references he maintained were 'as invariably right as Froude's are invariably wrong'.[92] Although a lesser target than poor Froude, Charles Kingsley found his appointment to the Regius Professorship at Cambridge greeted with derision by most historians, even though he regularly attracted far larger audiences for his lectures than most of his professorial rivals in the field.

This outright disapproval was reserved, though, for those felt to be intruders in the true community of historians. Where historians disagreed over interpretation or found a work dull, but nonetheless maintained a measure of professional respect, the author was not dismissed in the same way. Freeman clearly found Gardiner a struggle to read but was prepared to acknowledge him as a fellow scholar. 'With Gardiner, I have only got a little way into Charles I. He certainly does not tell his story like Macaulay. But he impresses me with the feeling that he is telling a true story [. . .] I have not yet marked any unfairness.'[93] A distinct sense of boundary was thus maintained around the discipline.

Historians in general had little time for antiquarian pursuits. Freeman, it is true, was an active member of the Somerset Archaeological and Natural History Society, and his friendship with J. R. Green dated from the time the latter delivered a paper on St Dunstan to the society in 1862. Stubbs was a

[89] B. Reynolds, 'James Anthony Froude', in *Some Modern Historians of Britain: Essays in Honour of R. L. Schuyler*, ed. H. Ausubel, J. B. Brebner & E. M. Hunt (New York, 1951) p. 49.

[90] J. Coll. Oxon. MS. 199, ff. 415–16, n.d. but Stephen *op. cit.* says end of 1869. For information on Palgrave, see Chapter 5.   [91] W. H. Hutton, *op. cit.* p. 102. 23 December [1865].

[92] W. R. W. Stephens, *op. cit.* II, 265. 17 December 1882, Freeman to Edith Thompson. Rosemary Jann has argued, however, that personal rivalry as much as professional standards were important in determining the exclusion of Froude from the inner circle of historians. See Jann, 'From Amateur to Professional: The Case of the Oxbridge Historians', *Journal of British Studies* XXII (1983) 2, 122–47 (pp. 132–3).   [93] *ibid.*, Stephens.

Fellow of the Society of Antiquaries and sat on its council in 1860. Montagu Burrows was a member of the Oxford Archaeological and Historical Society which in its early years had numbered Freeman among its active members. Notwithstanding these slight connections with the antiquarian world, historians tended to regard their own work as superior, and few sought to establish such connections, whether institutionally or socially. The common assumption that archaeology or antiquarianism was the 'handmaid' of history gained currency as the strength of the historical community grew. As Stubbs put it, 'all Chronological minutiae are the pebbles of the concrete in which the foundation of Histories must be laid'.[94] Green applauded Stubbs' inaugural lecture as Regius Professor of Modern History at Oxford because he thought it would at last 'demolish the "mere antiquary" notion' that he felt dogged the historical discipline.[95] Green regarded English antiquaries as living examples of Scott's Dryasdust parody. In a letter to Boyd Dawkins, he jests with an entertaining account of an imaginary archaeological society meeting.

The chair was taken by the celebrated Geologist – W. Boyd Dawkins, who after an Inaugural lecture on mud, called on the Revd. J. R. Green to read his paper "On Roman spoons and on the mode in use at that period of locking them up". Mr Dobbs [. . .] exhibited a fragment of a Roman or a Saxon teapot, the spout and body of which were lost.[96]

The compliment was returned, for antiquarians felt keenly their secondary status. Roach Smith railed at the choice of Lord Stanhope for the presidency of the Society of Antiquaries on just these grounds.

[Lord Londesborough] should have been President of the Antiquaries instead of one who does not care a rush for antiquities, or for the society, looking upon them as a matter-of-course tribute to his modern history publications.[97]

Earlier generations of historians had been less averse to acknowledging the intimacy of their interests. Hallam had been an active member and a Vice President of the Society of Antiquaries earlier in the century, and a personal friend of Albert Way. Lingard was a Vice President of the British Archaeological Association in the 1840s and knew antiquarians Thomas Wright and Thomas Pettigrew well. It was the historians of the new university schools some twenty years later who, on the whole, scorned such connections. Neither the British Archaeological Association nor the Archaeological Institute – both large national organisations – ever attracted more than a handful of members from amongst this historical community.

Nonetheless the historians were scarcely better trained or more scholarly in

[94] Bodl. MS. Eng. misc. e. 148, 13 April [1858]. Stubbs to Freeman. Also quoted in W. H. Hutton, *op. cit.* p. 42. He gives 'the stories' where I give 'Histories'.
[95] J. Coll. Oxon. MS. 199, ff. 310–14, February [1867].
[96] J. Coll. Oxon. MS. 198, ff. 68–71, 18 October 1861.
[97] B.L. Add. MS. 30297, f. 444. Corresp. Thomas Hugo II. Roach Smith to Hugo, 20 February 1860.

their intellectual approach. Freeman had chosen his family home at Somerleaze near Wells on distinctly antiquarian grounds.

It lay on what became the borderland of Welsh and English territory, after Ceawlin, the West-Saxon King had won the battle of Deorham in 577 [. . .] The special interest [. . .] of Somerset as a whole [. . .] was that in no other part of the country could the gradual growth of the West-Saxon kingdom which in time absorbed all England, be so clearly traced.[98]

Similarly Green, who was perhaps the unkindest of them all in his derision of antiquarian methods and forms of study, could quite candidly and cheerfully admit his own ignorance.

I didn't dare tell him [Joseph Burtt – an Assistant Keeper at the Public Record Office, and employed on the Westminster archives by the very man whom Green remembered as having imbued him with a love of history – Dean Stanley] the worst of the matter, namely that I had never seen a "Roll" or read a manuscript in my life [. . .] Of course, bore as it is, one must work at the "Rolls", but it seems to me that the Burtt and Hartshorne school forget that these may supplement and correct history, but that they never can *be* History.[99]

The recipient of this letter, Freeman, would have doubtless sympathised; his steadfast refusal to work in libraries and consequent ignorance of non-printed sources has often been remarked upon. An amateur ethos continued to prevail.

Freeman when he finally became Regius Professor at Oxford confessed to Goldwin Smith, 'Years ago to fill one of the historical chairs at Oxford was my alternative ambition with a seat in Parliament.'[100] And indeed, he had even planned to try for the Camden Professorship of Ancient History although that subject had never been one of his more prominent interests.[101] The principal ambition of many of these men was to gain public recognition, but not necessarily via historical eminence, hardly a surprising motive in an age which still had little to offer the professional academic. Their need to dissociate themselves from the amateur world of antiquarian interests hints at their relative insecurity. Not long before his death, Green felt he had finally won the acceptance he longed for.

What has cheered me most [. . .] has been the reception of The Making [of England]. I don't mean its sale and the praises of it, but the cessation at last of that attempt which has been so steadily carried on for the last ten years to drum me out of the world of historical scholars and get me among the "picturesque compilers".[102]

This acute sense of the value-laden distinction between the historian and the antiquarian was fundamental to the gradual development of a professional standing for the historian.

[98] W. R. W. Stephens, *op. cit.* pp. 250–1.

[99] J. Coll. Oxon. MS. 199, ff. 244–7, n.d. Charles Henry Hartshorne (1802–65), a Northamptonshire cleric and author of *Sepulchral Remains in Northamptonshire* (1840) and *Historical Memorials of Northampton* (1848) and other similar books. He was also a Fellow of the Society of Antiquaries.　　[100] W. R. W. Stephens, *op. cit.* p. 278, n.d.

[101] J. Coll. Oxon. MS. 192, f. 72, 17 July 1872. Freeman to Boyd Dawkins.

[102] J. Coll. Oxon. MS. 202, ff. 237–41, 8 May 1882. Green to Freeman.

IV

Archaeologists in this period formed a far smaller group. The casual and common assumption that antiquarianism and archaeology were identical, particularly in antiquarian circles where so many belonged to what were dubbed archaeological societies, hindered the formation and development of a separate self-image. In seeking an identification for this group, it is their concentration on artifacts and excavation that sets the archaeologists apart; they eschewed broad antiquarian concerns in favour of a more specific study of the material remains of the past. There were, as ever, exceptions: Canon Greenwell, primarily known as a barrow-digger, also wrote on Greek numismatics but for the most part early archaeologists – Thomas Bateman, Charles Warne, Austen Layard – were single-minded. Nonetheless as late as 1899, the dictionary *Men and Women of the Time* classified antiquarians and archaeologists, 'including Egyptologists' as a single category and historians as a further separate category. Thus Edward Peacock, author of *English Church Furniture* (1866) and *The Army List of Roundheads and Cavaliers* (1863), and Richard Ferguson, the Carlisle lawyer who wrote histories of Cumberland and Westmorland were classified alongside Flinders Petrie, Arthur Evans, Wallis Budge and Alexander Murray.[103]

However, the work in the East of Rawlinson, Layard and Loftus and that of J. T. Wood at Ephesus in the middle decades of the century, was never classified as antiquarian. Their physical removal from England lent them an exotic aura: Layard, in particular, was regarded primarily as a traveller. There was a romance attached to the great monuments of the world that the British barrow-digger could not hope to rival.

The record of the Human Past is not all contained in printed books. Man's history has been graven on the rock of Egypt, stamped on the brick of Assyria, enshrined in the marble of the Parthenon – it rises before us a majestic presence in the piled up arches of the Coliseum.[104]

Like the historians, archaeologists were a far less cohesive network either socially or intellectually than the antiquarians, although those working in the same region tended to know one another well. Henry Creswicke Rawlinson, for instance, was never actually involved in excavation, being a full-time official of the East India Company, but his valuable work on inscriptions and decipherment kept him in close touch with the excavations at Nimrud and Nineveh; both Loftus and Layard sent their finds to him when they required the particular skills of decipherment.

Archaeologists working in England at this time were all active members of

---

[103] Respectively a renowned Egyptologist, the discoverer of Minoan civilisation, a British Museum Egyptologist and a Keeper of Greek and Roman antiquities at the British Museum. V. G. Plarr, *Men and Women of the Time. A Dictionary of Contemporaries* (London, 1899).

[104] Charles Newton, 'On the Study of Archaeology', *Archaeological Journal* VIII (1851) 1–26 (p. 1).

archaeological societies, and frequently also Fellows of the Society of Antiquaries. Thomas Bateman, the foremost excavator of barrows in his day, was the local secretary of the Society of Antiquaries in his native Derbyshire; Charles Warne, the Dorset archaeologist, was active in his local archaeological society, the Dorsetshire Natural History and Antiquarian Field Club; and the eminent Sir John Evans, whose work with Prestwich had established the antiquity of the human race, was not only an active member of many societies but became President of the Numismatic Society (1874), the Anthropological Society (1878) and the Society of Antiquaries (1885). Those archaeologists working outside England – in Assyria, Greece and Palestine, for example – were rarely involved in societies other than those focused on their own area of work – the Egypt Exploration Fund, for instance, of which Petrie was secretary in the 1880s, or the Society of Biblical Archaeology, of which Peter le Page Renouf became President in 1887.

Unlike the historians, early archaeologists were rarely university educated; John Evans had been entered for Oxford but did not go, Flinders Petrie was educated at home, Rawlinson was schooled by the East India Company, George Smith had begun life apprenticed to a banknote engraving firm, and Pitt Rivers was sent to Sandhurst to follow in the footsteps of his military father. A remarkable number did succeed though, in making archaeology or more precisely excavation, a full-time occupation, if only for a portion of their adult lives. The most important exception is, of course, John Evans who ran a successful paper manufacturing firm in the Home Counties throughout his life, and found time for various trade organisations – the Society of Chemical Industry, the Paper-Makers Association – in addition to his celebrated archaeological work. Of those able to pursue their archaeological interests full-time, few were in teaching posts. Archaeological chairs were rare; there was little other than the Disney Chair at Cambridge before the 1880s. The Egyptologist Renouf compromised with the chairs of Ancient History and of Eastern Languages at the Roman Catholic University of Ireland in the 1850s. Excavation, rather, accounted for almost all the full-time work in archaeology, particularly for those working abroad.

In England, archaeology was more likely to remain an amateur preoccupation. Thomas Bateman, having inherited a vast family fortune, was able to dig barrows whenever he desired, but for most of those domiciled in England archaeology remained the more usual leisure-time pursuit. The first two incumbents of the Disney Chair were both practising clerics: John Marsden in Essex and Churchill Babington in Suffolk. Bateman's co-worker, William Greenwell, was also in holy orders as well as librarian to the Dean and Chapter of Durham Cathedral. George Clark, the contemporary authority on medieval military architecture, was an engineer and Sir John Maclean, who directed excavations of the Roman villa at Tockington, was a civil servant.

Abroad, most were reliant on public funding and had no livelihood other than their site work. A few, like Rawlinson, had permanent jobs outside England. George Smith was funded initially by money raised through the *Daily Telegraph* in 1873 to help him find the missing fragment of the Chaldean account of the Deluge. Thereafter his usual employers, the British Museum, paid his expenses until dysentery killed him in 1876.[105] John Turtle Wood who defected from his job as architect to the Smyrna and Aidin Railway to search for the Temple of Diana at Ephesus also received funding from the British Museum. So too did Austen Layard, after his first finds in Assyria, but he always regarded himself as badly treated by the museum. He wrote to Henry Ellis in 1849, 'I must [. . .] observe that the funds placed at my disposal for excavations and researches are much smaller than I could possibly have anticipated.'[106] Throughout his short career in excavation, Layard's relations with the Trustees of the British Museum were poor. Their apparent lack of interest and effort in shipping the treasures of Nimrud back to England – an arduous task – seemed to Layard symptomatic of their lack of sympathy with the manifold problems of excavation.[107]

The success rate of these excavators was remarkably high. Smith found the fragments of the Biblical legend within a few days; Wood spent four years at Ephesus but found the temple; Layard's finds were so rich that he became blasé, writing to Henry Ellis thus:

The expense [. . .] of digging through the immense mass of rubbish [. . .] is so considerable that I question whether upon the chance of finding more detached inscriptions or sculptures it would be very desirable to carry on extensive works.[108]

This emphasis on moveable antiquities was common to both those working abroad and in England. The interest stirred up by barrow finds often focused on the treasures found alongside the skeletons, making excavation a popular sport in mid-century England. The danger to artifacts thus increased with the broadening of its appeal. Both in England and abroad, the damage and desecration arising from careless excavation and primitive techniques was enormous. Layard and other 'experts' described wall-paintings fading before their eyes, and antiquities crumbling on exposure. Pottery, jewellery and skeletons alike all broke under the impact of a roughly handled spade as

---

[105] Seton Lloyd, *Foundations in the Dust. A Story of Mesopotamian Exploration* (London, 1947) pp. viii; 165.   [106] B.L. Add. MS. 38942, f. 1, 20 August 1849. Layard to Ellis.
[107] The best work on Layard is Gordon Waterfield's *Layard of Nineveh* (London, 1963) but see also N. Kubie, *Road to Nineveh: The Adventures and Excavations of Sir Austen Henry Layard* (London, 1965); R. Silverberg, *The Man Who Found Nineveh: The Story of Austen Henry Layard* (Surrey, 1968); Seton Lloyd, *op. cit.* Layard's description of the problems he encountered in moving the larger antiquities prior to shipping gives some idea of the enormity of the task. 'We encountered considerable difficulty in the operation owing to the rains which have recently fallen. Three hundred men, however, dragged the monster in three days through every obstacle of mud and sand', wrote Layard to Sir Stratford Canning in 1850. B.L. Add. MS. 38942, f. 24, 15 January 1857.   [108] B.L. Add. MS. 38942, f. 24. 15 January 1857. Layard to Ellis.

barrows and tumuli up and down England were explored.[109] Such damage was regrettable but unavoidable in the context of an age in which any interested party was free to excavate, and often to claim public money when doing so. David Hogarth, who became director of the British School of Archaeology at Athens in 1897, points out in his autobiography that when he was an undergraduate in the 1880s, universities offered no training in archaeology. He came to the subject through his travels in the East.[110] Some forty years earlier, the first major British excavator in Assyria had also acquired his archaeological interest through travel. The young Layard, bored after six years of legal work, left England on horseback bound for Ceylon and, he hoped, his fortune. Fascinated by the culture and politics of the East, he tarried in Baghdad where the nearby ruins of the Biblical cities of Nimrud and Nineveh captivated him.[111] He never got to Ceylon, but his excavating activities won him a good deal of acclaim – *Nineveh and its Remains* (1849) was an enormous publishing success. Having come to the attention of Stratford Canning, his short-lived archaeological activities were followed by a career in politics, a knowledge of the East being of considerable advantage at a time when the Eastern question was of more than a little interest to the Western powers.

A. H. L. F. Pitt Rivers who was perhaps the most important pioneer of the techniques which were to accompany archaeology into academic respectability was also, in this sense, an amateur. He had been an army officer for twenty-two years before becoming involved full-time in archaeology. His subsequent friendship with men such as Canon Greenwell and the anthropologist John Lubbock (who became his son-in-law in 1884 when he married Pitt Rivers' daughter Alice)[112] cemented his closely related interests in both evolution and archaeology. The excavations he undertook on inheriting the enormous Cranborne Chase estate derived from his practical experience both as a soldier and in fieldwork shared with men such as Greenwell rather than from any formal academic training. It was his rejection of the treasure-hunt aspect of archaeology which marked so momentous a turning-point, his insistence that common objects rather than the rare and the beautiful were the raw materials of the archaeologist.

Tedious as it may appear [. . .] to dwell on the discovery of odds and ends, that have no doubt, been thrown away by their owners as rubbish [. . .] yet it is by the study of such trivial details, that Archaeology is mainly dependent for determining the dates of earthworks.[113]

[109] Barry M. Marsden, *The Early Barrow Diggers* (Aylesbury, 1974) p. 25.

[110] D. G. Hogarth, *Accidents of an Antiquary's Life* (London, 1910). Introduction.

[111] Charles Lyell, the geologist, was another lawyer appalled at the prospect of a lifetime of litigation and the like. In his case, the doctrines of uniformitarianism rather than biblical archaeology were his escape route out of the legal profession.

[112] M. W. Thompson, *General Pitt-Rivers: Evolution and Archaeology in the Nineteenth Century* (Wiltshire, 1977) p. 33.

[113] A. H. L. F. Pitt Rivers. *Excavations in Cranborne Chase* (London, 1898) III. 9.

Petrie concurred with this view of the misplaced values of early archaeology. 'The science of observation, of registration, of recording was yet unthought of, nothing had a meaning unless it were an inscription or a sculpture.'[114]

As archaeology gradually emerged as an independent discipline, it shed its associations with antiquarianism and built up a network of men, skilled if formally lacking in training, familiar with one another and establishing for the first time communal standards of practice for the discipline. The boundaries of the community, by the end of the century, effectively excluded the antiquary.

V

In their differing attitudes to the institutional developments associated with their own sustenance, both intellectual and material, the three communities of antiquarianism, history and archaeology exhibited the characteristics which mark their separate existences. Archaeological societies remained a focal point for antiquarians both socially and intellectually throughout the century. Few did not belong at the very least to their local county society and, more often than not, to one or more of the national societies too. The historians, as their academic stature grew, held themselves aloof from these amateur organisations. Archaeologists were less inclined to dismiss antiquarianism than were historians, perhaps because of their own close and only gradually severed association with it. Even after the tentative establishment of a separate discipline of archaeology, antiquarian societies were not entirely spurned. Whilst Prestwich took his evidence of human antiquity – antediluvial flints and hand axes – to the Royal Society, it was to the Society of Antiquaries that John Evans presented the same findings in 1859. And it was largely an amateur impetus which led to the founding of the specialist societies later in the century.

Attitudes to the various government initiatives undertaken in this period also highlight the different nature of these three groups. The slightly brittle hostility of the Oxford school of historians towards those active in record research and administration differs markedly from the enthusiasm with which these ventures were greeted by the antiquarian community. For the archaeologists, the excitement over written sources was largely irrelevant. The only real archaeological advance sponsored by government in this period was the Protection of Ancient Monuments Act which, after the protracted efforts of Sir John Lubbock, was finally passed in 1882.[115]

The establishment of university courses in related disciplines was the other institutional field where differences between the three communities were obvious. The activity in such institutions where, from the 1870s on, an ever increasing number of undergraduate historians emerged, left antiquarians

[114] W. M. F. Petrie, *Seventy Years in Archaeology* (London, 1931) p. 19.
[115] See Chapter 5, p. 123.

unmoved. They clearly did not regard such developments as in any way relevant to their own interests and paid scant attention to the growth of university history. For the historians, however, this was the crucial development, the recognition of the serious worth of their studies. The increasing number of historians employed in the examining and teaching of undergraduates and the creation of new professorships spelled the possibility of financially secure full-time employment in the field, freed from the vicissitudes of seeking patrons or odd jobs. It is little wonder that historians actively applauded these moves and sought to extend them. Again, archaeologists were in a different position. Their relative lack of recognition in the university curriculum did nothing to bolster their sense of a collective image. Their coming together as a community and their absorption into academic circles were roughly simultaneous; chairs of archaeology began to be created and – more importantly – towards the close of the century to be filled by those worthy of the title. It is inconceivable that the first Disney Professor of Archaeology, the Reverend J. H. Marsden, doyen of the Essex Archaeological Society, could have filled that or any other academic post in archaeology at the end of the century.

By that juncture, however, antiquarians, historians, and even archaeologists had begun to form three distinct and separate communities. Any complete notion of community must embrace the social aspects of their intellectual pursuits and the social homogeneity arising from that. These are factors which reinforce the idea that these groups deserve to be seen separately as communities of scholarship and communities of interest. Specifically, such a definition rests not merely on the particular interests that they shared but on their agreement about the social value of their studies, and their own evaluation of themselves within that context. Their sense of a common purpose, their unity against those they felt undermined the security of interests which served to define the communities and their social intercourse as well as intellectual and institutional closeness – all these are factors which give shape and definition to these communities.

The idea of an 'invisible college' comprising informal networks within a specific area of study, in which collaboration, citation of one another's works and informal communication have been seen as tangible evidences of existence, is one which resembles the make-up of these groups.[116] All three of the historical communities fit this description: collaboration and collective work was lauded

[116] Derek J. de Solla Price & D. de B. Beaver, 'Collaboration in an Invisible College', *American Psychologist* 21 (1966) 1011–18; Diana Crane, 'Social Structure in a group of scientists: A Test of the "Invisible College" Hypothesis', *American Sociological Review* 34 (1969) 335–52; Derek J. de Solla Price, *Little Science, Big Science* (Columbia, 1963). David Allen in his work on British naturalists in the nineteenth century also found evidence, particularly in the field of botany, of what he called 'network research'. D. E. Allen, *The Naturalist in Britain: A Social History* (Harmondsworth, 1978) p. 110. In her recent work on the professionalisation of history in late Victorian and Edwardian Britain, Doris Goldstein has also made use of this model.; *loc. cit.* p. 23.

as a scholarly ideal, they cited and acknowledged one another's work freely, and the informal communications on their research they maintained with one another were important factors in determining their social and intellectual cohesion. Antiquarians corresponded with one another constantly, requesting information, passing on their discoveries, correcting facts; the meetings of the various societies frequently included contributions passed on by letter from those unable to attend but eager to exhibit their latest novelty. Amongst historians, collective efforts such as the *Lives* Green edited for Macmillans, Freeman's *Historic Towns* series for Longmans, the *Cambridge Modern History* and, of course, the *English Historical Review* are monuments to collaborative effort in a community where encroaching specialisation spelled the gradual introduction of a more competitive individualism. In archaeological circles, it was the joint efforts of excavator Layard and decipherer Rawlinson that fired the imagination of the British public for the treasures of the Persian deserts, whilst at home men such as Bateman rarely dug alone.

The relationship between these invisible colleges or communities of interest and the formation of élites is a palpable one. Arguing that science rapidly became a major cultural resource in Victorian England, Morrell and Thackray's description of their 'Gentlemen of Science's' own understanding and interpretation of the values of their studies, moral as well as intellectual, could equally describe the spiritual tones so often adopted by the nineteenth-century antiquarian or historian. Science, said Morrell and Thackray, 'came to be seen as [. . .] the guarantor of God's order and rule, the proper way of gaining knowledge, and the key to national prosperity and international harmony'.[117] History, too, was just such a cultural resource if William Gladstone may be considered a representative voice of educated opinion. Congratulating Stubbs on his *Constitutional History* Gladstone rehearsed just such sentiments:

I am convinced that the thorough [. . .] study of history is a noble, invigorating manly study, essentially political and judicial, fitted for and indispensable to, a free country. But rightly or wrongly, I go much farther than this; and I believe that it is the truly historical treatment of Christianity, and of all the religious experience of mankind, which [. . .] will supply under God effectual bulwarks against the rash and violent unbelief [. . .] rushing in upon us.[118]

Stubbs doubtless concurred; as he had stoutly declared some years previously, 'I do not believe that a Dissenter could write a History of England.'[119]

The creation of a closely defined élite, marked more by who was excluded than by who was embraced, was a means of limiting access to those deemed acceptable on both social and intellectual grounds. The high degree of social homogeneity amongst these groups, reinforced by the development of a genealogy through marriage and family ties, suggests that a process of

[117] Morrell & Thackray, *op. cit.* p. 96.   [118] W. H. Hutton, *op. cit.* p. 147. 27 December 1875.
[119] Bodl. MS. Eng. misc. e. 148, ff. 44–5, 3 November 1859. Stubbs to Freeman.

selection did indeed exclude the unacceptable. Such a selection operated on two levels; obviously the field was, in the first instance, open only to those with the education and leisure to enjoy it. At a secondary level, unconscious selection through this inexorable defining of boundaries further limited the field. Some, like William Lecky, kept deliberately apart from these networks of contact. Others – such as the Dissenters whom Stubbs feared so greatly – did surmount the barriers.[120] Nonetheless, social familiarity and ease were important qualifications – almost always necessary but seldom sufficient conditions for entry into the community.

The pattern of this development of self-defining élites changed discernibly over the century. T. W. Heyck has interpreted it as a shift, dating from the 1870s, from the dominance of the tradition of the 'man of letters' to that of the 'intellectual'.[121] In historical circles certainly, the shift was not so simple. The growing strength of historians and archaeologists derived from a whole range of factors. The creation of university departments in those fields, accompanied as it was by the emergence of a corps of full-time paid professionals had as its corollary an increasing emphasis on the fragmentation of historical and archaeological knowledge and the phenomenon of specialisation. This mapping out of the separate territories of archaeology and history, and their deliberate dissociation from the image of the polymath was associated with the development of techniques exclusive to each of the two disciplines. Archaeology became increasingly quantitative and reliant on technical testing – Petrie's *Inductive Metrology* (1877) is an early example of the new approach – whilst history simultaneously developed rigorous rules for the reading and interpretation of source materials. Moreover, the concentration of serious research into the universities not only channelled funds in that direction but also transferred the accompanying prestige to those institutions. Increasingly, 'localism' acquired pejorative overtones. Roy Porter noted in later nineteenth-century geological circles, 'the conflicts of interest between the élite and the weekend amateur' provoked by 'the narrowing specialisation and complexity of élite research'.[122] The antiquarian community suffered a similar fate to that of amateur geologists. Appropriation by the new professional communities meant that although the antiquarian network did not cease to exist, it found itself increasingly relegated to a back seat by the new historical and archaeological establishment primarily by virtue of its lack of an academic and thus professional identity. The growing precision of archaeological techniques, the rise of the professional historian and the university training associated with these developments made antiquarians redundant on the national scene by the end of the 1880s.

Thus did the historical communities of nineteenth century England define

[120] Although not always successfully – see Chapter 5 for the disastrous case of the Catholic W. B. D. D. Turnbull.   [121] T. W. Heyck, *op. cit.* p. 15.   [122] Roy Porter, *loc. cit.* p. 830.

themselves or find themselves defined through social and intellectual homogeneity. Fewer and fewer individuals could straddle the dividing lines between
them as the century wore on and the demarcation grew sharper and more
important. Correspondingly, taxonomic shifts were evident in the linguistic
separation of the terms 'historian', 'archaeologist' and 'antiquarian'. This was
a significant step for the three communities. The liberal use earlier in the
century of the three terms to mean roughly the same thing was nowhere
acceptable at the end of the century. The emergence of a more specific
application of the three words was the logical corollary of the shift in values: as
'historian' and 'archaeologist' came to signify the trained and respected
professional, 'antiquarian' acquired the sub-meaning amateur, and with it a
definite depreciation in value. By the 1880s, three separate communities thus
existed on the historical scene, each united not just in a recognition of common
enterprise and purpose but keenly aware of the social values and standing of
their discipline. The spirit of pure intellect was never to reign supreme in
Victoria's class-bound England: social and economic considerations were often
as much the determinants of exclusion from these fraternities as were
intellectual evaluations. Their sense of community was a strong one, and one
which as the boundaries grew more specific, they were ever more keen to
protect.

3

∽∽

Individuals in concert

Little popular county histories are to be found in every farmhouse in the country, where the editors or compilers have contrived, by mingling the *utile* of the directory with the *dulce* of historic memoranda, to stimulate the curiosity of every class.

(William Stubbs, Two Lectures on the Present State and
Prospects of Historical Study)

I

The learned society in both provincial and metropolitan England was a characteristic institution of the age, existing alongside a vast range of other voluntary and principally charitable organisations. Membership of such societies was often an entrée into educated and respectable social circles. Learned societies were primarily concerned either with scientific knowledge – and this included the many literary and philosophical societies which had sprung up in the late eighteenth and early nineteenth centuries – or with history and archaeology. The rapid and sustained success of the latter was such that, by the end of the century, few counties did not boast at least one antiquarian organisation devoted to the elucidation of the past of the locality.

Alongside these county-based societies there grew a host of printing clubs publishing hitherto inedited and inaccessible manuscripts relating to the history of England. At a national level there were also such bodies as the Society of Antiquaries which was nearing the centenary of its incorporation and the two rival organisations founded in 1843, the British Archaeological Association and the Archaeological Institute. Other more specialised organisations in these areas followed in later years, such as the Royal Historical Society (1868), the Society of Biblical Archaeology (1870), the Society for the Protection of Ancient Buildings (1877) and the Egypt Exploration Fund (1882). The history of these primarily amateur organisations is, however, a neglected chapter of social and intellectual history. 'It is characteristic of an organisation such as ours that its history should be somewhat uneventful.' The council of the Norfolk and Norwich Archaeological Society in its report for 1873 thus gave a clear indication of why antiquarian activities have failed to find favour with

40

posterity. These historical and antiquarian societies were obviously limited in their appeal, although their success in attracting large memberships was often impressive. They have largely escaped the notice of the historian, not simply because of their inevitably narrow appeal, but because of the seeming predictability of their interests and activities. Notwithstanding the general truth of that, they do remain an important if small phenomenon in institutional terms through their role as the collective voice of antiquarian concern.

The first open society to take root in England was the Surtees Society. This Durham-based society founded in 1834 to commemorate their late local historian Robert Surtees proposed:

The publication of inedited Manuscripts, illustrative of the intellectual, the moral, the religious, and the social condition of [these] parts of England and Scotland [. . .] which constituted the Antient Kingdom of Northumberland.[1]

The sceptics were quick to reply.

I assure you it is with much reluctance that I should appear to throw cold water upon [the] [. . .] project; [. . .] antiquarian researches are not sufficiently and generally interesting in the present enlightened alias darkened Age to perpetuate the proposed Society.[2]

Their pessimism proved unfounded. The success of the Surtees Society – and its continued existence more than 150 years after its inception – attests to the potential and actual depth of interest in the annals of the past. Its first anniversary celebrated in Durham in July 1835 boasted that 'the field of which [the Society] has taken possession has been hitherto totally unoccupied by any past or present association of literary men' and it looked forward to a time when 'no longer confined to the Saxon kingdom of Northumberland, it may consider the whole of Britain as the field of its labours'.[3] It began publication with a subscribing membership of 101, over half of whom were resident locally in the north-east of England; ten years later the membership had risen to 184.

The early English printing societies followed in the footsteps of the earlier Scots model and indeed James Raine, founder of the Surtees Society, had sought advice from the experienced Edinburgh antiquary David Irving on the setting up of a printing club. Justly proud of their own successes and cognisant of their intellectual pre-eminence in the latter half of the eighteenth century, the men of the Bannatyne were the model for the developments in England during the 1830s and 40s. The English community found their interests in such ventures much boosted, however, when the revelations of the Select Committee appointed to investigate the waywardness of the six Record Commissions were made public in 1837. The financial and editorial incompetence of these

---

[1] Surtees Society. Rules. 1834.
[2] Surtees Society MSS; Durham Cathedral, Dean and Chapter Library, Prior's Kitchen. Correspondence file 1. 1/37. L. G. Usher to James Raine, 14 May 1834.
[3] Surtees Society First Annual Report, 14 July 1835.

Commissions had caused considerable disquiet even before their disbandment in 1836. No alternative government initiative was offered until 1838 when the Public Record Office Act was passed and it is F. J. Levy's contention that the Camden Society founded in that year stepped into this gap in a desperate attempt to dispel the pessimism and apathy which seemed confirmed by the demise of the Record Commissions. Levy presents an overly gloomy prognosis. 'What evidence existed seemed to indicate that private printing of records would be a failure; the same evidence suggested that there was no real interest in serious historical research.'[4]

The Record Commissions had certainly encountered enormous difficulties in disposing of their publications, let alone in selling them. Not only did they resort on occasion to giving copies away but, in desperation, to selling volumes as waste for rendering into pulp or glue. The fault, however, lay not with the lack of enthusiasm suggested by Levy but with the actual publications the Commissions chose to sanction. Their editions were cumbersome, expensive, off-putting and moreover often poorly edited. Private printing certainly posed problems, principally practical in nature, but the demand for affordable and readable editions of ancient manuscripts existed in abundance. If the regional isolation of the Surtees Society in north-eastern England prevented it from acting as the catalyst, the Camden Society certainly assumed that rôle. Neither demand nor supply faltered; after the foundation of the Camden Society in 1838, the printing club – a logical extension of the tradition of subscription publishing – became a firmly established medium for the reception and distribution of editions of old documents. And as they proliferated, so the clubs sought more adventurous ground; by the later years of the 1840s societies devoted to ancient music, portraiture and early medical texts were all able to command a viable membership.

A few followed the example of the Surtees Society in limiting themselves to regionally specific publications. Of these, the Chetham Society – 'Remains Historical and Literary Connected with the Palatine Counties of Lancaster and Chester' – alone survived the century. Founded by the lawyer James Crossley and the Reverend Thomas Corser in Manchester in 1843 it commanded the support and influence of a considerable proportion of Manchester's business and professional classes whose reasons for subscribing often rested more on a sense of local pride and duty than a penchant for antiquarianism.[5] Similar attempts in Berkshire, Essex and Lincolnshire proved luckless, though the

---

[4] F. J. Levy, 'The Founding of the Camden Society', *Victorian Studies* VII (1964) pp. 295–305 (p. 305).

[5] J. Tait, 'The Chetham Society: A Retrospect', *Chetham Miscellanies* n.s. VII (1939) pp. 1–26 (p. 4). Tait suggests that the business and professional classes joined the society out of social considerations in the main. He lists bankers, landowners and lawyers as prominent amongst its editors between 1843 and 1883.

Berkshire Ashmolean Society produced three creditable volumes all edited by well-known figures.

Twenty-seven separate attempts to found printing clubs followed the evident success of the Camden and Surtees societies of which only five were outright failures. Many others foundered after the publication of a handful of volumes whilst some deliberately ceased functioning after successfully completing publication of a stated body of texts. (See Appendix II.) One such was the Parker Society founded in 1840 which set itself the specific tasks of

reprinting, without abridgement, alteration or omission of the best works of the Fathers and early Writers of the Reformed English Church [. . .] between the accession of King Edward VI and the death of Queen Elizabeth; secondly, the printing of such remains of other writers of the sixteenth century as may appear desirable [. . .] and thirdly, the printing of some Manuscripts of the same authors, hitherto unpublished.[6]

Under the aegis of the established Church, the Society commanded a list of subscribers in excess of seven thousand, the largest membership of any society in this period. Its appeal was unusual in antiquarian terms, being more concerned with the principle of devotion than with intellectual curiosity. In 1853, having issued fifty-four volumes it closed its proceedings, satisfied that it had successfully erected 'a bulwark against Popish Error'.[7]

The Parker Society frequently intoned the national importance of its venture. Such was the consciousness not just of this bastion of Anglicanism but also of the secular societies of the 1840s. Their argument that private enterprise was undertaking work of public and national significance in the face of government failure to fulfil its obligations in this direction lent the clubs a certain sobriety.

It was in the full conviction that this state of things ought not to continue, that a number of gentlemen formed themselves into a voluntary association, with the object of collecting and publishing all the materials for English history.[8]

The Anglia Christiana Society of 1836 which survived only three years similarly stressed the need for 'the aid of *individual* zeal and liberality'.[9]

Accessibility was the keynote of the societies' activities, albeit within carefully defined social boundaries. The ceiling on membership numbers imposed by some printing societies was a largely practical measure designed to minimise financial and accounting difficulties. Nevertheless, the texts published by, for example, the Anglia Christiana Society which were reproduced in Latin without translation, were a telling comment on the assumptions these societies made about their membership. Their appeal was to a monied and

---

[6] Parker Society Laws, 1840.   [7] Parker Society Prospectus, 1840.
[8] J. M. Kemble, 'Plan of the English Historical Society/Venerabilis Bedae [. . .] Stevenson', *British and Foreign Review* VII (July–October 1838) xiii, pp. 167–92 (p. 178).
[9] Anglia Christiana Society Prospectus, n.d. but Brit. Mus. catalogue suggests 1846.

educated readership. In 1838, 20% of the Camden Society's members were clergymen, 9% held legal qualifications and 36% were Fellows of the Society of Antiquaries of London.[10] Outside London, the Chetham with a membership of 341 in 1843 – its year of foundation – derived 91% of its members locally in Lancashire and Cheshire. 10.5% of its members were clerical whilst less than 2% claimed membership of the Society of Antiquaries.[11] The Durham-based Surtees Society, on the other hand, had a local membership only 50% of its total of 184 ten years after its foundation. Of that total, 25% were clerics and 10% Fellows of the Society of Antiquaries. They were catering, in short, for a manageable 'in house' community.

The enthusiasm generated by the clubs was not always matched by an expectation of exacting standards from contributors. Beriah Botfield, a well-known Northamptonshire antiquary, revealed the problem.

> I am afraid of making but a sorry editor of the Surteesian volume, but if you know of any works likely to throw light upon my darkness as regards the middle ages I hope you will not hesitate to indicate them.[12]

It was not want of remuneration which forced the societies' reliance on willing rather than able editors. Editors were rarely paid for their trouble, save the actual cost of transcription. The task was considered an honour in itself, and it represented, after all, an easy means of access for aspiring authors and editors.[13] The pioneering work of these societies was laying the groundwork of future expertise, but in the meantime a degree of inaccuracy for which later generations were to pillory their forerunners was unavoidable. A. Hamilton-Thompson commenting on the early publications of the Surtees Society noted that the Durham manuscript used for their first publication, Canon Raine's *Reginaldi*, had not been collated with any of the alternative manuscript versions. Of Joseph Stevenson's 1841 edition of the *Liber vitae ecclesiae dunelmensis*, he remarked: 'This text made no attempt to indicate handwritings and additions in

---

[10] No regional breakdown was available for this period, but other London-based societies of the same period suggest a common south-east preponderance. Percy Society (1840) – 74% London members; Historical Society of Science (1840) – 69% London members; Hakluyt Society (1846) – 62% London and south-east members.

[11] A figure which suggests that the newly wealthy industrialists of the north had little time for the traditional institutions of the metropolis.

[12] Durham Cathedral, Dean and Chapter Library, Prior's Kitchen. Surt. Soc. MSS. Corresp. File 2. 2/ 31. Beriah Botfield, 26 May 1835.

[13] When the London printer J.G. Nichols took over the treasurership of the Surtees Society in 1842, he was surprised to find that payments had been made to editors of the society's volumes contrary to the usual practice. A series of letters passed back and forth between him and his predecessor and James Raine, the founder, in which Nichols frequently expressed concern at this 'new branch of Expenditure termed Editing [which has] risen to such an amount as to form quite an important feature in the general distribution of the funds'. (3/7) It was an expenditure the society could ill afford and Nichols was quick to rid them of this unique feature. Surt. Soc. MSS. Corresp. File 3. See Chapter 7 for a discussion of this problem in the later years of the century.

the original, and often misplaces entries. It is further disfigured by a very large number of misreadings.[14] It was some time before high standards of editing became common. In 1870, the Reverend A. B. Grosart complained, 'I have the Camden Society's *King Johan*: but alas! alas! it literally swarms with errata.'[15]

After the flurry of the 1840s, the foundation of new societies devoted to publishing textual material slowed down. The opening of the new Public Record Office in Chancery Lane and the initiation of both the Rolls Series publications and the Historical Manuscripts Commission by the 1870s diminished the sense of urgency and duty which had fuelled their rapid proliferation. The societies welcomed government's entry into the field.

The Council beg to congratulate the Society on the important steps now being taken by the Master of the Rolls [. . .] for the promotion of English Historical Literature, by the publication of Calendars of our State Papers and editions of our early Chronicles [. . .] Whilst these publications are in progress some portion of the original design of the Society will probably fall into partial abeyance [. . .] But this is not a circumstance which will be in any degree detrimental to the Society. On the contrary, the limitation of our operations to Documents, Letters, Diaries and Poems, and other works not contemplated by the Master of the Rolls, will probably tend to advance the interest and popularity of the Society's publications.[16]

Only two new publishing societies were founded in each of the two decades of the 1860s and 1870s. In 1864 Frederick Furnivall formed the Early English Text Society and in 1869 came the genealogical and heraldic Harleian Society. In the 1870s the tradition of regional publishing was strengthened by the foundation of the William Salt Archaeological Society in 1879 (which in 1936 became the Staffordshire Record Society) and the Lancashire and Cheshire Record Society in 1878. 1883 saw the emergence of the Pipe Roll Society. All these still function today and the popularity of this form of organisation showed no signs of waning. From their early years on, none had memberships of less than two hundred.

II

The middle years of the century also saw the foundation and growth of the county archaeological societies alongside the printing clubs. Often there was a considerable overlap in membership between the two, but the county societies embraced very different objectives and in consequence demanded a different

[14] A. Hamilton-Thompson, 'The Surtees Society, 1834–1934', *Publications of the Surtees Society* 150 (1939).
[15] RHS Library, UCL Lib. Camd. Soc. MS. C4. Miscellanea. Interleaved in J. G. Nichols, *Descriptive Catalogue of the Works of the Camden Society* (London, 1862) between pp. 2 and 3. Poor editing was not confined to the private sector, however. Chapter 5 details similar problems of scholarship in government-backed projects of this type.
[16] Camd. Soc. Council Report for 1857. Vol. 70, pp. 3–6 of insert.

type of membership. Whereas subscribers to bodies such as the Camden Society, the Hakluyt Society or the Musical Antiquarian Society were required only to exchange their subscription for the annual publications of the club, the county societies encouraged and depended upon a more active and participatory membership. They all held annual summer excursions, generally of two or three days duration and most held quarterly or monthly meetings in addition, where papers were read and objects exhibited.

Marinell Ash, describing the early Scottish printing clubs, spoke of their 'fusion of conviviality and utility', a unity which their English successors in the publishing field had failed to maintain but which passed to the county societies instead.[17] Other than their annual general meetings, bodies such as the Surtees or Granger Societies were anonymous publishing outfits, generally not even maintaining a library for the use of members. For the more peripheral of their number – the bulk of the subscribers – the distribution of the annual volumes was their sole contact with the societies. In the county organisations by contrast, the members were bound together specifically by their dedication to the promotion of local history and by the social ties created through these endeavours. The encouragement of personal investigation and exploration was directed through the issue of sets of 'queries' designed to assist the observer. The results of these inquiries were intended as the first stage in the collection of material for projected county histories which were often the principal aim of such institutions. The Bedfordshire Architectural and Archaeological Society opened the first volume of its journal in 1867, twenty years after its formation by stating: 'From the Commencement of this Society, it has been the primary object of its supporters to provide a more perfect County History than has hitherto been attempted.' The 'Queries and Directions for the Assistance of Correspondents' published by the Essex Archaeological Society in the first volume of its annual transactions gave careful instructions on the correct method for cleaning brass, taking rubbings and removing whitewash. It also remarked rather archly that 'plans and elevations accurately drawn, with measurements, are more valuable than picturesque sketches of buildings &c.'. The Wiltshire Archaeological and Natural History Society, founded in 1853, divided up its queries under the following heads: Parochial History; Ancient Buildings, Monuments and Antiquities; Traditions and Customs; Idiom and Dialect; the Church; the Churchyard; questions on Ornithology, Entomology and Geology.

The particular attention to ecclesiastical architecture typically displayed by the societies was prompted primarily by the growth of the ecclesiological movement in the 1830s and 1840s which demarcated the battlelines of the debate over theology and aesthetics, the principles of which came to represent

---

[17] Marinell Ash, *The Strange Death of Scottish History* (Edinburgh, 1980) p. 59.

for these early societies a crusade of moral importance. This doctrinal element exerted a powerful influence on the course of their development. Ecclesiology was virtually coterminous with the Cambridge Camden Society founded in 1839. The society promulgated a devotion to the architecture of the English Middle Ages as representing the truest expression of the Christian religion and an embodiment of the virtues it promoted. Many of the county societies echoed the principle. In a self-congratulatory address to the Leicestershire Architectural and Archaeological Society in 1869, James Thompson enunciated the doctrine.

The [. . .] Society has [. . .] exercised a wholesome influence in the formation of a correct taste [. . .] If the medieval spirit, as embodied in the stone walls, and towers, and details of its cathedrals, its churches, its castles, and its home was one that spurned deceit and enkindled self-sacrifice [. . .] then let us thank that spirit.

The Cambridge Camden Society was contemporary with the popular resurgence of interest in the Middle Ages and in Gothic architecture, but its involvement in doctrinal questions – over the functional and aesthetic requirements demanded by Protestant forms of worship – and the influence of the Tractarian element on its governing committee led to its identification as the artistic and aesthetic concomitant to theological Tractarianism.[18] Not surprisingly, a sister society was founded in Oxford where the Tractarian movement was at its strongest – the Oxford Society for Promoting the Study of Gothic Architecture. Both societies assumed a militant Protestantism when the issue of secession became urgent in the 1850s. Benjamin Webb, secretary of the Cambridge Society, wrote to his Oxford counterpart in 1852.

In cases of secession we have generally removed the name of such persons [. . .] Sometimes seceders have resigned of their own accord. We have always considered that the Law requiring Members to be members of the Church of England, implied that on their ceasing to be members of the Church of England they *ipso facto* ceased to be members of the Society.[19]

When ecclesiology moved outward from the ancient universities, and the Tractarian furore began to peter out, two types of society ensued; those concentrating exclusively on architecture and maintaining ecclesiological principles and those which, either from the start or latterly, combined architectural with archaeological interests in a more secular manner[20] (see Appendix III). Most of the archaeological societies continued to devote considerable attention to architecture, and in particular to ecclesiastical architecture but it was only the directly architectural and militantly

[18] J. F. White, *The Cambridge Movement: The Ecclesiologists and the Gothic Revival* (London, 1962) pp. 70; 136.

[19] Bodl. Lib. Oxford Architectural & Historical Society MSS. Dep. c. 589, f. 424. Benjamin Webb to Secretary, OAHS, 11 March 1852.

[20] Archaeological interests were, of course, taken to mean those of local history and topography at this juncture. See Chapter 4.

ecclesiological societies who restricted their membership to Anglicans, and invested their government in the local clergy. One such was the Architectural Society of the Archdeaconry of Northampton founded in 1844 whose rules stated explicitly

that the society be composed of [. . .] Ordinary Members to consist of Clergymen and Lay members of the Church, [and] that Rural Deans within the Archdeaconry [. . .] be ex-officio Members of the Committee, on their signifying an intention to become Members.

Of its 120 original members, 77% were clerics. In Lincolnshire, 64% of the 112 members of the local society in 1850 were in holy orders. Rule IV in the rules of the Architectural and Archaeological Society for the County of Buckingham laid down a membership charge of 5/- but exempted 'all persons holding the office of Churchwardens in any Parish of the County'.

In general, the non-denominational county societies were far less stridently Anglican than the ecclesiological societies. By the close of the century, the latter had largely disappeared or cast aside their overtly religious tendencies, although there were exceptions. The Worcestershire Diocesan Architectural Society had expanded to include archaeology within its province in 1876 but retained its diocesan and therefore Anglican position until 1910. This religious factionalism in the early years was partly a form of retrenchment in the face of what was seen as the danger of encroaching Catholicism. The pull of the medieval revival and the rallying call of Gothic as a national and Christian style were of major importance and it was this aspect of the architectural debate to which the county archaeological societies responded; they were able to do so because the effect of the move out of the universities had been to replace much of the aesthetic preponderance with an antiquarian bias. Ecclesiology in provincial society was more specifically about the past, and in practical terms therefore it was largely concerned with ensuring that the monuments of the past – churches in particular – were not destroyed.

The most immediate catalyst for the wave of county archaeological societies which began to appear after 1845 was the Archaeological Association founded in December 1843, 'for the encouragement and prosecution of researches into the arts and monuments of the early and middle ages'. The Association had been rapidly torn asunder by a petty internal squabble and had re-formed as two separate groups, the British Archaeological Association and the Archaeological Institute. They published two separate but similar journals and undertook work of a very close affinity. Before the rift the original Association had issued the first volume of its house journal, the *Archaeological Journal*, a title retained after 1845 by the Archaeological Institute. The new British Archaeological Association called their publication the *Journal of the British Archaeological Association*. This first undivided issue had laid down the principles on which the new organisation intended to proceed. Albert Way (the figure around whom the seceding faction clustered) expounded these ideas in his introduction, noting 'an increasing attention [. . .] paid to ancient memorials of a national and medieval character'. He unfolded a plan for exploiting that interest, a plan which was to serve both societies after their separation.

A central and permanent Committee has been formed of persons resident in London, and proposing to hold meetings every fortnight during the greater portion of the year [. . .] The primary intent of the Committee is to collect and impart [. . .] information; it is therefore desirable to organise a system of local correspondence.[21]

In practice, that network of correspondents never materialised. Enthusiasm tended to focus itself around the local bodies whose formation had been prompted by the two national associations rather than around the associations themselves. Both organisations continued to hold itinerant annual congresses, varying the venue each year though never holding them in London, an idea culled from the practice of the British Association for the Advancement of Science.[22]

The British Archaeological Association and the Archaeological Institute maintained a predominantly south-eastern membership, as figure 1 illustrates. Between 1838 and 1886, 30% of their summer congresses were held in towns in south-east England and another 27% in the south-west. Other than the excitement generated by their annual summer congresses, however, they exercised little influence over the local societies which followed in their wake. The stir caused by their annual meetings was largely due to the opportunities they offered for local antiquaries to congregate with like-minded men from elsewhere in the kingdom, and to display their familiarity with the antiquities and curiosities of their own locale. It was not awe but rather a sense of shared enthusiasm which guaranteed their appeal.

The Society of Antiquaries of London, the oldest established of the national antiquarian associations, was not held in high regard in the middle years of the century. It had a membership of 708 in 1838, the greater part of which was nominal. Of its members 14% were titled; for the aristocracy, the fellowship was merely one more honour to which their lineage entitled them. There were notable exceptions amongst whom Albert Conyngham, Lord Londesborough, Viscount Mahon (Lord Stanhope) and Lord Talbot de Malahide stand out as three men genuinely enthusiastic about antiquarian matters and active in the affairs of the society. For the most part, active membership in this period was confined to the same 'inner circle' of antiquarians who organised the two new archaeological bodies: men such as Albert Way, Thomas Wright, Thomas

[21] Albert Way, 'Introduction', *Arch. Jnl.* i (1844) pp. 1–6, (p. 1).
[22] The Wiltshire antiquarian John Britton adverts to this debt in his inaugural address to the new Wiltshire society in October 1853. In the account of the evening conversazione given in the first volume of their magazine in 1854, he maintains that archaeological societies have 'followed in its wake and imitated some of its principles and regulations'. (p. 47). In their book on the British Association for the Advancement of Science, however, Morrell & Thackray show how thoroughly a small élite managed to oust that ideal. Morrell & Thackray, *op. cit.*

Figure 1. British Archaeological Association and Archaeological Institute, 1845:
Regional membership as percentage of total

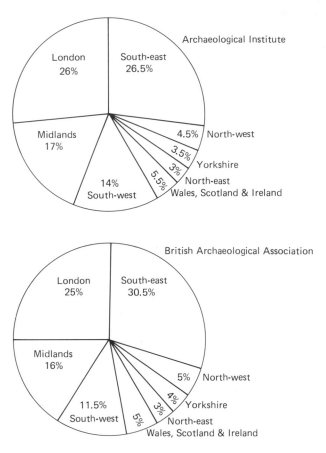

N.B. Oxfordshire and Northamptonshire have been incorporated as part of the midlands, Lincolnshire as part of the north-east and East Anglia has been included with the south-east.

Pettigrew, W. J. Thoms, Thomas Crofton Croker. They were also active in the foundation of many of the printing clubs; Crofton Croker was associated with the Camden Society, Wright with the Caxton and both had helped set up the Percy Society.

The intellectual bankruptcy of the Society of Antiquaries, amusingly described by Charles Hartshorne in a letter of 1839, made both the national and local new societies further determined to rekindle enthusiasm and advance the reputation of their pursuits.

I went to the Antiquaries for admission on thursday week, and came away not vastly impressed with the talents of the body assembled [. . .] All these men, no not all, but the powers that be are vastly behind the time. It is quite ridiculous to see how they copy and borrow from each other how thoroughly conventional they are what little freshness of mind they possess.[23]

As the provincial societies grew in strength and number, a separation from rather than a partnership with these national bodies emerged. When the London and Middlesex Society was founded in 1855, it was at pains to distinguish its own local functions from those of the national bodies also resident in the capital.

There are, indeed, three[24] institutions in London which devote their attention to archaeological pursuits; but they possess no local character whatever. They are like the staff of an army; they are not attached to any regiment, but they exercise a power and an influence over the entire system of operations. I apprehend that our object will be entirely and exclusively local.[25]

The encouragement to active participation built into the structure of the archaeological societies made them unlike both the printing clubs where membership was no more than an annual subscription and the national societies, too large in scope and scattered in membership to be more than repositories of information.

Communications to the national societies came frequently in the form of letters intended to be read aloud, for few non-London members could afford to visit the metropolis regularly. Thus, the overwhelming utility of a local society pursuing similar interests. The advantages of confining those interests to the immediate area was that not only could members meet and socialise locally but that their investigations would not involve them in the difficulty and expense created by being away from home. The localism which was so prominent a principle of the county societies was fuelled partially by the practical gains to be accrued from such an arrangement.

Unlike the printing clubs, archaeological societies did not ccasc to proliferate after the first flush of enthusiasm. Some were purely archaeological bodies, some architectural and archaeological in scope, some combined natural history and archaeology and others styled themselves as historical or antiquarian. Between the 1840s and the 1880s new societies sprang up all over the country and by 1886, there were forty-nine county and local societies in England (see Appendix IV).

Stuart Piggott has classified the county societies as the product and reflection

---

[23] Soc. Ant. MS. Corresp. C. H. Hartshorne to Albert Way. Copy of a letter in the possession of Mrs R. Wyatt of Sussex, 30 April 1839.

[24] *i.e.* Society of Antiquaries of London, British Archaeological Association and Archaeological Institute of Great Britain and Ireland.

[25] Sydney Smirke, 'Report of proceedings at inaugural meeting, 14 December 1855', *LAMAS Trans.*, I (July 1856) 1, pp. 10–11.

of a rural Anglican England distinct from the industrial midlands and the north where a scarcity of leisure and a well-established non-conformist tradition were less likely to stir strong feelings about ecclesiastical architecture. Charles Delheim has recently modified Professor Piggott's contentions in an attempt to account for the emergence of societies in industrial areas later in the century.[26] Both Piggott and Delheim, however, both over-emphasise the dominance of the south-east, a claim that would have carried more conviction if applied to the printing clubs. The south-east was certainly active during the 1840s and 1850s when ecclesiology was still a significant catalyst. From the 1860s, however, the impetus moved elsewhere as interests other than an Anglican-based architecture took precedence. Societies sprang up all over the country, both rural and urban in character and of the twenty-five local societies founded between 1860 and 1886, only two were located in the south-east. The dominance of the south-east was far more apparent in the membership of the specialised societies of the post-1870 period. The Society of Biblical Archaeology, founded in that year, claimed 59% of its membership from the capital alone and the Society for the Protection of Ancient Buildings, founded in 1877, culled 68% of its membership from London and the south-east. They were thus similar in membership structure to the national antiquarian bodies based permanently in London which exhibited a dominantly south-eastern profile throughout the century, and like those organisations were ostensibly national in representation.

Often it was a sense of local pride and a competitive spirit which motivated the formation of the new provincial societies.

Without wishing to draw any invidious comparisons between this county and other parts of England, I may say that I know scarcely any district so rich as ours – it is a perfect epitome of history.[27]

Such rivalry was, on the whole though, a mild affair. Little concrete jealousy existed between the societies.

We do not interfere, and do not intend interfering, (except as auxiliaries) with any existing society. We are collateral with several, but identical with none. We have our own specific duties to perform, and it will be sufficient for us to perform them fully.[28]

Collaboration and a sense of community were far more evident than animosity; a spirit of co-operation based on an appreciation of common objectives prevailed. Internal scandals there were, but little inter-society rivalry. Most of

---

[26] Stuart Piggott, 'The Origins of the English County Archaeological Societies', *Ruins in a Landscape: Essays in Antiquarianism* (Edinburgh, 1970) pp. 171–95 (p. 191); C. J. Delheim, 'Medievalism in Modernity. The Victorian's Encounter with their Inheritance' (unpublished PhD dissertation, University of Yale, 1979) pp. 46–7.

[27] S. Herbert, 'Address', *Wilts ANH Mag.*, II (April 1855) iv, pp. 3–5 (p. 5).

[28] Report of Council, *HSLC Proc. & Papers* I (1848–9) 6.

the societies were 'in correspondence' with one another exchanging publications on a regular basis. In addition, some societies arranged combined sessions. The London and Middlesex and Surrey Archaeological Societies instituted a joint series of monthly evening meetings in September 1860. The four Lancashire and Cheshire societies met together from time to time. The Durham and Northumberland and the Cumberland and Westmorland societies joined forces for excursions occasionally as did the Essex and Suffolk societies. The establishment in 1850 of the Associated Architectural Societies cemented many of these informal links. Initially twenty-four societies joined 'to obtain a larger circulation for their papers and transactions, greater economy in the publication, and generally those advantages which result from combined action'.[29] The association issued an annual volume in which each society paid the typesetting costs of setting up its own contribution. In practice, the Association became a voice for the smaller societies who found joint publication a far less costly business. The larger members such as the Sussex Archaeological Society and the Archaeological Institute had little need of a collective publishing medium, so the annual volume generally consisted of reports from smaller societies such as the Worcester, Sheffield and York architectural societies.

The culmination of all this collaborative activity was the Congress of Archaeological Societies which first met in November 1888. It was organised nationally by the Society of Antiquaries in response to a memorial 'from a large number of leading archaeologists and members of Archaeological Societies, to discuss the great question of the better organisation of archaeological research'.[30] The aims of the Congress differed little from those propounded by the British Archaeological Association back in 1843. It proposed to make the Society of Antiquaries a central body where information gathered countrywide would be collated and stored, and it was undeniably more effective in this than the earlier effort had been. By 1890 the secretary of the Congress was able to report that an archaeological survey with nationwide aspirations had been set in motion in the counties of Cumberland, Westmorland and Surrey, and that a Record Committee and a Parish Registers Committee were at work.[31]

III

In his book on the British naturalist, David Allen contends that certain preconditions need to exist in combination before a field science can 'take off'.

[29] 'Introduction', *Associated Architectural Societies* I (1850).
[30] *Proc. Soc. Ant* 2nd series, XII (November 22, 1888) p. 233.
[31] *Surrey Archaeol. Collns.* X (1891) p. xxxv.

They are popularity, a common social code, standardisation of techniques and the existence of an overseeing institution.[32] These are the selfsame conditions which define the working of the nineteenth-century antiquarian community – what Allen describes is an efficient mechanism of consensus and one that was bolstered very considerably, in the case of the archaeological societies, by their homogeneous social composition.

The men – and occasionally women (always referred to as a separate category of lady members) – involved in antiquarian pursuits were largely derived from a class where education was an unquestioned privilege and leisure an ample commodity. Their shared social referents as well as intellectual predilections made the assumption of consensus far easier. The organisational impetus which thus surfaced within antiquarianism in the mid nineteenth century suggests this strong sense of community amongst like-minded scholars. The idea of a community based on a code of practice defining exclusion and inclusion suggests a shift within antiquarian circles away from the individual private collector to the more convivial society in which the county museum and county history acted as symbols of shared access. The priority awarded to these collective aspects of their aspirations committed the societies to a sense of corporate duty. The contribution of the individual was valuable insofar as it fulfilled the corporate requirement, and when men dishonoured that ideal the community was quick to act. In 1854, Mr Bridger, treasurer of the Surrey Archaeological Society, was found to have been embezzling the society's funds. His resignation having been accepted, the society continued harmoniously.[33] Similar events shattered the calm of the London and Middlesex Archaeological Society in 1857 over the conduct of their Honorary Secretary, the Reverend Charles Boutell.[34] Petty pilfering was uncommon in these organisations, but its occurrence signalled a rupture in the community aspect so dear to antiquarian bodies. Dishonesty was hardly unique to the antiquarian community but in that context it represented a dishonouring of the important ideals of trust and reciprocation.

The Royal Historical Society was another which suffered from internal problems. Its founder, the Reverend Charles Rogers, had engineered the finances of the society such as to ensure that not only had the cost of building his house been borne by the Society, but that he was also in receipt of a substantial salary for his vaguely defined duties as its 'Historiographer'. In 1879, complaints against him and his mismanagement of the society's affairs began to amass. The *Athenaeum* printed a number of articles critical of the society and membership began to fall off. Finally, after threatening resignation

---

[32] D.E. Allen, *The Naturalist in Britain: A Social History* (Harmondsworth, 1978) p. 120.
[33] A. W. G. Lowther, 'A Brief History of the Society', *Surrey Archaeol. Collns.* Centenary volume, LIII (1954) pp. 1–34 (pp. 10–11).
[34] London Museum, LAMAS MSS. Minutes of General Meetings, 27 November 1857, pp. 37–9.

twice, Rogers left the society but furiously circulated indignant pamphlets detailing his persecution. Once rid of him, however, the society's fortunes improved rapidly, consensus having once again been achieved within the community.[35]

The antiquarian community was a compact body where familiarity frequently served as an important reference point. The testimonials recommending membership of the Society of Antiquaries show the same few names over and over of the active core anxious to ease the passage of their fellow enthusiasts into the community.[36] Lacking the encumbrance of a professional hierarchy, they had no need to retreat into a jealous solitude. 'The present age is distinguished by a tendency towards combination and union of effort in every department of human activity. Archaeology has partaken of the same impulse.'[37] Few membership lists specify profession or occupation but we can glimpse the lifestyle behind the names and titles. The archaeological societies swelled their ranks with clerical members as had the earlier architectural societies. Sixteen of those founded before 1880 (for which figures are available) had a high clerical element in their membership with between 20% and 40% of their members in holy orders[38] (see Appendix V). The figures are largely unaffected by region or by date. By the nineteenth century, parish clergy were often men of some considerable education and frequently sometime-fellows of Oxford and Cambridge colleges, retired into college livings after having fulfilled their requisite tutorial and collegiate duties. The percentage of society members with masters' degrees closely mirrors the percentage of reverends. The intellectual activity thus offered to men of active mind by the archaeological societies is one factor in explaining their extraordinary preponderance. The persistence of ecclesiological principles in many of the societies which led to a good deal of emphasis in their activities on ecclesiastical architecture and history contributed to the archaeological interest displayed by so many nineteenth-century clerics. It was rare for a volume of transactions not to contain a handful of articles on these subjects.

The church is always a building of importance, and very often the only one, in a parish. It is a repository of parish history. It is [. . .] in the power of the residential clergy [. . .] to put these things down.[39]

The clergy were powerful men with a wealth of antiquarian information in their direct keeping, from brass rubbings and gravestones through parish registers to the very fabric of their church buildings.

---

[35] RHS Lib, UCL Lib. RHS MSS. Minute Book 1880–6; MS. H3/1.I, Treasurer's Corresp. 1879–81; Rev. Charles Rogers, *Parting Words to the members of the RHS in a letter to the President* (9 July 1881); letters from Rogers to the RHS, 15 December, 22 December 1880, 5 May 1881; *Athenaeum*, 22 November 1879, 28 May 1881; R. A. Humphreys, *The Royal Historical Society, 1868–1968* (London, 1969) pp. 14–19.

[36] *e.g.* Soc. Ant. MS. Minutes (Meetings), 1838–41.

[37] James Picton, 'Inaugural Address at Plymouth Congress, 1882', *Jnl. BAA* 39 (1883), pp. 1–3, (p. 2). [38] See Chapter 2. [39] J. E. Jackson, 'Address', *Wilts ANH Mag.* I (1854) p. 37.

Another factor explanatory of their numerical strength lay in the still dominant interpretation of history as a Providential plan. Addresses delivered before such bodies were often more akin to sermons than to academic lectures. The secular idiom was barely acceptable. The voice of clerical domination rose above all others when the Bishop of Oxford, opening the meeting of the Archaeological Institute at Chester in 1857, declared that 'there was far more than the mere gratification of a somewhat idle curiosity when archaeologists ransacked the dust of antiquity. They were carrying out the great plan of the Creator and Ruler of the world.'[40] History was invested with divine intention. 'He who thus takes up the proofs of History set before him, and who learns the truth [. . .] surely becomes more and more reverential and is strengthened in holy faith and kindles into high and holy hope.'[41] Religious elements further cohered the social fabric and consensus was achieved. Dr Buckland, addressing the Somersetshire Archaeological and Natural History Society, endorsed

the wise provision of this institution [. . .] which forbade all discussions on subjects of a religious or political character. Here they met as brethren, as subjects of one common government, and children of one common God; and it was their business to investigate the works of the Almighty in creation and the works of Man in the ages long gone by.[42]

The classlessness after which Dr Buckland strived was, of course, utopian. The relative formality of the proceedings of most societies with their monthly or quarterly meetings, their emphasis on the acquisition of property in the form of a museum or library, their soirées and conversaziones – all such trappings of polite society set them apart from the bulk of the population. The Architectural, Archaeological and Historic Society of Chester was unusual in its attempts to woo the labouring classes. It introduced three categories of membership, ranging from Quarterly members who paid one shilling per quarter and gained free admission to meetings, lectures and exhibitions, through ten shilling per annum Associate members who gained additionally the use of the library and occasional invitations to the Society's excursions to Full members, whose annual subscription of one pound gave them the right to stand for election to Council.

The admission of Quarterly members upon such low terms [. . .] would, it was hoped, be the means of opening new sources of information and amusement to that large class of young men who were engaged in the shops and offices of the city as well as to the industrious and intelligent artisan who might there acquire a knowledge of the true principles of that art which his labour was employed to shape into practical effect.[43]

Their membership lists indicate little success; of their forty original members, 12.5% were titled and 32.5% clerical. The sprinkling of M.Ds and Justices of the

[40] Bishop of Oxford, 'Address to Congress, July 21 1857', *AAHCh Jnl.* II (1864) p. 239.
[41] P. Hookins, 'On Some Uses of Archaeology', *Archaeological and Natural History Society for North Oxfordshire Trans.* I (1853–5) pp. 1–13 (p. 12).
[42] Dr Buckland, 'Speech', *Som. ANH Proc.* I (1849–50) p. 12.
[43] Report of first meeting, 31 December 1849, *AAHCh Jnl.* I (1857) p. 11.

Peace as well as Fellows of the Society of Antiquaries does little to dispel the image of antiquarianism as a pursuit of the socially confident.

In their appeal to working men the societies frequently rehearsed the common Victorian dedication to self-improvement. Their censorious tones, reminiscent of the minister's sermons, were unlikely to have much appeal to a class with neither ready money nor leisure, overawed as much by the formality of the language as of the proceedings. The Chester Society was unusual in its concern, however hierarchical that might have been. For most of the societies accessibility meant little more than availability within the existing community and they were not in general evangelical across class or cultural boundaries. Charles Delheim has accused the Sussex Archaeological Society of 'Home Counties snobbism' for its open courting of the aristocracy.[44] Doubtless the Sussex men were impressed by the aristocratic birthright; 9.5% of their first year's members were titled, but the vice was not a regional one.

It was agreed that the Society's circular be sent to the persons comprised in the following Classes [. . .]: Rectors; Members for the Counties and Boroughs; Borough and County Justices; Peers, Baronets, Knights, and all of the legal rank of Esquire; beneficed Clergy; Select List of Dissenting Ministers; Select List of Medical and Legal Professions; Past and Present Councils of Literary &c. Societies; Authors connected with the district; Inventors; Mayors and all who have passed the Civic chair; Present and Past President of Liv[erpool] Library and Athenaeum; Principal teachers; Principal Borough Officers; Consuls; Certain gentlemen of the Press; Fellows of Metrop[olitan] and Local Societies; Past and present High Sheriffs; Officers of the Chancellor of the Duchy and similar offices in both counties; Select List of Merchants &c.[45]

The Historic Society of Lancashire and Cheshire, so concerned with the pedigree of its members, charged a correspondingly high rate of subscription, at one guinea per annum for members residing within seven miles of the Liverpool Exchange and a half-guinea for non-residents. Some societies charged only five shillings per annum, but most levied a ten shilling or ten-and-sixpenny subscription. The printing clubs generally charged a one pound or one guinea membership. This was hardly the working man's milieu, more particularly since there was also a myriad of additional payments without which active participation in the societies' activities was impossible. The annual summer excursions invariably involved the costs of rail travel and communal dining while entry to the various semi-social events was generally by purchase of a ticket. When the London and Middlesex and the Surrey Archaeological Societies established their joint monthly evening meetings in 1860, participation cost an additional subscription of five shillings.

Nonetheless, the societies constantly wrestled with the problem of insufficient funds. The collection of subscriptions was a source of constant irritation;

[44] Delheim, *op. cit.* pp. 46–7.
[45] Liverpool Central Library, HSLC MSS. Minute Book I, December 1847 to October 1854; 24 March 1848, p. 9.

councils were forever exhorting their members to prompt payment. For most societies, the annual subscription was the sole form of income available (at least until any investments began to pay dividends) out of which they had to finance the annual volume as well as all other activities. The first publication which the society for Buckingham could afford to produce, eleven years after its foundation, could refer with long experience to the hampering effect of 'the deficiency of funds which from the small amount of the subscription [5/- per annum] can scarcely ever suffice to carry out any important object'.[46] Council business was invariably dominated by financial problems, by the fear of losing members with its grave financial consequences as well as with the ubiquitous problem of arrears. The formal structure of the societies, their need for a venue for meetings and often for a permanent office, library or museum plus the minor but constant expenses of correspondence and organisation dictated their relatively high financial requirements.

At a Special General Meeting of the Surrey Archaeological Society in 1855, rebel members issued an ultimatum. The society had no money left with which to proceed with publication and the Secretary's contention that the arrears of eighty-nine of its members were to blame brought an angry response.

And there are eighty-nine who never will pay until something has been published. They say faith has not been kept with them. There have been meetings of the Society at Chertsey, Guildford and elsewhere; and to attend them involves an expenditure of time and money, which many members cannot afford [. . .] I am satisfied, Sir, that unless something is printed [. . .] which will prove the vitality of the Society, the Society will sink to nothing.[47]

There was a constant and precarious balancing of what the members could – and would – afford against what the societies could afford. Proposals to raise the subscription of the Somerset society in 1875 precipitated many doubts amongst the officers of the society.

I am not at all sure whether it would be wise to double our yearly sub[scription] – there are a great many members, one fifth at least who care very little about the Soc[iety] – and who never exercise any rights of membership & they w[ou]ld I think be unwilling to be called upon for a larger sub[scription]; besides these, there are a good many who are not over well off in the world – poor parsons &c.[48]

Although the officers of the societies were rarely paid for their labours, it was common to employ a paid collector for the onerous task of rounding up outstanding subscriptions. The collectors' books of the Society of Antiquaries for the late 1840s exhibit the lengths to which even the wealthiest members went to avoid payment.

---

[46] *Records of Buckinghamshire* I (1858) p. 11.
[47] Guildford Castle, SAS MSS. SAS 8/3/4. Minutes of Proceedings at a Special General Meeting, 30 October 1855.
[48] Somerset Record Office, Taunton. Som ANH MSS. DD/SAS/ C/2646.3. Corresp. 1, 75–7. Hunt to Malet, 30 June 1875.

Monday April 19, 1847, Lord A Conyngham. Serv[an]t said Lord A was not at home. I saw LA leave the house directly after [. . .] Saturday July 10 Mr Thoms, 2nd call. not got his chekbook but going to pay but as he was going into the Country directly w[oul]d not said he should be short of money for it [   ] Saturday Feb 12, 1848, Mr T. Wright, 3 call. was thinking about it & not having it now would bring it.[49]

IV

The growth of more specialised societies towards the end of the century heralds the twin phenomena of professionalisation and specialisation so characteristic of later nineteenth-century intellectual developments. As antiquarianism found itself caught more and more in a grey area between the interests of the professional historian and those of the professional archaeologist, so bodies catering for narrower and less general interests grew.

The energy that fuelled the success and trenchancy of the county societies was nonetheless channelled into a militant localism which defied the encroachment of a metropolitan culture. Local pride was the driving force behind the activities of the county societies, a localism born not of any sense of inferiority but whose determinants were located very firmly in a sense of place which bore little relation to legal boundaries.

We are not the British Archaeological Association [. . .] ours is a County Society. We are specifically concerned with the records and history of this County, and the question at once suggests itself, what is a County, and why should we have a County Society? Now it may be said that we have County histories and they will give us the answer [. . .] But it may be asked is a County history on true historical lines, really possible? I think it is. At present indeed we only know of a County as a unit for certain purposes of civil administration and political organisation, as sending members to Parliament, as imposing rates, and so on; while increased facilities of communication are tending more and more to level down any peculiar characteristics which still survive to mark off one county in England from another, whether in speech, or in ideas, or in customs.[50]

It was the expression of an overpowering sense of loss in the face of this process of levelling. It was not merely a simple protest against the loss of a rural way of life or the imposition of an ever more centralised power structure, but an affirmation of the rôle of provincial culture in a society increasingly prone to defer to the central authority of the urban and the metropolitan. But romantic nostalgia played no part in this. Despite these doubts, pride in modern achievements was common currency and the fruits of civilisation were constantly lauded.

Few of us can observe such indications of the habits and physical conditions of the earliest inhabitants of this island as are afforded by the remains of their rude dwellings, and by the rude implements occasionally found, without a sense of thankfulness that

[49] Soc. Ant. MS 323. Collectors' Books, 1847–9.
[50] Lord Edmond Fitzmaurice, 'Inaugural Presidential Address', *Wilts ANH Mag.* xxi (1848) p. 7.

our lot has been mercifully cast in times of improved knowledge, of advanced civilisation, and more refined habits.[51]

Knowledge became appropriately enough an expression of property. Fascination with the past in this period stemmed largely from an acknowledgement and approval of the modern and the curios and objects which were so popular a contribution to the meetings of the societies were simply the concrete form of this appropriation. In consequence, the cataloguing and collecting instinct remained prominent; the work and method of these societies was overwhelmingly empirical. The amassing of historical facts culled perhaps from documents, perhaps from the tangible facts of settlement – the pot, the flint – unearthed by excavation, accounted for the bulk of their activities. The prospectus of the Society for the Publication of Collections from the Public Records,[52] dated 1840, saw its primary function as 'collecting the historical evidence accumulated in our Record Repositories and of printing them in a classified form'. Their aim was considered justified because

they furnish unerring data elsewhere wholly unattainable. Not only may we collect the numbers of inhabitants of various towns of England, and their trades and occupations, together with the wages of labour and prices of food and commodities, but even the ages of certain classes are detailed with accuracy sufficient to yield an average of the duration of life compared century by century.

They revelled in the sheer weight of detail, in 'a fanatical obsession with the historical significance of the individual object'.[53]

It was an attempt both to reappropriate a heritage and to rationalise knowledge into categories. Coupled with fierce local pride, the conditions for the upsurge of antiquarianism were ripe. The societies flourished in an age when property conferred status and the antiquarians could claim virtue and duty as their moral motives.

It is the duty of all those who venerate the soil they live upon, and the memory of past times which shed a lustre upon the plains and hills [. . .] that shall never be effaced from the page of History, to promote [. . .] the interests of a Society which [. . .] would [. . .] shed a more hallowed reminiscence.[54]

The voice of piety led on occasion to a clash between the guardians of sobriety and the defenders of pleasure. The bishop of the diocese, addressing the Bristol and Gloucestershire Archaeological Society, was 'glad that mere pleasure-meetings were not a part of their programme' for

scientific meetings of late had been a little spoiled by junketings and picnics [. . .] A pleasant reunion after a day of honest labour was a most permissible and even natural conclusion, but mere picnic-work was certainly to be deprecated.[55]

[51] Earl of Devon, 'Inaugural Address at Exeter Congress, 1873', *Arch. Jnl* xxx (1873) p. 206.
[52] There is no evidence to suggest that the society ever got beyond the stage of publishing its prospectus.   [53] Delheim, *op. cit.* p. 53.
[54] *Shropshire Archaeological and Natural History Society Trans.* I (1878) p. v.
[55] *B & B Trans.* I (1876) p. 15.

Over in the east of England, life was obviously more relaxed for the Sussex society took a decidedly hedonist view of their amusements.

Some of the hypercritical sort taunt us with undervaluing archaeological science by this cheerful conviviality – they think forsooth that we ought to be constantly plying the spade and pickaxe, or turning over the musty leaves of chartularies and chronicles. But while the pickaxe and the spade are at all due places and times in requisition by those who can wield them [. . .] why should we obstinately repudiate picturesque scenes, the joyous expression of kindly feeling, the wine and the venison?[56]

Belonging to the locality was to be in possession of an identity and of a genealogy, and to explore and uncover the past of the county was to enrich that genealogy. 'It is not to be forgotten that this is a Local Society, and that its main and primary duty is to set forth [. . .] ancient glories.'[57] The reconstitution of the past was a means of consolidating and realising place and identity in a landscape increasingly unfamiliar. A historical landscape peopled with events, buildings and figures from the past and verified by historical fact was a triumph of possession. Nostalgia provides an insufficient explanation for the popularity of organised antiquarian pursuits. It was rather an alternative cultural force of amazing vigour, an attachment to local identity motivated in many ways by the same sentiments as that civic pride which spurred on the town hall and sewer builders of the later nineteenth century. It asserted a sense of provincial dignity and of distinctiveness and provided a crucial link between past glories and present triumphs.

A problem which often arose where societies espoused this overt localism was that of avoiding small-scale 'colonialism' within the county. The establishment of headquarters in a county town frequently brought about complaints from members situated elsewhere in the region about the inaccessibility of the meeting place, more particularly in the more rural counties of England. It is thus that the summer excursions to a variety of spots throughout the county were adopted so uniformly. Some societies chose tortuous methods in an attempt to mitigate the accusation. The Bristol and Gloucestershire Archaeological Society decided to establish two libraries, one at each of their centres dividing the volumes equally between them though allowing donors the option of naming the place of deposit.[58] The decision of the Historic Society of Lancashire and Cheshire to introduce a resident and non-resident subscription was another attempt to deal with this predicament as was the practice of instituting local committees and local secretaries. In most cases, the establishment of a museum and library dictated the need for a single focal centre of activity but the summer excursion – the highlight of the year's activities – always remained itinerant.

---

[56] M. A. Lower, 'Address', *Sussex Archaeological Collns* x (1858) p. x.
[57] Preface, *AAHCh Jnl.* ii (1864).
[58] Bristol Record Office, B & G AS MSS. Minutes Book II, 1881–4. Report of Committee of Deposit of Books &c., 5 April 1881.

Some societies sought to acquire prestigious property; in Somerset, Surrey and Sussex the purchase of castles sat as comfortably with the social aspirations of the membership as with their historical leanings. Others were less concerned with social position and image. The Architectural and Archaeological Society of Durham and Northumberland, founded in 1861, boasted that it was constituted differently from all other archaeological societies. It remained firmly committed to its aim of effectuating a 'steady increase of practical knowledge' by confining its activities solely to excursions.[59] It could thus claim in 1890 that

within the limit of the two counties with the antiquities of which the Society is concerned, no place which possesses architectural and archaeological features of sufficient interest to warrant an examination has been left unvisited, and those features have been more or less fully explained.[60]

The promotion of local identity which thus dominated the activities of such societies did not, however, render them unmoved by the nationalism so prominent in this period. Love of county was matched by a patriotism and a pride which found expression through religious interpretation. A divinely-suffused view of a nation 'entrusted with [. . .] vast powers and empires',[61] gave them licence to claim that 'the true patriot becomes of necessity the antiquarian'.[62] Theirs was 'accumulated wealth brought to the common store'.[63] The history of the counties was the history of England: 'the history of Kent is, in a measure, the history of our common country'.[64] The notion of a sense of national identity rooted in history was as strong as the sense of local identity. Heritage and history had culminated in 'a wonderful story of development and progress – from darkness to light, from slavery to freedom, from ignorance to knowledge, from short-sighted folly to long-sighted wisdom'.[65] The antiquarians were the nation's flag-bearers.

The study of the past history of the English people must, I think, produce in every well-ordered mind a deep feeling of thankfulness to the good providence of God for the many blessings which, as Englishmen, we now enjoy.[66]

It was not surprising, then, that they succumbed to the proprieties of the day. Guardians of the nation's heritage, they obviously felt constrained to honour its modesties. The decision taken by the Camden Society in 1873 to publish the Prideaux Correspondence was accompanied by agonies of indecision as to which of the letters would have to be sacrificed in the name of modesty.[67] The revelation that they were 'a pleasing mixture of literature,

---

[59] Preface, *Architectural and Archaeological Society of Durham and Northumberland Trans.* I (1870).
[60] *ibid.* III (1890) p. v.   [61] Introduction, *Archaeologia Cantiana* I (1858) p. 19.
[62] Rev O. Freire Owen, 'The Archaeology of the County of Surrey', *Surrey Archaeological Collns* I (1856) pp. 1–13 (pp. 2; 3).   [63] *ibid.*
[64] Introduction, *Archaeologia Cantiana* I (1858) p. 7.   [65] James Picton, *loc. cit.* p. 3.
[66] Lord Chichester, 'Address at Lewes Congress, 1883', *Arch. Jnl.* XL (1883) p. 441.
[67] These were the letters of Humphrey Prideaux, Dean of Norwich, addressed to Under Secretary John Ellis, 1674–1722.

religion, gossip and smut' was hastily followed by a query 'as to whether whore and such words are to be printed in full, or whether the decency (?) [his question mark] of the nineteenth century refuses to know anything about them'.[68] Propriety won the day, for in accepting E. Maunde Thompson's offer to edit the letters, Alfred Kingston, secretary of the Camden Society, requested him

before parting with the Copy to mark all passages which you consider as questionable – I mean any in which force of character or vigor of language might make one hesitate as to the propriety of sending them forth under the sanction of the worthy Dean's name.[69]

Historical fact thus gave way under the pressure to conform to the standards of Victorian morality.

The antiquarian community although convinced of the high value of its activities was nonetheless apologetically self-conscious. The siege mentality displayed so markedly in the 1830s was never wholly discarded and the societies were constantly reiterating their high-minded belief in the intrinsic value of their work.

I am aware that many persons of great wit and acuteness have amused themselves by ridiculing Topographical works, as altogether dull and worthless compilations; mere collections of legendary tales, long successions of rectors or vicars, or lists of the mayors and bailiffs of country towns.[70]

The societies claimed always to have replaced such trivia with 'a pursuit [. . .] elevated to the rank of a science',[71] but instances of this type of work were still printed in abundance. The first volume of the *Sussex Archaeological Collections* in 1848 contained an article on *The Names of the Sussex Gentry in 1588*. In 1885, the Chester Society printed *An Original Manuscript List of Mayors* in the third volume of their journal.

The breadth of interests which characterised their investigations often extended into the realm of natural history as well. A host of field clubs and natural history societies flourished alongside the specifically antiquarian institutions. One survey conducted in 1873 listed 167 local scientific societies in Great Britain and Ireland,[72] a proportion of which saw no contradiction in combining natural history and archaeology with their shared emphasis on regular outdoor excursions and on the collecting and cataloguing of finds. Antiquarianism had always encompassed an interest in the physical remains of the past, whether in the field or in the form of objects, buildings and the like, and societies such as the Bath Natural History and Antiquarian Field Club (1868), the Eastbourne Natural History and Archaeological Society (1867) and the Penzance Natural History and Antiquarian Society (1839) put this combination into practice. Topography provided the link between the two disciplines

---

[68] Camd. Soc. MS. C 3/1. Secretary's Corresp. E. Maunde Thompson to Kingston, 30 January 1873.
[69] Camd. Soc. MS. C4. Miscellanea. Letter book. Kingston to Thompson, 6 March 1873.
[70] E. J. Willson, 'Opening Address', *Lincolnshire Topographical Society Papers* (1843) p. 11.
[71] Mr Scrope, 'Presidential Address', *Wilts ANH Mag.* I (1854) p. 9.
[72] D. E. Allen, *op. cit.* p. 170.

but additionally the religious element brought harmony to this partnership of natural and human history. They were two logically related features of a Providential Plan. The phenomena of nature and the events and remains of history were both proof of the unfolding of a pre-ordained scheme.

The oldest history itself insensibly fades off into a time when man either did not exist, left no records behind him, and the only history of which we can take any cognizance at all is consequently the history of nature.[73]

The natural historians and the antiquarians were nonetheless rarely the same people, nor of similar social class.

Local antiquarians were often wealthy collectors of *objets d'art*, for whom the subject was an exercise in Taste, rather than a scientific study [. . .] The 'Ants' [. . .] were always stoutly Tory, whilst the 'Nats' according with the radical inclinations of science, tended to be more liberal in outlook.[74]

This was a tendency which diminished as much with the encroachment of professional science as with professional history but it is not without significance that the Bath Natural History and Antiquarian Field Club, always primarily naturalist in its attentions, claimed no titled members in its first membership in 1868. The field clubs conducted their business in a far less formal manner than was common in archaeological societies. Their wholly itinerant existence served to lower their social prestige. Correspondingly, they were under far less financial constraint as well. 'They hold no property such as libraries and museums, but they *do* hold field meetings.'[75]

In archaeological societies, the social element – the dinners and soirées – were an important social feature. One contemporary wit described archaeologists as divisible into four classes.

(1) The Archaeologist proper, (2) the Harkaeologist, who comes to listen, (3) the Larkaeologist, who comes for the fun of things, (4) the Sharkaeologist, who comes for the luncheon.[76]

Their conviviality was not simply one of shared field experience but of a shared social milieu. Whereas the field clubs stressed intellectual consensus, the archaeological societies consciously and deliberately combined social and intellectual interests.

All the societies – as indeed all institutions of whatever character – carried many sitting members who rarely participated in the programme of activities laid on. It was a committed core of enthusiastic and active men and women who offered up their leisure hours *gratis* to administer the business of the societies. The small budget at their disposal had to cover the cost of an annual

[73] Lord Fitzmaurice, *loc. cit.* p. 6.   [74] Allen, *op. cit.* p. 163.
[75] G. S. Brady, 'Naturalists' Field Clubs; their Objects and Organisations', *Natural History Trans. of Northumberland and Durham* I (1867) pp. 107–14 (p. 108).
[76] Leslie Dow, 'A Short History of the Suffolk Institute of Archaeology and Natural History', *Proc. Suffolk Institute of Archaeology and Natural History* XXIV (1949) pp. 129–43 (p. 142).

journal as well as all the expenses of more quotidian organisation. Council reports, the reports of the committed to the 'lay' members, tell of their disappointments.

The Council has to mention with regret [. . .] the failure in point of attendance at the public meeting held with the last Annual Meeting. The advertisments, hire of room, and general expenses incidental to such a meeting were considerable, and it was very disheartening [. . .] to find the splendid collection of seals and brasses exhibited [. . .] so little attractive to their Huddersfield friends.[77]

The same report recounted, however, that on their summer excursion to Wakefield, 110 tickets were distributed resulting in a profit of three shillings. Despite such setbacks, the societies were remarkably successful as the continued survival of so many of them suggests. In addition to the astonishing rapidity of their success, the ability to sustain their numerical strength and a high degree of enthusiasm reflects the liveliness maintained by provincial cultures in this period. The willingness to entertain payment of an annual subscription was in many cases, of course, far greater than the subsequent commitment to participation. The Surrey Archaeological Society members and visitors book gives some idea of attendance. Between summer 1854 and summer 1865, the lowest recorded attendance of members was the nine who appeared for the Annual General Meeting in 1865 and the highest recorded was 209 – this in a society of around 420 members. Average attendance was sixty, though perhaps not always the same sixty. The meetings were itinerant, ranging in venue from Lambeth Palace and Southwark in the London area to Godalming, Guildford and Chertsey, and each locale would probably have provided a new audience.[78] Their collaborative monthly evening meetings with the London and Middlesex Archaeological Society showed a steady rise in popularity in the 1870s with numbers rarely dropping below thirty-five even given the additional subscription required of participants.[79]

Three months after their formation the Norfolk and Norwich Archaeological Society had attracted 180 members; the Sussex Archaeological Society jumped from an initial fifty members to ninety in the three weeks between their founding meeting and their first general meeting. At the end of their first year, their membership had reached 218. In 1888, they had increased to an enormous 564, and even then were not the largest of the county societies. The societies themselves, never quite able to throw off their sense of inferiority, subscribed to the myth that the 1880s ushered in a fall in membership numbers, variously attributed to the agricultural depression,[80] the growth of new leisure pursuits and the encroachment of the professions on antiquarian

[77] Report for 1869, *Yorkshire Archaeological and Topographical Jnl.* I (1870) p. 344.
[78] SAS MSS. SAS 8/1. Members and Visitors Book.
[79] LAMAS MSS. Monthly Evening Meetings: Members and Visitors Attendance.
[80] Report 1885–6, *B & G AS* XI (1886) p. 186 – commenting on a fall in numbers from 510 to 495.

territory. The figures, however, show roughly the same number of societies increasing in membership in the 1880s as decreasing. No regional pattern is observable nor a direct connection between such changes and the age of the society. Generally, the increases are more marked than the declines; comparing the earliest available membership lists with one for the 1880s for each society, the average drop in numbers over this period is only 86 where it does occur, whereas the average rise is 153.5, proof indeed of an unquenchable vitality.

Despite the tremendous level of support which the societies – printing and county clubs alike – had clearly received over the years, some still failed to maintain the impetus. The English Historical Society quietly disappeared after a publishing life of twenty years. The Cabot Society was swallowed up by the successful Hakluyt Society as was the similarly conceived Columbus Society. Other unsuccessful clubs were the Leland Society for the promotion of British Topography, Genealogy and Biography, the Essex Morant Society with its regional bias and the clumsily named Society for the Publication of Collections from the Public Records. The Wiltshire Topographical Society, forerunner of the successful Wiltshire Archaeological and Natural History Society, finally admitted defeat after eleven unsuccessful years in which only four of their fifteen projected volumes had come to fruition. There were numerous other cases of societies which, after a few volumes, simply ceased publishing. It was not a lack of demand which led to these failures nor a saturation of the market, for the army of successful societies exhibited a marked overlap in membership. The London circle of antiquarians, in particular, tended to be members of most of the printing clubs, collecting editions of medical manuscripts and art reproductions along with the more orthodox texts available in these series. In the case of the English Historical Society, the Leland Society and the Society for the Publication of Collections from the Public Records, their aims were too much akin to those of the Camden Society whose early successes had established its supremacy in the field.

The Wiltshire Topographical Society failed, significantly enough, because it was regarded as an imposition on the county by outsiders. Although its founder, John Britton, was a local county historian, he was also closely involved with the metropolitan antiquarian fraternity and he took with him into the Wiltshire society many of his London friends and colleagues more eager to support the publication of manuscript material in whatever form than to enhance the history of the county. The society was thus not born from the same co-operative sense of local interest and regard which actuated the successful formation of the Wiltshire Archaeological and Natural History Society in 1853. In the case of the local publishing ventures, there seemed little enthusiasm (except in the north-west where the successful Chetham was followed in the 1870s by the Lancashire and Cheshire Record Society) for locally specific printing clubs despite the overwhelming support for the more

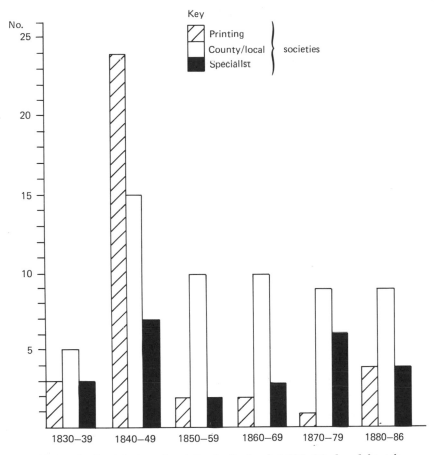

No.

Key
Printing
County/local } societies
Specialist

1830–39 1840–49 1850–59 1860–69 1870–79 1880–86

Figure 2. Foundation of societies in England, 1830–86: decadal totals

participatory county institutions. The anonymity of the printing clubs prohibited the introduction of the social elements on which county societies relied and which were so attractive a feature of their programmes.

In Oxford and Birmingham in the 1880s specifically and exclusively historical societies were founded for the first time. The Oxford Historical Society, founded in 1884 with a membership of 503 and rather akin to the printing clubs than the archaeological societies, issued notes for the guidance of its editors. These dictated that 'every editor is to prepare for the press the best text of the work on which he is engaged, using for purposes of collation the principal manuscripts available'.[81] The omissions of Canon Raine nearly fifty

[81] Oxford Historical Society, *General Suggestions for the Guidance of Editors* (March, 1885).

years previously were not to occur again. Accuracy and integrity were stressed and they regarded their approach as based upon scientific principles. Thoroughness had ousted enthusiasm, and not because of a preponderance of Oxford scholars amongst the membership. London and the south-east contributed 32% of the total membership, Oxfordshire 21% and the university 23%. The Birmingham Historical Society, founded in 1882, published transactions rather than editions of texts. The first transactions included articles on North American history and on European ethnography as well as the more staple fare of English life before the industrial revolution and discussions of medieval political history.

These historical societies showed a visible shift in favour of the political aspects of history, away from the more general interests of the antiquarians. It is interesting to compare their preferred interests with those which J. R. Green saw as characteristic of antiquarianism in the 1860s.

I have been immensely struck – in going over ye "Som[erset] Arch. Ass." to find how all their attention has been concentrated on a few periods. On the British (so-called) and Medieval times. Roman Somerset attracts very little attention, Saxon ditto none, there is not a paper on the Roman period, nor on the Reformation, only one on the Great Rebellion time, none on the Monmouth rebellion, or thence to our own day.[82]

Sir John Seeley delivered the inaugural address of the Birmingham society, dwelling at length on the intellectual significance of its foundation.

There could scarcely happen a more important or a more encouraging occurrence for historical study in England than the formation of this Society [. . .] it will assert by its very existence that history is as serious a pursuit as science or as politics; no mere entertaining diversion.

The new historians thus inherited from the antiquarians their self-conscious need for justification. It was still deemed necessary to promote the gravity and worthiness of the subject legitimated as much in the new as in the old societies by institutional form.

History [. . .] needs [. . .] that the assertion should be made in this particular way, that is, by creating for history an organisation similar to that by which science is maintained in its seriousness and in its rigour.

The institution remained the most important form of public recognition. At root lay the desire for social and intellectual assimilation. The celebration of the past *always* embraced the present.

The comparison of the present times with those which are gone by, renders us more satisfied with the present age, and more content with the lot in which it has pleased Providence to place us.[83]

---

[82] J. Coll. Oxon. J. R. Green. MS. 198, ff. 75–80. Green to Boyd Dawkins, 15 January 1862.
[83] Richard Brooke, *HSLC Proc. & Papers* I (1848–9) p. 8.

These organisations, whether predominantly antiquarian or historical in their aims, were not the tail end of the Romantic movement fleeing from utilitarianism but a proud expression of the predominantly acquisitive culture in which they flourished. Their possessions – symbolised by the artifacts and manuscripts which graced the showcases of their museums – were knowledge and the nation's memory. Knowledge in their hands became a commodity through which they took possession of their own genealogies. For some, it was family pedigree; for others, association through the locality; and on a grander scale, it was England and the national personality. This was a local movement of national proportions enshrining all the paradoxes of Victorian England.

Their activities were not always high-minded however; moments of relief were provided by such bodies as the Noviomagians, a gourmandising offshoot of the Society of Antiquaries. Their tongue-in-cheek teasing of their fellow antiquaries at their monthly dinners regarded nothing and no-one as sacred. Their light-hearted interpretation of the acrimonious split between the Archaeological Association and Institute, the two factions headed by Thomas Wright and Albert Way respectively, put into perspective the absurd tragedy of this petty wrangle.

The recent proceedings of the British Archaeologicals were discussed, and the pacific and emollient tendency of the study of Antiquities was triumphantly proved by reference to the various acts of the most eminent of this body. It was proposed that as a cure for squabbling, or fussy, or overbearing dispositions, the parties should be compelled to join the British Archaeological Association, where nothing is eaten but honey, and nothing drunk but the milk of human kindness. A premium was offered for a new pun, on the names of the rival disputants, and a fresh Way to set all Wright, was anxiously worked for, but not found.[84]

[84] Soc. Ant. MS. 705. Meetings of the Noviomagian Society. Session 1844–5. 'Noviomagio Triumphans. Minutes of the 5th Ordinary Meeting, Wednesday 19 March 1845'. (p. 56).

4

Past history and present politics

and soon they floated
Through desiccated forests; mangled myths
And argued easily round megaliths.
(Siegfried Sassoon, Early Chronology)

history is a pattern
Of timeless moments. So, while the light fails
On a winter's afternoon, in a secluded chapel
History is now and England.
(T. S. Eliot, Little Gidding)

Towards the end of the nineteenth century, the practice of applying the terms archaeology, history and antiquarianism indiscriminately to all and any studies of the past became noticeably less common. As the three historical communities grew anxious to cordon off their own specific territories of investigation and study, the value of a more precise terminology became obvious. The three disciplines had never been synonymous. In method as much as in materials, they had always differed considerably and though many practitioners straddled more than one of the three subjects, the blurred taxonomy which presided was more indicative of image than of actual practice. But as professional specialisation increasingly imposed itself upon the historical disciplines, the differences became more pronounced and more important. Specialisation did not bring about these differences; it simply emphasised their significance.

I

Antiquarianism, rather than confining itself to one specific type of source material had attempted to marry the literary and material evidences of past ages; 'to collect, to preserve, and to transmit the memory of the past, "of the men of old, men of renown", such is the task of the modern Antiquary'.[1] The method of the antiquarian had been and remained one of collection and

---

[1] A. J. Dunkin, *Prospectus for a New History of Kent* (London, 1874?).

classification on a descriptive basis, regardless of chronology and embracing both text and artifact.[2] H. N. Humphreys, introducing his *Stories by an Archaeologist and his Friends* (1856) sketched the popular conception.

When archaeological pursuits, and their votaries are spoken of among the uninitiated, the idea generally suggested is that of a small number of well-meaning gentlemen, invariably advanced in years, if not in science, respectable individuals who make it their business to collect small pieces of old iron which they agree among themselves to term fibulae or armillae or prigiones; and that they occasionally vary their labours of research by giving amusing prices for similarly small fragments of broken crockery which they proceed to label and describe. (p. 1)

Humphreys' satire was more than a simple stereotyping. The reputable antiquary J. R. Planché described his own initial disillusionment.

My constant attendance at the evening meetings of the Society of Antiquaries had cruelly dissipated the illusion that I was under previous to my election. I felt humiliated by the conviction that the ridicule and contempt which had been so plentifully heaped upon professed antiquaries were not so undeserved as I had imagined. The owl-like solemnity of the scanty conclave [. . .] the ponderosity or triviality of the papers – an account of the price of eggs and butter in the reign of Queen Elizabeth – wearied and disgusted the few fellows [. . .] who came.[3]

Whilst descriptive classification, whether of Elizabethan food prices or fragments of pottery, remained the mainstay of antiquarian study, its most singular characteristic was its promiscuous mix of sources, its use of both literary and material evidence. Few antiquaries before the advent of a specific archaeological method would have seen any need to treat exhumed burial remains differently than a town charter or a church font. They were as comfortable editing medieval poetry as they were inspecting Roman remains. Thomas Wright's published work varies from his *Archaeological Album* (1845), a diverse compilation which included essays on an ancient bedstead in Lancashire, on symbolism in ecclesiastical architecture, on illuminated manuscripts and on Saxon barrows, to the volumes of Latin poetry he edited for the Camden Society. Joseph Hunter, best known for his works on his native Yorkshire, also produced topographical descriptions of Norfolk towns and large-scale transcripts of medieval pipe-rolls under the Record Commission.

The typical if ambitious product of antiquarian research was the county history which acknowledged the significance of both material remains and of municipal manuscripts. The ideal county history was one which embraced accounts of local superstitions and customs alongside discussions of medieval land holdings, of monasteries dissolved under Henry VIII and transcripts of epitaphs on old tombs. In his preface to the *History and Topography of*

---

[2] A. Momigliano, 'Ancient History and the Antiquarian', in *Studies in Historiography* (London, 1966) 1–39 (pp. 3; 25).

[3] J. R. Planché, *The Recollections and Reflections of J. R. Planché: A Professional Autobiography* (London, 1872), p. 92.

Ketteringham in the County of Norfolk (1851), Joseph Hunter outlined his views on the best way to compile a good local history.

Two qualifications are essentially requisite to the proper execution of a topographical work [. . .] First, a just apprehension of the nature and objects of topographical writing [. . .] and a knowledge of the deposits of [the] evidence [. . .] And secondly, a familiar acquaintance with the district [. . .] and an intimate historical acquaintance with the persons who have resided within it.

His emphasis on the physical acquaintance as well as the intellectual understanding of his subject matter is significant. In the absence of photographic reproduction, detailed descriptive material was an important feature of antiquarian studies. The range of such antiquarian studies even where confined to a small locality is indicative in large part of method. Defending its scope, Thomas Pettigrew described the skills and talents necessary to the antiquarian.

To render his labours effective, he must possess no little acquaintance with heraldry, with genealogy, with various languages in which inscriptions are to be found either on monuments or in manuscripts, with numismatics, with history in general, and particular manner and customs, and a variety of other attainments.[4]

So broad a range of topics encompassing such a disparate collection of sources was representative, although specialisation did not leave antiquarianism entirely untouched. The growth of carefully designated specialist areas in the sister disciplines of history and archaeology robbed antiquarianism of much of its primary material. Writing in 1890, the local historian Richard Saul Ferguson commented on the effects of the changes of fifty years.

The time has gone past for writing a history [. . .] of any county, on the old-fashioned lines and scale. The work is now sub-divided; the *fauna* and the *flora*, the pedigrees and the geology, the ecclesiology, and the everything else, are dealt with by specialists in little books devoted exclusively to one subject.[5]

Antiquarianism was lapsing fast into obscurantism, and when Sir John Seeley praised its advances in 1891 he saw them, significantly, as confined to the 'illustration and elucidation of the minor monuments of the last nine centuries'. Antiquarianism was becoming an adjunct to the mainstream academic disciplines, rather than a companion study and the marginalisation of the antiquarian community was complete before the end of the century.[6]

Despite the constant abjuration of anything removed from the purely factual, antiquarians were wont to embellish their researches in imaginative fashion, a habit hardly consonant with the academic rigour increasingly

---

[4] T. J. Pettigrew, 'On the Study of Archaeology', *Jnl. BAA* VI (1851) 163–77 (p. 163).

[5] R. S. Ferguson, *A History of Cumberland* (London, 1890), preface.

[6] J. Evans, 'The Progress of Archaeology', Opening Address of the Antiquarian section of the Edinburgh meeting of the Archaeological Institute, 11 August 1891. *Arch. Jnl.* XLVIII (1891) 251–62 (pp. 261–2).

demanded of the new history and archaeology. Writers such as John Brent and Edward Peacock turned their hand to historical fiction as well as more sober antiquarian tracts. They were not given, as was Carlyle, to recounting the details of everyday life and conversation in their antiquarian works, but rather sought to present their researches 'in forms full of quaint and original features, which impart a picturesque and striking character to such fitful glimpses of the romance of life in other ages as are thus revealed'.[7] Untrammelled by the narrowing considerations of the professional academic, antiquarians often clothed their work in a prose style and a language more commonly associated with poetry. The romantic influence was clearly still strong when Charles Hartshorne wrote his funereal discourse on Northamptonshire.

I would prevail on you to accompany me to the narrow resting-places of the dead. Let us enter reverently [. . .] and contemplate the silent sanctuaries where the great and the good lie entombed [. . .] The hoary hand of time has spread mildew on the busts.[8]

Hartshorne's indulgent Gothic prose was composed in 1840 at the height of the ecclesiological revival and it reveals a greater emphasis on empathy than on analysis, a stress which Rosemary Jann has suggested was emblematic of conceptions of historical writing in this period.[9] Charles Hardwick showed a similar fondness for poetic imagery in his history of Preston.

Unrecorded time passeth. Twilight glimmerings succeed, followed by brighter flashes of historic truth. Huge oxen and deer browse beneath umbrageous oaks [. . .] Time passeth, and more light penetrates the semi-gloom.[10]

The deliberate use of the archaic past tense to evoke a sense of the long sweep of history may seem far removed from the subject matter of his work but the magisterial style he adopted was not uncommon. Frequently, as is explicit in Hartshorne's work, such language was intended to convey the religiosity of the work. The many volumes on churches and ecclesiastical trappings which account for so substantial a portion of antiquarian work were frequently motivated by religious sentiment.

Nor if we enter these holy places with a sober and chastened mind, shall we fail to gather therein some godly reflections, which will teach us to moralise on the vanity of earthly greatness.[11]

The language of antiquarianism maintained a strong affinity with that of the pulpit.

Alongside this religious motivation lay a strong sense of English pride, expressed both as nationalism and as a fondness for the locale.[12] The

[7] Anon (H. N. Humphries), *Stories by an Archaeologist and his Friends* (London, 1856) I, 3.
[8] C. H. Hartshorne, *A Discourse on Funeral Monuments in Northamptonshire* (Cambridge, 1840) p. 2.
[9] R. Jann, 'From Amateur to Professional: The Case of the Oxbridge Historians', *Jnl of British Studies* XXII (1983) 2, 122–47 (p. 123).
[10] Charles Hardwick, *A History of the Borough of Preston and its Environs; in the County of Lancaster* (Preston/London, 1857) p. 511. [11] Hartshorne, *op. cit.* p. 2. [12] See Chapter 3.

concentration amongst antiquarians on local history and on British antiquities reflects this partisan approach.

All men naturally feel more interest in the historical associations of their own race than they do in any other portion of mankind [. . .] The dullest familiar scene is encircled with a sacred halo.[13]

The Victorian reverence for the home, both as a symbol of the domestic ideal and as a homeland, found an outlet in the national pride of the antiquarian community. It served thus to heighten the moral significance which was read into past events and to assert the essential rightness of a god-fearing England. Charles Roach Smith's description of Kent establishes the coalescence of the moral and the historical.

Here the first Anglo-Saxon Kingdom was established, and here the standard of Christianity was first raised in Britain by Augustine [. . .] Who can view unmoved the shores and fields which witnessed the transaction of events so momentous? Who, save the ignorant and the apathetic, can behold without emotion the venerable monuments from times in which were involved the destinies of kingdoms, empires and ages?[14]

It was a simple step from such sentiments to a teleogical assertion of natural progress: if the England of yesteryear could boast so fine a profile, how could the present nation be anything other than an improvement? 'Civilisation is a process which, year by year, age by age, and century by century, is gradually unfolding itself.'[15] The notion of a pre-ordained historical process reaching its pinnacle in Victorian England was consonant with the religious beliefs so commonly espoused in antiquarian work. Past Providence and present satisfaction deserved pious praise: in a universe of classified and categorised factual information the task of the antiquary was the preservation of information to be honoured by posterity.

Man no sooner emerges from that barbarous state of existence, in which food, shelter and clothing, form the sole desiderata of his existence [. . .] than he indicates a strong and earnest desire to collect, to perpetuate, and to transmit, some records of his own and preceding generations.[16]

In consequence, their interest lay in the systematic collection of a body of factual knowledge culled from both manuscripts and antiquities, the corollary of which was a hostility to theory. The view that the fanciful theories of earlier antiquarians were responsible for the latter-day ridicule suffered by the community was widely held. Charles Roach Smith, in introducing the first volume of his *Collectanea Antiqua* in 1848, defended this stern empiricism.

The notion that a record of *facts*, copiously illustrated, and but sparingly dilated with theory, would be acceptable to the antiquary and to the historical inquirer, is proved to have been well-founded. (p. v).

---

[13] Hardwick, *op. cit.* p. viii.
[14] C. Roach Smith, *The Antiquities of Richborough, Reculver and Lymne in Kent* (London, 1850) p. iv.
[15] Hardwick, *op. cit.* p. vii.   [16] Dunkin, *op. cit.*

Montagu Burrows, Chichele Professor of History in the University of Oxford made the same point – though with different intention – nearly forty years later. 'Facts, naked, unadorned facts, are the objects of the love and reverence of the rigid antiquarian.'[17] Antiquarian method thus focused upon a thorough factual grounding rather than on theoretical application. This factual grounding did not in any way dilute the didactic purpose of historical study so prevalent in this period however; antiquarianism no less than history proper was emphatic in drawing on the past for moral exhortation.[18]

II

Whilst antiquarianism directed its energies in so many diverse directions, historians in England were seeking simultaneously to define their aims and interests more and more minutely. Their traditional reliance on sundry written sources for their material often rendered them heavily and problematically dependent on specifically narrative sources. In the middle decades of the century, the move away from such 'chronicle history' towards a more rigorous 'record history' received an important fillip from governmental initiatives.[19] Historians active in this and later generations differed significantly from their predecessors in their devotion to state papers, a preference which resulted in a marked concentration amongst English historians on national and specifically political history. The new schools of history emerging at the same time in the English universities also stressed these areas, and this institutional voice aided professional historians in imposing a uniform standard of scholarship based on such sources.

One of the most important steps in achieving this was the establishment of an academic apparatus unique to historical skills. Freeman had denied its existence in a bantering letter to his friend William Boyd Dawkins.

[17] M. Burrows, *Antiquarianism and History. A lecture delivered before the University of Oxford, May 26 1884* (Oxford, 1885) p. 7.

[18] Rosemary Jann has suggested that the distinction between antiquarianism and history can be identified within this area of the moral fable. 'In Victorian eyes, historical study would amount to little more than unscientific antiquarianism without some attempt to organise and systematise it, and the historian would be morally remiss if, out of a misplaced devotion to objectivity, he merely recorded events without comment.' Jann. *loc. cit.* p. 125. The explicitly didactic position of antiquarians and historians alike does not really allow of such a means of defining their differences; the text-artifact division still seems a more satisfactory approach.

[19] P. B. M. Blaas in his *Continuity and Anachronism. Parliamentary and Constitutional Development in Whig Historiography and in the Anti-Whig Reaction between 1890 and 1930* (The Hague, 1978) makes this distinction (p. 51). However, his concentration on the Rolls Series as the lynch-pin of governmental activity led him to regard the mid-century as a period of 'chronicle' rather than 'record' history. It is equally plausible, though, to argue that the calendaring of the state papers was the key activity, and one which encouraged 'record' rather than 'chronicle' research (p. 154). See Chapter 5.

But O professor of earth and bones, don't beguile yourself into thinking that arbitrary names of your own making answer to the names of early English kings [. . .] History has no technical terms – I half wish it had, just to frighten away fools.[20]

His was a distinctly old-fashioned view, however. By the 1870s when university history courses appeared, historians had begun to develop a critical approach both to their sources and to their analysis; Carbonell has maintained that in France, the 1860s saw the birth of the long erudite preface and of a minute attention to critical detail. 'En trente ans, on est passé de l'édition passive, simple copie et paresseuse reproduction, à l'édition critique.'[21] English historians were quick to follow suit and the corollary of the particulars of this new critical approach was a re-affirmation of that empiricist stance which derived its values from an assumption that theory was a luxury inimical to the English temperament.

In his inaugural lecture at Oxford, Stubbs had identified the function of his professorial post as one of 'simple sheer work'. Modern History, he asserted, was a subject in which the student could hope for nothing more than to be a 'patient learner rather than [a] theorist'.[22] Victorian attitudes both to the contemporary world and in their interpretation of past events found any form of determinism fundamentally unacceptable as much on moral as on methodological grounds. Unfolding the bounty of Providence was a very different prospect from cataloguing humanity into a pre-ordained development, even if that development did assume the name of progress. There was a tacit and subtle distinction between Victorian beliefs that the English were a chosen people whose evangelism was to have a civilising effect on the world, and a universe in which even hard-won English liberties were no more than part of a system beyond the control of a peculiarly English divinity.

In such a climate historians like Buckle, attempting to introduce a Comtean perspective, became the butt of much antagonism. Men as temperamentally and intellectually diverse as Froude and Stubbs agreed on this. Addressing the Royal Institution in 1864, Froude attacked Buckle's theoretical premise on the grounds that it gave too little prominence to the individual[23] whilst Stubbs hardly thought Buckle's ideas worth consideration. His dismissal of Buckle is particularly interesting in the light of his respect for the scholarship of Ranke. Doris Goldstein has made the important point that for Stubbs, it was the method rather than the philosophy of the German thinker which commanded his

---

[20] J. Coll. Oxon. MS. 192, f. 132. 1 May 1880. On the question of access to which Freeman refers, see Chapter 5.

[21] C. O. Carbonell, *Histoire et historiens: une mutation idéologique des historiens français, 1865–85* (Toulouse, 1976) p. 116.

[22] J. Coll. Oxon. MS. 199, ff. 310–14, n.d. (1867?).

[23] B. Reynolds, 'James Anthony Froude', in *Some Modern Historians of Britain: Essays in Honour of R. L. Schuyler* (New York, 1951) pp. 49–65 (p. 51).

interest.[24] His complete neglect of Ranke's philosophy was such that he could write unselfconsciously to Freeman from his vicarage in Navestock: 'Have you seen Buckle on Civilisation, Vol 1? [. . .] I do not believe in the Philosophy of History, and so do not believe in Buckle.'[25] As it remained for the antiquarians, factual content, albeit subjected to a more critical battery of tests, was paramount for the historians.

Certain topics continually exerted a fascination over English historians and proved to be their most popular and tenacious areas of study.

There are few periods in the world's history that attract the minds of Englishmen so strongly as the era of the Reformation [. . .] For upwards of two centuries this period has been the chief battle-ground of religious controversialists.[26]

There were many who shared Edward Peacock's interest in the Reformation; historians as diverse as J. S. Brewer, J. A. Froude, Frederic Seebohm and Rawdon Brown. The controversies surrounding dissatisfaction with papal power in the sixteenth century and earlier received growing attention in the light of the religious controversies of the period; such issues were still hotly debated and highly contentious. Hatred of Catholicism was still a common English prejudice.

The most indecorous actions of a London brothel shrink to nothing, when compared with these idolatrous receptacles of filthy friars and consecrated nuns.[27]

Although the days when the institutions of Catholic England could be thus compared to orgiastic gatherings and found wanting were receding, suspicion lingered on fanned by the flames of Tractarianism. Proud Protestantism found justification in the pages of English historical texts.

The English Civil War was another popular topic, combining religious preoccupations with contemporary politics. The turbulent events of the seventeenth century were near-contemporary in their significance and highly relevant; as William Lecky remarked in his *The Political Value of History* (1892), 'We are Cavaliers or Roundheads before we are Conservatives or Liberals.'[28] Religious and political allegiances merged in a perspective culled partly from a historical appreciation and partly from layers of myth. The proclamation of English liberty, both spiritual and constitutional, had as its guarantor the struggles of the seventeenth century; it sustained its contemporary relevance as long as religious categories remained so enormously influential.[29] It was not,

[24] D. S. Goldstein, 'The Professionalisation of History in Britain in the Later Nineteenth and Early Twentieth Centuries', *Storia della Storiografia* (1983) 3, 3–26 (p. 11).
[25] Bodl. MS. Eng. misc. e. 148. 8 November (1857?), Stubbs to Freeman.
[26] E. Peacock, *English Church Furniture, Ornaments and Decorations at the period of the Reformation* (London, 1866) p. 12.
[27] Major Samuel Dales, *An Essay on the Study of the History of England* (London, 1809) p. 25.
[28] Quoted in J. W. Burrow, *A Liberal Descent: Victorian Historians and the English Past* (Cambridge, 1981) p. 14.   [29] *ibid.* p. 15.

however, merely the devotional aspects of the crisis of seventeenth-century England which made it so great a focus of attention but its topical significance in the light of parliamentary changes. The Reform Act of 1832 whilst affecting the structure of government and representation only minimally had called forth much rhetoric about the sacred heritage of English constitutionalism. Identification with a parliamentary system of great antiquity, defended in the Stuart period with bloodshed, was an attractive argument for tradition.[30]

There was a logical path from such a view to that major historical interest in the constitution pursued by historians such as Stubbs and Freeman, Gardiner and Maitland. This debate over the origin of the English constitution dominated professional history overwhelmingly in the later years of the century. Early historians of Parliament such as Francis Palgrave and John Allen were succeeded by a great wave of interest following the substantial impact of 1832. P. B. M. Blaas contends, very plausibly, that the roots of this new analysis were to be found in the experience of growing bureaucracy. Administrative history, he said, was 'the child of contemporary experience' pulled into the centre of the stage by the burgeoning machinery of government necessitated by an industrialising society.[31]

The constitutionalism which was thus so central to historical debate in this period had focused on erudite discussion of the Middle Ages. Alongside its more arcane cousin, there was a more popular revival of interest in medieval England which had taken its cue from the ecclesiological and romantic interests in medieval society. The propensity to see in medieval England the ideal of a purer social organisation in which mutual obligation and a simpler faith in God subsisted was a powerful political mechanism.[32] Longstanding grievances about ancient Saxon liberty trampled underfoot by the Norman invasion, although never successfully quenched, cemented the emotional commitment implicit in so much historical writing at this juncture.[33] The antiquity of the parliamentary system and the antipathy to the absolutism symbolised by the Magna Carta story represented jointly a celebration of English pride and a

---

[30] See, for example, T. W. Mason, 'Nineteenth Century Cromwell', *Past and Present* 40 (1968) 187–91; C. H. George, 'Puritanism as History and Historiography', *Past and Present* 41 (1968) 77–104; J. W. Burrow, *op. cit.*

[31] Blaas, *op. cit.* p. xv.

[32] A. Chandler, *A Dream of Order. The Medieval Ideal in Nineteenth Century English Literature* (London, 1971).

[33] Alongside this essentially Whig view of history, some commentators have also pointed out the alternative political use of this myth. Christopher Hill's essay on the Norman Yoke in his *Puritanism and Revolution* (London, 1958) and T. W. Mason's article on 'Nineteenth Century Cromwell' *loc. cit.*, both talk of the radical tradition which asserted the rights of the common people. In Hill's essay, the theory of lost rights, of liberties plundered by the Norman conquerors is paramount. Mason points out the very varied purposes to which Cromwellianism lent itself, and not just within the sphere of 'radical, working-class and socialist politics' (p. 188). See too Asa Briggs, *Saxons, Normans and Victorians* (Sussex, 1966) in which he underlines the invocation by radicals and moderates alike of this forceful myth.

means of linking the two major fields of historical interest, the troubles of the Stuart years and a discussion of the constitution generally pitched in an earlier period.

The popular and persistent belief in the imposition of an alien Norman culture after 1066, masking the antiquity of English institutions and customs was particularly important. The 1830s and 1840s had seen the growth of historical philology and in particular, the study of Anglo-Saxon. When the *Saturday Review* spoke of Henry III's famous proclamation of 1258 as 'our one native oasis in a howling wilderness of French and Latin, a philological and constitutional ewe-lamb to be tended with the most religious care', the suggestion of a Norman corruption of English innocence – linguistically and constitutionally – was strong. English nationalism found fodder for outrage in the French and Latin customarily used for royal proclamations and legal transactions after the Norman invasion.[34] The origins of the English nation were identified with the small localised communities in North Germany, underlining the strong contrast between these idealised small and local units as opposed to the centralised administration deemed to have been introduced under ruthless Norman rule. Blaas's point about the experience of centralising forces in government would seem a strong one.[35]

Such work was paralleled by a new approach to the study of Old English which began with the philological work pioneered in England in the 1830s and 40s by J. M. Kemble and Benjamin Thorpe. In common with other historical fields, it was based extensively on the exploitation of manuscript material. Both Thorpe and Kemble were prodigious editors of Anglo-Saxon manuscripts for the new printing clubs. Their emphasis on language as the medium – both within a grammatical and an etymological framework – through which historical developments were best understood had important ramifications. Teutonism expressed itself not just in the quest for the Northern forerunners of the English race, but in a deliberate and self-conscious Saxonism in language. The common dictum that the Anglo-Saxon should be preferred over the Latin reached its apotheosis in the prose of that arch-Teuton Edward Freeman.[36] His attempts to expunge his writing of words of Latin descent and to employ a purely English vocabulary reflect his strong emotional attachment to Teutonism. Fowler's *Modern English Usage* (2nd edition, 1965) dates this linguistic purism to the first half of the nineteenth century; the earliest example given is *bodeful* as an alternative to *ominous*. In the *Oxford English Dictionary* the earliest citation given is foreword, the Saxon substitute for preface.

One of the attractions of asserting a Germanic descent was the association which could thus be drawn with the growth of Protestantism. Zealous churchmen, amongst them Charles Kingsley, were drawn to the Teutonic

---

[34] PRO 8.14. Press Cuttings. *Saturday Review*, 27 March 1869.   [35] P. B. M. Blaas, *op. cit.*
[36] For a description and discussion of Freeman's style, see J. W. Burrow, *op. cit.* pp. 211–2.

interpretation by the idea of the shared religious principles of the Northern German states and England. Kingsley's essays on *The Roman and the Teuton* dwell lengthily on the moral righteousness and nobility of the Northern tribes drawing an explicit contrast with the decadence into which he saw Rome and its Empire plunging. The moral prescription inscribed in the doctrine of Saxonism was explicit.

We have at last awaked to the fact that Greece and Rome do not exhaust the world's stock of wisdom and greatness [. . .] that the soil of Teutonic Christendom has brought forth as deep and enduring systems [. . .] We have at last learned where to look for our own fathers [. . .] The inheritance of those principles on which the whole scheme of modern arts and literature and manners and government are primarily formed and to which we owe that the thrones of the North stand firm amid the convulsions of Europe, that peace and order still reign supreme in the realm alike of Harold Hardrada and of Harold the son of Godwin, while the land of the Conqueror is tossed to and fro by intestine broils.

The date of publication of Freeman's *Thoughts on the Study of History* is telling. It appeared in 1849, as did Kemble's two-volume *The Saxons in England*, the preface of which expressed remarkably similar sentiments: 'On every side of us thrones totter, and the deep foundations of society are convulsed.' Kemble's description of the European uprisings of 1848 which had left England comparatively unscathed carried with it, like the work of Freeman, the conviction that English stability derived from Saxon roots; the continuity of English institutions obstinately and fundamentally undisturbed by the Normans and defended so stoutly against the encroachment of absolutism in the seventeenth century formed the basis for this view. The celebration in that year of the Jubilee of King Alfred at his birthplace of Wantage crowned the triumph of such traditionalism. It is significant that 1866 saw no similarly lauded full-scale commemoration of the Battle of Hastings.[37]

The new philologically-oriented Saxonism was one of the first areas in which the growing divisions between historians and antiquarians became apparent. Hans Aarsleff has identified the chief difference between the two groups as the claim, on the part of the advocates of the new Continental philology, that their studies were scientifically conceived and based on a systematic understanding of grammatical structure.[38] Their dismissal of antiquarian dilettantism was to become the rallying cry of the self-conscious historical community for the remainder of the century.

Amongst those [. . .] who are engaged in the study of the past there will always be, as there have always been, the men of simple research, delighting in the multiplication of facts, in the chain of positive sequence, not only undeterred by the dryness of mere facts as facts, but positively revelling in them.[39]

[37] Briggs, *op. cit.* p. 12.
[38] H. Aarsleff, *The Study of Language in England, 1780–1860* (Princeton, 1967) pp. 165; 195.
[39] M. Burrows, *op. cit.* p. 6.

Both antiquarians and historians were anxious to claim empiricism for their own, but it was the historians who successfully appropriated the value-laden terms which afforded them their intellectual pre-eminence.

There are men who busy themselves with buildings or primaeval monuments or actual objects and relics of early times [. . .] but whose interest ends in the objects themselves [. . .] Unless it [. . .] goes on to their higher value as forms part of a greater whole [. . .] antiquarian study is a mere matter of curiosity; it cannot be allowed to claim the rank of a science [. . .] The value of a local history is the way in which it illustrates general history.[40]

For all their assumed superiority however, historians owed much to the forms of antiquarian study. The frequent insistence, notable in the Oxford historical school, on a physical acquaintance with the geographical area of study was reminiscent of the emphasis laid by the topographer and local historian on descriptive material.[41] John Burrow has made the crucial point that Whig historians attached considerable significance to the organicist analogy of the ancient building as an 'image of endless renewal [. . .] compatible with the essential integrity and continuity of the structure', a preoccupation reminiscent of the central importance attached to architecture and particularly to church architecture, in the work of the archaeological societies.[42] The symbolism that historians invested in ancient buildings was given concrete expression by antiquarian practice. Nor can it be claimed that exclusively scholarly considerations were always paramount even amongst established historians. The attack on picturesque history which Rosemary Jann has identified as a central dividing point between amateur and professional was only a gradually acquired consensus.[43] Freeman's plans for his *Norman Conquest* in the late 1860s make clear that, despite the careful distance historians maintained from the antiquaries, they did not yet see themselves catering exclusively for a professional or even a knowledgeable readership.

I have to make for my text a narrative which I hope may be intelligible to girls and curates, and in an appendix to discuss the evidence for each point in a way which I hope may be satisfactory to Gneist and Stubbs.[44]

Freeman's comments to fellow historian George Kitchin express the widely held idea that history should play a vital role in uniting the disparate classes of English society into a racially welded whole.[45] The organisation of consensus

---

[40] E. A. Freeman, 'Address to the Historical Section of the Annual Meeting of the Archaeological Institute held at Cardiff', *Arch. Jnl* xxviii (1871) 177–95.

[41] See Chapter 2. p. 27.   [42] J. W. Burrow, *op. cit.* pp. 179; 217.

[43] Jann's assertion (*loc. cit.* p. 131) relates specifically to university history but clearly has ramifications which reach well beyond the confines of the ancient universities.

[44] Bodl. MS. Eng. lett. d. 74, ff. 106–9. 24 November 1867.

[45] See Morrell & Thackray, *Gentlemen of Science: The Early Years of the British Association for the Advancement of Science* (Oxford, 1981) p. 17, and J. H. Plumb, *The Death of the Past* (London, 1969) for the idea of the rôle of men of knowledge as promoters of class unity.

and social cohesion around a national solidarity was as strong a force in nineteenth-century historical writing as in its antiquarian counterpart. The combination of 'fervent patriotism with a respect for tradition', as David Douglas has pointed out, encouraged historical writing but at the same time licensed the use of polemic.[46] Nineteenth-century historians coloured their works with a nationalist hue and presented the events of the past as proofs of the unchallengeable primacy of the English with a certainty that this was their function as historians.[47] 'The supreme question was always what rôle did an event play in the development of the English nation?'[48]

This emphatic insistence on the pre-eminence of the English meant that historians frequently chose to concentrate as we have seen on topics pertinent to England; such expressions of patriotism hardly serve to distinguish history from moral didacticism in this period. Few historians did not view the events of the human world as ultimately subservient to an omnipotent creator, and as such were tempted to draw moral lessons from historical example. One of the most potent metaphors of this historical court of appeal was the decline – invariably conceived in moral terms – of the Roman Empire. The fall of Rome, attributed to decadence, luxury and indulgence, was cited as a great object lesson by innumerable commentators and used to fuel the spirit of jingoism. Kingsley in his *The Roman and the Teuton* contrasted the simple healthy vigour of the northerly Teutons with the sickly pallor of Roman degeneration. So too the antiquary Charles Hardwick, solemnly intoning the wreckage of a great empire. 'Luxury and vice have done their work; the power of the once "almighty Rome" is broken.'[49]

The contrast between the British and the Roman empires lent endless opportunity for this commonplace comparison to be turned to patriotic advantage.

Another empire has sprung into being, of which Rome dreamt not [. . .] Her empire is threefold that of Rome in the hour of its prime. But power is not her brightest diadem. The holiness of the domestic circle irradiates her literature, and all the arts of peace flourish under her sway. Her people bless her. We may [. . .] learn [. . .] on the one hand to emulate the virtues that adorned her [Rome's] prosperity, and on the other to shun the vices that were punished by her downfall. The sceptre which Rome relinquished, we have taken up. Great is our Honour – great our Responsibility.[50]

The differing tones employed when fondly describing England and when cataloguing the disastrous consequences of vice are distinctive. Nineteenth-

[46] D. Douglas, *The Norman Conquest and British Historians* (Glasgow, 1946) p. 8.
[47] J. G. A. Pocock, 'The Origins of the Study of the Past: A Comparative Approach', *Comparative Studies in Society and History* IV (1961–2) 219–46.
[48] M. E. Bratchel, *Edward Augustus Freeman and the Victorian Interpretation of the Norman Conquest* (Ilfracombe, 1969) p. 15.   [49] C. Hardwick, *op. cit.* p. 511.
[50] J. C. Bruce, *The Roman Wall: A Historical, Topographical and Descriptive Account of the Barrier of the Lower Isthmus* (London/Newcastle, 1851) pp. 40; 49.

century historians tended to adopt an affectionate almost wistful tone when talking of English soil, customs or people.

No spot in Britain can be so sacred to Englishman as that which first felt the trod of English feet. There is little indeed to catch the eye in Ebbsfleet itself [. . .] but taken as a whole the scene has a wild beauty all of its own. To the right, the white curve of Ramsgate cliffs looks down on the crescent of Pegwell Bay; far away to the left, across grey marsh-levels, where smoke-wreaths mark the sites of Richborough and Sandwich, rises the dim cliff-line of Deal.[51]

J. R. Green had obviously visited Ebbsfleet in person and his vivid description captures not just the landscape but his excitement and love of its historical associations. It was more often than not an emotional rather than an intellectual appreciation of historical continuity which thus motivated the historian.[52]

England and English history were central fixed points in a universe judged invariably by Christian and English standards. Historians whose work lay outside that sacred field often found it necessary to justify their efforts by reference to their value for national or at least Western historical knowledge. Sidney Owen's history of India was prefaced with just such an explanation.

It was attempted to survey this revolution not as an isolated and abnormal series of occurrences, but as forming, not the less because its actors bore strange names and had [. . .] dark complexions, an essential portion of the history of the world; [. . .] a portion suggestive of striking and instructive analogies to the leading circumstances, characters and events of European annals [. . .] and hence [. . .] both claims and repays the attention of the general student of history and politics.[53]

Truth in this period was never a neutral and value-free arbiter. It was contained in and defined by those facts which lent weight to the dominant values of society. Truth for the historian was primarily also that which furnished proofs of English pre-eminence. The past had an ideological import in supporting the claims of contemporary English values. J. H. Plumb has distinguished between the past as a 'created ideology with a purpose' and a critically-oriented historical scholarship, and P. B. M. Blaas has similarly identified a 'traditionalist' and a 'historical' consciousness.[54] Both writers have crucially differentiated ideology from history as a species of disinterested scholarship. Throughout the nineteenth century, history was a central weapon in the armoury of political and moral values and its practitioners had no wish to liberate it from that involvement.

Historical investigation whether historical or antiquarian in method was

[51] J. R. Green, *A Short History of the English People* (London, 1874) p. 7.
[52] J. W. Burrow, 'The Village Community and the Uses of History in Late Nineteenth Century England', in ed., N. McKendrick, *Historical Perspectives. Studies in English Thought and Society* (London, 1974) pp. 255–84 (p. 267).
[53] S. J. Owen, *India on the Eve of the British Conquest. A Historical Sketch* (London, 1872) pp. iii–iv.
[54] Plumb, *op. cit.* p. 17; P. B. M. Blaas, *op. cit.* p. 32.

intrinsically connected in this period with the urgent need to make sense of a changing society. The identification of past events with current structures and their use as a justification for and explanation of those structures, was a means of establishing not just a common consensus but a sense of both individual and collective purpose. Historians sought to establish an organic continuity with the English past wherein present conditions could claim to be not just the only logical but the best outcome of a revered and celebrated past.[55] History was thus, though hardly consciously, a useful tool; the promotion of ideals, the creation of a consensual contentment made it a valuable addition to the gentlemen's education.

Its integration into the *status quo* of Victorian society is highlighted by the frequent historical allusions which accompanied political and specifically parliamentary debate. A wide range of government business was conducted with reference to historical comparison. Olive Anderson has argued that its impact was often great enough to influence directly the creation of government policy; 'one of the *sentiments-clefs* of the well-to-do in the 1850s was faith in the accessibility and value of the past'.[56] A large number of active historians and antiquarians sat in the Commons during the course of the century; Macaulay, Alexander Kinglake, Stanhope, J. E. Thorold Rogers, E. P. Shirley, Beriah Botfield and Lord Londesborough for example, and Disraeli's Young England derived much of its philosophy directly from that most tenacious of Victorian mythologies, the idealisation of the Middle Ages. The attraction of an ideal of social cohesion based on the *noblesse oblige*, the evocation of a land in which freedom and responsibility were ineluctably yoked together was a compelling image of powerful cultural force in a society as radically divided as Victorian England.

Changes in attitude to a particular event or person similarly reflect the accommodation of history to ideological purpose. Blaas has plotted a significant shift in the appraisal of Cromwell; dismissed at the start of the century as a 'detested hypocrite', he was later lauded by Carlyle, became a commonplace of parliamentary debate and in time one of the favourite subjects of historical artists.[57] There was no perceived incompatibility between the ideals of truth and the discipline of history; the latter revealed the former in the honours due to English soil.

[55] Plumb has identified the changeover from this attitude to the past to the idea of a critical historiography in his *The Death of the Past*. Michel Foucault, recognising the same disjunction, talks of the establishment of a new central historical concept, that of discontinuity (*The Archaeology of Knowledge* (London, 1972)). Both writers convey the sense that the 'new' history had as its corollary a break with the past.

[56] O. Anderson, 'The Political Uses of History in mid Nineteenth Century England', *Past and Present* 36 (1967) 87–105.

[57] Blaas, *op. cit.* p. 142; Roy Strong, *And When Did You Last See Your Father? The Victorian Painter and British History* (London, 1978) pp. 44–5; A. O. J. Cockshut, *Truth to Life: The Art of Biography in the Nineteenth Century* (London, 1974) p. 56.

It cannot be without advantage for us to learn how a State so favoured as our own has set about the great work of constitution and solved the problem, of uniting the completest obedience to the law with the greatest amount of individual freedom.[58]

Kemble's words of 1849 record precisely that coalescence of freedom and responsibility which was glorified as England's finest and most treasured heritage. J. R. Green's emotive description of Magna Carta evokes the power and strength which national pride could summon.

It is impossible to gaze without reverence on the earliest monument of English freedom which we can see with our own eyes and touch with our own hands, the great Charter to which from age to age patriots have looked back on as the basis of English liberty.[59]

History was the tangible proof of English glory, a monument to the power of tradition and stability, a metaphor of pious belief.

History was contained within a religious, specifically Christian framework which necessarily assumed an immanent divinity. The stress on continuity rather than on disjunction or conflict was consistent with an epistemology which emanated thus from the Christian tradition. Thus could Anglican historians such as Stubbs argue the 'continuous and self-contained existence' of the English Church 'which successfully resisted all attempts by the medieval papacy to encroach upon its primitive and native authority'.[60] The religious influence on historical thinking was more than merely ecclesiastical in content, however.

History has been selected by Revelation itself as the chosen vehicle of its teaching in a manner which can be asserted of no other human pursuit; we may fairly say that it has set on it the especial stamp and seal of Divine approbation; a portion of history is given us on the highest sanction, as a sample of the true and religious treatment of the whole.[61]

Freeman's evidence, it must be assumed, was epiphanic but the spiritual vindication of the study of history, and in particular that pertaining to the English and their established religion, was a persuasive comment on its suitability for Victorian consumption. It was no accident that William Stubbs relinquished his professorship at Oxford to take up a bishopric. His friend Green described his inaugural professorial lecture at Oxford as suffused with a 'religious glow', and summarised its climax as 'the old simple lesson that the world's history led up to God, that Modern History was but the broadening of His light in Christ'.[62] Green had his own doubts about the reception which awaited such sentiments, but Stubbs' appointment in 1866 came at a time when Gladstonian liberalism was proclaiming the moral aspects of good government.[63] Stubbs simply transferred that view to the groves of Academe.

[58] J. M. Kemble, *The Saxons in England* (London, 1849) p. vi.   [59] J. R. Green, *op. cit.* p. 123.
[60] H. G. Richardson & G. O. Sayles, *The Governance of Medieval England from the Conquest to Magna Carta* (Edinburgh, 1963) p. 9.
[61] E. A. Freeman, *Thoughts on the Study of History, with reference to the proposed changes in the Public Examinations* (Oxford/London, 1849) pp. 10–11.
[62] J. Coll. Oxon. MS. 199, ff. 310–14, February (1867?).
[63] See Chapter 2 on the coalescence of Stubbs' and Gladstone's views.

It was inevitable that such views would produce a strongly teleological reading of history; tradition and topicality were twinned essential elements in history throughout this period. The fashion for castigating nineteenth-century historians for an anachronistic presentation of their findings and a tendency to linear representation seems an inappropriate response. The fusion of process and progress was an obvious and tempting solution in a society whose dominant moral code was coterminous with Christian tradition and whose long-held fear of conflict and revolution thus favoured a doctrine of continuity. A society experiencing change at so great a pace was as anxious not to lose power over its own past reflections as it was to understand and thus control its metamorphosis. The tension between 'the need for permanence and the conviction that change was inevitable'[64] was resolved by this exaltation of national and religious consensus however frail the reality. The 'doctrine of the splendid present', as Galbraith put it, which successfully integrated past and present in a continuum of gradual progress was a necessary and sometimes desperate attempt to pin down a workable and profitable epistemology. There was, of course, an unresolved paradox inherent in the stance they chose; the empiricist antagonism to the determinist philosophies of the period did not rest easily with the assertion of a Providentially administered universe. The solution was the glorification of individual freedom: the liberty of the individual within a sphere ordained by God and couched in the language of redemption.

Latter day historians have commented critically on the 'backwardness' of their nineteenth-century predecessors in England.[65] European nations, France and Germany in particular, had seemingly moved closer to the construction of a specifically academic history prior to their English counterparts. In methodology and in institutional establishment both these countries acquired the apparatus of the modern professional academic world earlier than England. The social and political context of their 'advance' is revealing, for again ideology played a major rôle in the mode of development apparent in those nations.[66] Dismissing the English experience as 'two centuries late in accomplishing the equivalent of the scientific revolution of the seventeenth century' is to miss the point.[67] England did not lag behind developments on the

---

[64] R. Jann, 'The Art of History in Nineteenth Century England: Studies in Victorian Historiography', (unpublished PhD thesis, Northwestern University, 1975), p. 222.

[65] Writers as diverse as Herbert Butterfield and Gareth Stedman Jones have adopted that same teleology in assuming a finality for contemporary historical scholarship. See H. Butterfield, 'Some Trends in Scholarship 1868–1968, in the Field of Modern History', Trans. Royal Historical Society 5th ser. XIX (1969) 159–84; G. Stedman Jones, 'History: "The Poverty of Empiricism"', in ed. R. Blackburn, Ideology in Social Science. Readings in Critical Social Theory (Glasgow, 1972) 96–115.

[66] W.R. Keylor, Academy and Community. The Foundation of the French Historical Profession (Harvard, 1975); F.K. Ringer, The Decline of the German Mandarins. The German Academic Community, 1890–1933 (Cambridge, Mass., 1969).   [67] Butterfield, loc. cit. p. 159.

Continent – its experience was barely comparable either in the cultural or the political context.

Victorian historians did, however, attempt the definition of a methodology. Their desire to distance their work from the collecting instinct they labelled as antiquarian represents one attempt. Most important, though, was the change in the status of the text as the key source of historical investigation. Textual authority became the fundamental tenet of Victorian historical writing. The abundant schemes, both private and public, for publishing editions of manuscripts, early books, catalogues of records and collections attests to this new dominant faith in the text. Archival research had, by the turn of the century, become the *sine qua non* of the professional.[68] It was from this belief in the verification through original sources that English empiricism derived its strength. The reliance of ancient history on commentary, albeit of the stature of Herodotus or Livy, added further weight to the claims of the modern historians who could point to the pipe rolls and inquisitions post mortem that were becoming their stock-in-trade. Literary history receded and textually based accounts took precedence over form. The overtly diplomatic and political content of much orthodox historical writing reinforced the contrast between history proper and the popular historical fiction of the day.

III

Archaeology was freed from some of these problems by its exclusive concentration on material remains. Modern archaeologists can define their subject succinctly as 'the systematic study of antiquities as a means of reconstructing the past'.[69] For nineteenth-century students, however, such simple delineation was hampered by a multitude of considerations. The desire to understand all recognised aspects of the subject was strong, since specialisation was so clearly a corollary of professionalisation. Charles Newton, the first Yates Professor of Classical Archaeology at University College London from 1880, wrote an essay 'On The Study of Archaeology' in 1851. The archaeological ideal he describes requires an intellectual paragon of rare worth and sensitivity.

He who would master the manifold subject-matter of Archaeology, and appreciate its whole range and compass, must possess a mind in which the reflective and perceptive faculties are duly balanced; he must combine with the aesthetic culture of the Artist, and the trained judgment of the Historian, not a little of the learning of the Philologer; the plodding drudgery which gathers together his materials must not blunt the critical acuteness required for their classification and interpretation.[70]

---

[68] Men such as Freeman and Green had thus been ousted, at the end of the century, by meticulous scholars such as Maitland, Gardiner and others.

[69] G. Clark, *Archaeology and Society. Reconstructing the Prehistoric Past* (London, 1968) p. 17.

[70] C. Newton, 'On the Study of Archaeology', *Arch. Jnl.* VIII (1851) 1–26 (pp. 25–6).

They had inherited from classical civilisation what Momigliano has described as 'the notion of a science called archaeology dealing with subjects which today we would call of antiquarian interest'.[71] The failure to distinguish between the two terms neither aided the community's own sense of unity nor made clear the significance of the break between textual and material analysis. The acquisition of specific methods appropriate to the examination of antiquities was vital to the development of the archaeological approach. The most characteristic activity which classified archaeology throughout the century was excavation: 'the difference between antiquarianism and archaeology is excavation, or largely so'.[72] And it was undoubtedly the work of the excavators that first fired the public imagination – Bateman and Greenwell's digging often attracted large crowds of spectators whilst the public flocked to the British Museum for the exhibition of winged lions and bulls brought from Nineveh by Layard.

Excavation was hardly innovatory however; many eighteenth-century antiquarians had been keen barrow-diggers and the early nineteenth-century investigations conducted in Wiltshire by Sir Richard Colt Hoare had resulted in an expensively-mounted publication. One of the foremost of Colt Hoare's successors was dismissive of the earlier man's work however. His own work, he claimed, contained

a greater amount of information respecting the primeval sepulchres of Britain, derived from actual excavation than has ever appeared in a single work, except perhaps in the costly folios of Sir Richard Hoare's Ancient Wiltshire which are in a great measure useless to the scientific student, from the absence of any Craniological Notices or Measurements.[73]

Colt Hoare's work was rendered incomplete by its lack of a classificatory framework. Classification was, of course, also regarded as the hallmark of antiquarian study and it would not be unreasonable to suggest a sustained and direct relationship between the two disciplines on this basis, more particularly since an identifiably antiquarian mode of classifying antiquities, founded on classical notions of the archaeology of art, proved tenacious in archaeology. The new Department of British and Medieval Antiquities created in 1860 from the old general Department of Antiquities in the British Museum continued to divide its collection among two dominant classifications – Sculpture and smaller remains, including coins and medals.[74] In similar vein, the Rev. J. H. Marsden, first Disney Professor of Archaeology in the University of Cambridge, told the audience at his introductory lectures in 1852 that his task as an

---

[71] Momigliano, *loc. cit.* p. 3.

[72] G. Daniel, *Cambridge and the Back-Looking Curiosity* (Cambridge, 1976) p. 5.

[73] T. Bateman, *Ten Years' Digging in Celtic and Saxon Grave Hills in the Counties of Derby, Stafford and York from 1848–58* (London, 1861) p.v.

[74] G. E. Daniel, *A Hundred Years of Archaeology* (London, 1950) p. 82.

archaeologist was 'to collect, analyse and classify those relics of the past which form a very important portion of the materials of history'.[75] It was another twenty years, however, before men such as Petrie and Pitt Rivers could assert with any authority that the application of such techniques would best be achieved by 'the mathematical and mechanical study of antiquities'.[76]

In common with both the antiquarian and the historical communities, archaeologists were anxious to found their discipline on a pragmatic basis.

I will only add, that theory, the bane of nearly all the older Antiquarian books, has been avoided, and that the very few deductions I have ventured to make from recorded facts are either demonstrable, or such as may be fairly inferred.[77]

Bateman nonetheless added, with a recognition of the methodological infancy of his subject:

we look forward with confidence to the time [. . .] when the immense mass of valuable facts and observations already accumulated, compared and generalised, and subjected to a process of induction, shall yield conclusions on questions that have hitherto been merely subjects of hopeless speculation.[78]

The most significant change to affect nineteenth-century archaeological technique was perhaps the shift from *a priori* deduction to inductive analysis in which the publication in 1877 of Petrie's *Inductive Metrology* was an important milestone. In his introduction, he made much of this epistemological transform-ation. 'The historical sciences seem to pass through two stages in the course of their development – the literary and the monumental – the deductive and the inductive.'[79] Significantly enough, inductive techniques were pioneered largely in the province of technical method. Again, Petrie was one of the earliest archaeologists to broach this new area; having studied the skills of surveying at Stonehenge during his teens, Petrie applied broadly similar methods to his investigations at Gizeh in the 1880s. His mathematical analysis of the construction of the pyramids and temples, with its work 'involving co-ordinates, probable errors and arguments based on purely mechanical considerations' was intended to appeal to 'separate classes: the antiquarian [and] the surveyor and geodetist'.[80] His work was such that by the end of the century David Hogarth could confidently claim that 'the excavator, from being a random hunter for treasure has become a methodical collector of evidence'.[81]

Unlike antiquarianism or history, archaeology benefited greatly from

[75] J. H. Marsden, *Two Introductory Lectures upon Archaeology delivered in the University of Cambridge* (Cambridge, 1852) p. 5.
[76] W. M. F. Petrie, *The Pyramids and Temples of Gizeh* (London, 1883) p. xiii.
[77] T. Bateman, *op. cit.* p. vi.   [78] *ibid.* p. iii.
[79] W. M. F. Petrie, *Inductive Metrology* (London, 1877) p. 2.
[80] W. M. F. Petrie, *op. cit.* (1883) p. xiii.
[81] D. G. Hogarth (ed.), *Authority and Archaeology. Sacred and Profane. Essays on the relation of monuments to biblical and classical literature* (London, 1889) p. x.

simultaneous advances in various scientific fields. John Evans had at an early stage collaborated closely with the geologist John Prestwich in examining remains uncovered in the gravel pits of the Somme and it became increasingly common for archaeologists to defer to the expertise of scientists in other areas. Pitt Rivers frequently asserted their value for archaeological analysis. 'Firstly we have to put into requisition the services of the geologist [. . .] Then comes the palaeontologist who examines [. . .] the [. . .] bones [. . .] After this [. . .] we are dependent entirely on the labours of the physical anthropologist'.[82]

Older classically bound notions of archaeology continued to exert a hold however, and were central to the definition of the broad boundaries of the discipline. In 1866 Samuel Birch of the British Museum's department of General Antiquities described archaeology thus:

By archaeology is understood the study of the monuments of antiquity of all times and places, and it divides itself into several branches as palaeography [. . .] epigraphy [. . .] and the study of figured antiquity, or of the shapes and meaning of sculpture, painting and symbolical representations.[83]

The idea of archaeology as fundamentally connected to artistic values was widely held. Birch rounded off his description by asserting that the value of archaeology was that it 'aids in the formation and cultivation of public taste by directing it to the selection of the good and useful'.[84] John Marsden on his appointment to England's first chair of archaeology at Cambridge, talked of 'the close connexion between the antiquary and the poet'. Marsden's use of the term antiquary itself suggests the lack of specific definition; he had in mind one 'whose occupation [is] among objects which he can touch, and handle, and pry into, and weigh, and measure'.[85] Like the poet, the work of the archaeologist fired the imagination. 'Few things excite the imagination more forcibly than the relics of the past.' Marsden's contemporaries in archaeology all spoke interchangeably of the antiquary and the archaeologist: Thomas Bateman, William Greenwell, Samuel Birch, Churchill Babington and John Evans. The coalescence of the two fields, both institutionally and individually, derived principally from their similar interest in artifacts and their classification. Most antiquaries sought their evidence not only in antiquities but in documents, combining the perceptions of the historian and the archaeologist. It was to the notice of the antiquarian community rather than the nascent archaeological network that the pioneering work of the Danish archaeologists Thomsen and

[82] A. H. L. F. Pitt Rivers, 'Address to the Antiquarian section at the Annual meeting of the Archaeological Institute held at Lewes', *Arch. Jnl.* xli (1884) 58–78 (pp. 59–63).

[83] S. Birch, 'Inaugural Discourse delivered in the section of General Antiquities at the Annual Meeting of the Archaeological Institute in London, July 1866', *Arch. Jnl.* xxiv (1867) 1–12.

[84] *ibid.* p. 1. And yet Birch condemned the foundation of the Egypt Exploration Fund in 1882 for its promotion of what he dubbed 'emotional archaeology'. See Margaret S. Drower, 'The Early Years', in ed. T. G. H. James, *Excavating in Egypt. The Egypt Exploration Society 1882–1982* (London, 1982) 9–36 (p. 14).   [85] J. H. Marsden, *op. cit.* p. 59.

Worsaae, architects of the controversial Three Age system first came, and it was institutions such as the Society of Antiquaries who welcomed them. Worsaae's *The Primeval Antiquities of Denmark* was translated by the antiquarian W. J. Thoms, a clerk at the House of Lords, and published by the Oxford antiquarian, J. H. Parker. Archaeologists hardly formed a separate community at this juncture and certainly could not boast a separate institutional identity before the 1870s.

Churchill Babington's description of the 'qualifications [. . .] necessary for an archaeologist' with its see-sawing terminology indicates this important lack of any real sense of differentiation.

Like the naturalist, the antiquary must in the first place bring together a large number of facts and objects [. . .] The hunting out, the securing, and the amassing facts and objects of antiquity [. . .] are the field sports of the learned [. . .] Nimrod. In a certain sense every archaeologist *must* be a collector; he must be mentally in possession of a mass of facts and objects [. . .] but he must also, when there are sufficient data, proceed to reason upon them. He puts them together, and considers what story they have to render up [. . .] He must be a man of learning [. . .] Another thing very desirable [. . .] is an appreciation of art.[86]

His stipulations were as descriptive of the requirements of the topographer or local historian as of the archaeological worker and many, of course, combined the two. John Evans, in an address in 1891, paid tribute to those who over the century had helped lay the foundations of archaeology. In British excavation he cited Charles Roach Smith, J. Yonge Akerman, John Brent and John Collingwood Bruce; for popularising heraldry he praised the Rev. Charles Boutell, and in the field of numismatics he singled out Edward Hawkins, Keeper of Antiquities at the British Museum from 1826 to 1860.[87]

Both historians and archaeologists often expressed the opinion that archaeology, like antiquarianism, was ancillary to the broader discipline of history. The notion that archaeology was the 'handmaid of history' did not always or necessarily involve the subjugation of artifact analysis to textual analysis. Thomas Hodgkin, addressing the Historical section of the Archaeological Institute in 1891 suggested that, whereas historical method was 'extensive', that of the archaeologist was one of 'intensive' cultivation; 'the Archaeologist *collects* facts relating to the past and the Historian *arranges* them'.[88] The distinction is, of course, similar to that drawn between the antiquarian and the historian. Thomas Wright certainly did not regard the antiquarianism he professed as a subordinate discipline.

Antiquarianism as a science allied to history, belongs to a more advanced state of intellectual refinement [. . .] To bring [the historian's] means together, and to arrange

---

[86] C. Babington, *An Introductory Lecture on Archaeology delivered before the University of Cambridge* (Cambridge, 1865) pp. 63–6.   [87] J. Evans, *loc. cit.* pp. 259–61.

[88] T. Hodgkin, 'Opening Address of the Historical Section at the meeting of the Archaeological Institute at Edinburgh', *Arch. Jnl.* XLVIII (1891) 263–73 (pp. 265; 267).

and make them intelligible, has been the work of the English historical antiquary for the last three centuries.[89]

In the tussle for academic status, such hierarchically conceived assumptions were the necessary expression of the professional dynamic. In reality, the three disciplines were closely related throughout this period. The work of the historians Freeman and Green in particular, owed much to archaeology. The 'new kind of history, embodying a new sense of the significance of landscape' was particularly evident in their work on town histories which invariably embraced an appreciation and analysis of physical remains. John Burrow describes Freeman as having 'an archaeologist's fascination with the superimposition of cultures and with reading history – above all, through architecture, as a palimpsest'.[90] It was well into the twentieth century before specialisation effected a radical intellectual break between these two academic subjects.[91]

Throughout the Victorian period, no training in archaeological method existed either within the universities or elsewhere. The few full-time archaeologists culled their expertise principally from that remarkable degree of self-motivation so characteristic in Victorian intellectual circles. Petrie describes how, from the age of fifteen, he read regularly at the British Museum and attended sales of antiquities and coins at Sothebys. In 1875 at the age of twenty-two, he undertook 'long survey tramps of a month at a time [. . .] working over a district to survey the earthworks and stone circles'.[92] It was experience rather than formal training that typified the nineteenth-century archaeologist.

Active and devoted archaeologists worked both in England and abroad on projects of major importance throughout the period and their efforts often involved personal financial outlay and considerable discomfort.[93] J. T. Wood, excavating the Temple of Diana at Ephesus, suffered great inconveniences during his stay in Turkey.

I had at that time no house at Ephesus, but lived alone at the hotel at Boudjah [. . .] a few miles from Smyrna. I had to walk a mile and a half to meet the train which started from Smyrna at six o'clock in the morning [. . .] The fifty miles between Smyrna and

---

[89] T. Wright, 'Antiquarianism in England', *Edinburgh Review* LXXXVI (October 1847) CLXXIV, pp. 307–28 (p. 308). Although the article was anonymous, the *Wellesley Index* assigns it to Wright.

[90] J. W. Burrow, *op. cit.* pp. 202; 188.

[91] In his *Histoire et historiens* (*op. cit.*) Carbonell suggests a distinction between 'historiens–archéologues' and 'archéologues–historiens'. His rather forced division is based on the assertion that the former group wrote narrative histories of, for example, churches based as much on archival research as on descriptions of the antiquities. The latter group Carbonell identified as those whose works were purely descriptive and without a chronological framework. No such distinctions can be drawn in the case of English writers and in any case the latter category does not represent at all the interests or mode of work of the archaeological community who dominate Carbonell's largely semantic configuration.

[92] W. M. F. Petrie, *Seventy Years in Archaeology* (London, 1931) pp. 14; 13.

[93] G. Waterfield, *Layard of Nineveh* (London, 1963) p. 191.

Ayasalouk [the nearest village to his site, at a distance of three miles] occupied nearly three hours and a half. There were no first-class carriages [. . .] and the second-class carriage had no sun-blinds [. . .] The whole day's work occupied between fourteen and fifteen hours.[94]

Pioneers such as Wood at Ephesus or Layard at Kuyunjik were dependent on local hired labour; beyond the perceived problem of dishonesty it mattered little however, for both in England where local workmen were also hired and abroad, the spadework of excavation was regarded as nothing more than simple manual labour. Petrie left his labourers at Gizeh digging while he applied himself to measuring tombs, sifting the earth they had dug and supervising their efforts.[95] J. T. Wood describes his typical daily routine, 'studying the ground and superintending the workmen [. . .] taking notes and measurements [. . .] drawing everything that was found'.[96] The important class distinction between manual and primarily intellectual effort remained paramount with team work developing only in the twentieth century.[97]

Despite the novel techniques which began to distinguish the archaeologist from the antiquarian in this period, they continued to share common sentiments as to the value and function of their researches. A strident nationalism marked archaeological narrative as distinctly as it did the historical and antiquarian. In the excavations in Biblical lands, English and French rivals were often involved in unseemly scrambles to grab at new discoveries they could then claim for their own nations. Unfavourable comparisons were drawn between the generous state funding to which the French archaeologists had access and the meagre finances available to English adventurers. The very fact of funds being diverted into projects abroad stirred the indignation of the champions of indigenous archaeology however. 'We dispatch expeditions to Asia Minor for Lycian marbles, we send to Egypt and Assyria for their antiquities [. . .] and is it too much to request that a certain degree of this care should be extended to our native remains?'[98] The arguments for a greater concentration on British antiquities were essentially the sentiments of national affirmation employed by historians and antiquarians. Thomas Wright had maintained that 'man [. . .] is anxious to become acquainted with the history of his own country and [. . .] the place in which he was born'.[99] He had constantly asserted the wealth of treasures awaiting the British excavator. 'There is hardly a corner in our island in which the spade or

---

[94] J. T. Wood, *Discoveries at Ephesus including the site and remains of the Great Temple of Diana* (London, 1877) p. 24.

[95] Griffith Institute, Oxford. MS. Journals of W. M. F. Petrie, Egyptian excavations, 1880–5.

[96] J. T. Wood, *op. cit.* p. 24.

[97] See Chapter 5 pp. 127–8 for a discussion of the manual–intellectual division as it affected the staff of the new Public Record Office.

[98] A. H. Rhind, *British Archaeology: Its Progress and Demands* (London, 1858) p. 25.

[99] T. Wright, *On the early history of Leeds in Yorkshire, and on some questions of prehistoric archaeology agitated at the present time: a lecture read before the Philosophical and Literary Society of Leeds, April 19 1864* (Leeds, 1864) p. 3.

the plough does not, from time to time, turn up relics of its earlier inhabitants.'[100] And Churchill Babington, taking up his professorial post at Cambridge in 1865, expressed a similar view.

What man is there, in whose breast glows a spark of patriotism, who does not view the monuments of his country [. . .] which connect the present with the remote past [. . .] with feelings deeper and nobler than any exotic remains . . . could either foment or engender?'[101]

Much of this national pride inevitably derived from religious belief. The relationship between religion and archaeology in the nineteenth century was a complex and uneasy one. Proofs of human antiquity which rendered a six thousand year old universe absurd and which conflicted with the Mosaic account of the creation were adduced by geologists, evolutionists and archaeologists alike in the middle decades of the century. It was the coalescence of proofs from human and natural history which were to prove, in the long term, so devastating to Creationist theories. Archaeological proofs of antiquity preceded the specifically geological evidence; the early discoveries of John Frere at Hoxne in 1797 and the excavations of Kent's Cavern, Torquay in the 1820s had suggested the need for a reappraisal of conceptions of time. William Bynum has asserted that it was only with the dawning of a sustained point of contact between geological and historical time that the intellectual impact of these separate discoveries became fully apparent.

What was missing from the concepts and frameworks of these geologists was any real grasp of the idea of human pre-history. Civilisation for them was virtually co-existent with man.[102]

For archaeology, that distinction between history and prehistory was to be immeasurably influential in shaping the new discipline. The emphasis laid on distinguishing documented societies from essentially non-literate ones widened the conceptual gap between textual and artifact analysis. The differentiation of history and prehistory was represented as literacy. Glyn Daniel defined the domain of prehistoric archaeology as 'that period of recent time between geology proper and history proper'.[103] The denial of a fundamental reading of Genesis implicit in an acceptance of the very concept of prehistory thus exacerbated that important disparity by casting doubt on the accuracy of literary and primarily Biblical models of the past.

The Danish Three Age system which plotted human development by its successive use of stone, bronze and iron artifacts was the first real attempt to instigate a theory of prehistory. From the start, it attracted opposition, with

[100] T. Wright, *The Celt, the Roman and the Saxon* (London, 3rd edn., 1875) p.v.
[101] Babington, *op. cit.* p. 8.
[102] W. Bynum, 'Time's Noblest Offspring: The Problem of Man in the British Natural Historical Sciences, 1800–63' (unpublished doctoral dissertation, University of Cambridge, 1974) pp. 277–82.   [103] G. E. Daniel, *Hundred Yrs. Arch.* (London, 1950) p. 32.

authorities such as the antiquarian Thomas Wright maintaining that archaeology was an essentially historical discipline with no place for the application of stratigraphical geology.[104] Wright dismissed the alliance of geologists and archaeologists as another example of the ills attached to overtly theoretical work and accused 'those who advocate this extreme antiquity' of 'building upon assumptions without any real foundation'.[105] His opposition to the Three Age system centred on his contention that 'history [. . .] cannot be treated as a physical science, and its objects arranged in genera and species'.[106]

Naturally enough, the infant discipline of prehistory approached its radical findings with some hesitancy. Early practitioners were reluctant to establish a definitive time-scale; tentative forays in that direction thus involved an attachment to the vague and less controversial term 'primaeval'. The *Archaeological Journal* and the *Journal of the British Archaeological Association* carried no more than a handful of articles on primaeval antiquities or remains during the century. *The Archaeological Journal* published three in the 1840s, none in the 1850s, one in the 1860s, three in the 1870s and two in the 1880s. No such articles appeared in the *Journal of the British Archaeological Association* before the 1850s when there was one. Nothing more was heard of the primaeval in its pages until the 1870s when five relevant articles were published. Three more found their way into print in the 1880s. The authors of these papers rarely risked dating their finds. Sir John Lubbock, addressing the section of Primaeval Antiquities at a London meeting of the Archaeological Institute in July 1866, erred on the side of safety and defined the prehistoric epoch – without dates – as that stretching from the first appearance of the human race on earth to the commencement of Christianity. Richard Kirwan writing in the *Archaeological Journal* of 1872 on the 'Prehistoric Archaeology of East Devon' confined his attention to the sepulchral remains of the Ancient Britons.

The first use of specific prehistorical dating, as distinct from the vaguer 'primaeval', came in the *Archaeological Journal* of 1870 with the use of the term megalithic, and in 1877 in the *Journal of the British Archaeological Association* again with a reference to the megalithic period. The two journals bore articles referring to the palaeolithic for the first time in 1880 and 1881 respectively. The gradual integration of prehistory and its eventual elevation to an almost defining rôle within archaeology was thus of major importance in determining the development of the subject in an academic context.

The difficulties associated with determining an accurate time-scale invited a mystical approach to prehistory. Charles Warne's *Ancient Dorset* of 1872 dealt with Celtic, Roman, Saxon and Danish antiquities. It sported an introductory essay on the primaeval ethnology of the county in which William Wake Smart elaborated this magical element.

[104] *ibid.* pp. 83–4.   [105] T. Wright, *op. cit.* (1864) p. 6.   [106] T. Wright, *op. cit.* (1875) p. vii.

. . . that still darker region into which the touch of history throws no gleam at all, and which with a strange fascination is ever alluring us into its mysterious labyrinths, and ever baffling our steps!

It was the religious controversy stirred up by the idea of prehistory which had the most profound effect on the new discipline however. The increasing association of archaeology with prehistoric studies necessarily brought the subject into conflict with prevailing Christian orthodoxy. It was only when the process of secularisation had reached a point where the book of *Genesis* could be read as a symbolic, or even mythical account of the Creation, that archaeology could hope to assert its academic respectability. Controversies over doctrine as well as institutional declarations of belief (in Parliament and at the universities) were current throughout most of the century. A discipline which threw doubt on the traditional beliefs of the Anglican establishment was unlikely to win status in an age in which casting doubt on the accuracy of the Pentateuch could prompt the deposition of a colonial bishop. Coupled with the impact of biblical criticism, archaeology was to have a profound effect on religion, and in so doing its development was to be hampered. It was only when religious issues were freed of so emotive and fundamental an ideological content that disciplines like archaeology could become really acceptable. Their development acts, in one sense, as an index of the fortunes of the Church.

Archaeologists were hardly in conscious and deliberate opposition to accepted beliefs and teachings however. As with the scientific community archaeologists were largely Anglican worshippers,[107] and many of the most ardent proponents of evolutionary theory were devout churchmen as well. Pitt Rivers, also a thorough-going evolutionist, regarded archaeology as instructive if not definitive of an appropriately Victorian morality.

I cannot myself see how human conduct is likely to be affected disadvantageously by recognising the humble origin of mankind. If it teaches us to take less pride in our ancestry, and to place more reliance on ourselves, this cannot fail to serve as an additional incentive to industry and to respectability. Nor are our relations with the Supreme Power presented to us in an unfavourable light by this discovery, for if man was created originally in the image of God, it is obvious that the very best of us have greatly degenerated. But if on the other hand we recognise that we have sprung from inferior beings [. . .] we are encouraged to hope that with the help of Providence [. . .] we may continue to improve in the long run as we have done hitherto.[108]

But it was precisely the tenacity of this religious dominance which retarded the formation of academic archaeology and of an archaeological community. As the separately conceived stature of archaeology grew and its public profile attracted greater attention, the methodological divisions between biblical, classical and British archaeology deepened. The most spectacular of nine-

---

[107] See Chapter 2, p. 9.
[108] A. H. L. F. Pitt Rivers, 'Inaugural Address to the Annual Meeting of the Archaeological Institute held at Salisbury', *Arch. Jnl.* xLIV (1887) 261–77 (p. 276).

teenth-century excavations were without doubt those carried out in the ancient biblical lands. Biblical archaeology was awarded this degree of attention not simply because of its exotic mien, nor its importance in establishing the international reputation of English archaeologists,[109] but because it represented an attempt to restore the veracity of the Bible in the face of the higher criticism and the adoption of a fluvialist geology. Ironically, it was the vindication of Old Testament authenticity offered by Layard's work at Nineveh and Nimrud that lent biblical archaeology one of its chief attractions. 'Archaeology is worthily employed in illustrating every kind of ancient literature; most worthily of all does she occupy herself in the illustration and explanation and confirmation of the sacred writings, of the Book of books'.[110] In consequence, the *Daily Telegraph* had no problem in rapidly raising £1,000 to fund George Smith's search at Nineveh for the missing fragment of the Chaldean account of the flood. As Layard remarked, 'the names of Nineveh and Assyria have been familiar to us from childhood', a fact which made the popular assimilation of biblical archaeology easier than that of classical archaeology.[111]

The dominance of the classical tradition in the educational curriculum and in the classification of antiquities was nonetheless considerable. Educated Englishmen were schooled in ancient history as a matter of course and their view of the nobility and glory of ancient Greek civilisation invariably coloured their assessment of contemporary conflicts in the East. For men who alluded as easily to Greek mythology as to the English past, or indeed the Bible, the classical tradition retained its significance. The Disney Professorship of Archaeology was established at Cambridge in 1852 as a chair of classical antiquities. Its first incumbent remarked of Athens: 'the scantiest gleanings of her soil are superior to that which constitutes the pride and boast of others'.[112] Nonetheless, classical archaeology remained primarily aesthetic in method, and excavation lay largely dormant until late in the century, as English archaeologists preferred the exploitation of sites in the East or at home. Neither Italy nor Greece could be 'colonised' in quite the manner possible in Arab countries at this juncture.

In England an unprecedented degree of interest was simultaneously aroused by the activities of men such as John Collingwood Bruce and Thomas Bateman. Barrow-digging had long been a spectator sport and there had been a rapid growth of consonant interest in Roman Britain. The excavation of Roman villas, the discovery of Roman coins, the exploration of the Roman wall and of Roman roads testify to the extent of interest in this aspect of Britain's early

[109] G. E. Daniel, *The Origins and Growth of Archaeology* (Harmondsworth, 1967) p. 113 pointed out the dominant rôle of English scholars, particularly in the period 1849–60.
[110] Babington, *op. cit.* p. 31.
[111] A. H. Layard, *Nineveh and Its Remains* (London, 1849) p. xx; K. Hudson, *A Social History of Archaeology. The British Experience* (London, 1981) pp. 73–4.   [112] Marsden, *op. cit.* p. 7.

history. Roman Britain has been described as 'the playground of the amateur
[. . .] the man who, whatever his abilities, has had no training at all'.[113] The
powerful symbolism of an empire guilty of its own destruction had obvious
resonances for the Victorians, engaged in their own pursuit of colonial power.
Indigenous interest was not confined to the evidences of Roman occupation
however. All aspects of native archaeology were eagerly exploited. Both Glyn
Daniel and Kenneth Hudson have suggested that this interest was a substitute
for the study of classical antiquities and Hudson has gone so far as to suggest
that, in the mid century, excavation sites being rare and country houses very
much in private occupation, churches were the only architectural antiquities
available for investigation.[114] These assertions seem a little glib in the face of a
nationalism powerful enough to exert so great a hold over the past. Although
the Teutonism which informed so much of the historical writing of the period
never really gained a foothold in archaeology, English pride was nonetheless
paramount. 'We are surrounded on all sides by an archaeology which is
emphatically an archaeology of progress, and we may justly be proud of it as
Englishmen.'[115]

The influence of anthropology and ethnology echo in Babington's statement. The tempting comparisons between modern 'primitives' and early
Britons dovetailed comfortably with contemporary ideas about English
superiority fuelled as they were by colonial exploitation. The common Victorian
habit of yoking prehistory to progress and evolution was as much an
archaeological as an historical or antiquarian peccadillo.[116] For all its
damaging and potentially secular implications regarding the antiquity of the
human race, archaeology could still service the presumptions of progress and
superiority so fundamental to the maintenance of the Victorian *status quo*.

It was during the later years of the nineteenth century that archaeology
became quite distinctively 'the systematic study, classification, and
chronological ordering of ancient artifacts and monuments',[117] and in essence,
of course, both text and artifact may be seen as documents of the past. David
Dymond has stressed the physical evidences to be derived from documentation
and has suggested areas such as architectural history and heraldry in which
the co-ordination of the relevant texts with the monuments has yielded
valuable information.[118] It is significant that the examples he chooses are those
that were popular in the mid-Victorian period before the formulation of a

---

[113] F. Haverfield, *The Roman Occupation of Britain* (Oxford, 1924) p. 87.
[114] G. E. Daniel, *Hundred Yrs. Arch.* p. 52; Hudson, *op. cit.* pp. 46–7; 69.
[115] Babington, *op. cit.* p. 60.   [116] G. E. Daniel, *The Idea of Prehistory* (London, 1962) p. 50.
[117] J. Rodden, 'The development of the Three Age System; Archaeology's first paradigm', in G. E.
Daniel (ed.) *Towards a History of Archaeology. Being the papers read at the first Conference on the
history of archaeology in Aarhus* (London, 1981) 51–68 (p. 51).
[118] D. P. Dymond, *Archaeology and History. A Plea for reconciliation* (London, 1974) pp. 56; 109.

definitive archaeology. It was precisely the antiquarian mix of text and artifact which proved irresistible, and antiquarian influence on archaeology was correspondingly strong. Inscriptions, the mark of a literate society, were particularly favoured. Roman Britain, Egypt and the biblical lands all offered such material in abundance; their popularity remained constant over the century.

The relation of archaeology to Egyptian history deserves especial notice. We have not here, as in pre-historic Europe, a mere multitude of uninscribed and inconsiderable remains; but we have colossal monuments of all kinds – temples, gateways, obelisks, statues, rock-sculptures – more or less over-written with hieroglyphics.[119]

The absence of the text–artifact division was apparent in the pages of the *Archaeological Journal* and the *Journal of the British Archaeological Association*. They were to become exclusively archaeological in the twentieth century although never entirely concerned with pre-literate societies. In the nineteenth century, however, they were more interested in examples and exhibits of manuscripts, wills, charters and other textual remains. Papers on and descriptions of antiquities – covering everything from seals and brasses to rings and pottery, but excluding coins – almost always accounted for the bulk of their contents. Essays on manuscripts did exceed those on antiquities in the *Archaeological Journal* in the 1860s. However, if ecclesiastical antiquities – tombs, effigies and the like – are included, their domination of the pages of these two journals becomes unchallengeable. There was little change before the 1920s when the number of articles in each issue began to diminish; few issues had less than twenty major contributions in either journal from their inception, but in 1922 the *Archaeological Journal* carried only six substantial articles. A new intellectual discourse was in preparation.

Antiquities, both to the antiquarian and the archaeologist, tended to connote moveable antiquities, those that could be easily displayed and indeed owned. Antiquarians and archaeologists alike castigated the commercial aspect of possession as 'an increased spirit of selfishness – a proneness to test the value of everything by the scale of the trader – a dogged utilitarianism'.[120] For these groups, ownership of such objects was rarely a deliberate commercial investment; collectors such as Thomas Phillipps were permanently in debt as a result of their insatiable habit. Theirs was an appropriation of knowledge, and given the intellectual climate in which they lived, of the principles of truth and progress. Their reverential view of the past, and in particular of the English past, lent the antiquities and documents of bygone times a hallowed significance and one which could not but affect their methods of work. Petrie criticised his predecessors for their over-riding interest in the moveable

[119] Babington, *op. cit.* p. 24.   [120] C. Roach Smith, *Collectanea Antiqua* I (1848) p. viii.

antiquity, but he was nonetheless aware of the interest that it aroused. 'I waited till the heat moderated and [. . .] went off to hunt chipped flints [. . .] as I found them so much appreciated at home.'[121]

Victorian conceptions of the past, like all others, cannot be dissociated from the social context in which they were fostered. Francis Haverfield pointed out that during the earlier Napoleonic Wars

nothing perhaps declares so eloquently the confidence of the British nation and the security enshrined by its island home, as the unbroken series of peaceful antiquarian notes and letters [. . .] printed in the Gentleman's Magazine throughout this terrible age.[122]

The historical tradition of English stability and wisdom was invoked frequently in the nineteenth century as a specific political device. J. H. Plumb has remarked that 'the most remarkable aspect of Western ideology is its leechlike addiction to its past'.[123] Without an understanding of that addiction, with its moral and religious as well as related political import, nineteenth-century historical studies are liable to be dismissed as worthless or immature. A new critical approach, unshackled by loyalties to the church or state, was apparent if embryonic towards the end of the century, but the institutional attachments through which much of that recognition had been won, left the historical communities with an ideological legacy. At no point in the nineteenth century did these groups deviate markedly from the expression of the values of their educated and comfortable world. There were occasional freethinkers and radicals, but for the most part these groups were amongst those whom tradition and stability favoured. Conservatism, whatever the party label, was the essential creed of the English and naturally enough was thus reflected in its dominant intellectual expressions. It was only when a genuine pluralism began to affect the power structure that such conceptions could be seriously challenged from within. Studies of the past – historical, archaeological and antiquarian – were institutionally and individually wedded to that power structure and in consequence imbibed the values it inscribed.

To everyone who looks back on his past life, it presents itself rather through the beautifying glass of fancy, than in the faithful mirror of memory [. . .] Among nations [. . .] the same feeling prevails; they also draw a picture of their infancy in glittering colours; the fewer traditions they have the more they embellish them; the less trustworthy these traditions are, the more they sparkle in the brilliancy which fancy has lent them, the more the vainglory of the people, will continue to cherish, to ennoble and to diffuse them from generation to generation through succeeding ages. Man's ambition is two-fold; he will not only live in the minds of posterity; he will also have lived in ages long gone by; he looks not only forward but backwards also; and no people on earth is indifferent to the fancied honour of being able to trace its origins to the gods, and of being ruled by an ancient race.[124]

---

[121] Griffith Institute, Oxford. MS Journals of W. M. F. Petrie, 1881–2. 15 October 1881.
[122] Haverfield, *op. cit.* p. 80.   [123] Plumb, *op. cit.* p. 51.
[124] Benjamin Thorpe, *Northern Mythology* (London, 1851), Introduction.

5

The rôle of government

Few of those who frequent the comfortable and convenient Literary Search Room at the Public Record Office in Fetter Lane, have any idea of the inconveniences which attached to those who, like myself, used to search twenty-five years ago in a long unpleasant room, with low tables and high backless forms, which cramped the searcher's legs if he were anything above a dwarf in stature. A searcher then had to pay a shilling for each search [. . .] and though the bad old days of extortion were over, those of civility and help had not yet come.

> W. Rye, *Records and Record Searching. A Guide to the Genealogist and Topographer* (London, 1888)

I

On the eve of the Public Record Office Act of August 1838, England's public records lay scattered in fifty-six separate record repositories, each of which was separately administered.[1] At the Chapter House Westminster, the Keeper of records was a salaried employee of the Treasury whilst at both the Tower of London and at the Rolls Chapel, one of the two keepers in each repository was paid exclusively out of the revenue derived from fees levied for searches amongst, and copies of, the records kept there. Court records, on the other hand, were under the exclusive jurisdiction of the court judges.[2] This lack of a centralised administration and the extortionate fees likely to be charged by a man dependent upon them for his livelihood, were but two of the serious abuses which the Record Commission at the turn of the century had been established to consider. Charles Abbott, Member of Parliament for Helston in Cornwall,

---

[1] The term record deserves some attention. Admissibility as evidence in a court of law constitutes the correct legal use of the term. The *Encyclopaedia Britannica* (11th edition, 1910–11) defines a record as 'a document regularly drawn up for legal or administrative purpose and preserved in proper custody to perpetuate the memory of the transaction described in it'. Under the terms of the Public Record Office Act of 1838 a record 'shall be taken to mean all rolls, records, writs, books, proceedings, decrees, bills, warrants, accounts, papers and documents whatsoever of a public nature belonging to Her Majesty, or now deposited in any of the offices or places of custody before mentioned'. See John Cantwell, 'The 1838 Public Record Office Act and its aftermath: a new perspective', *Journal of the Society of Archivists* 7 (1984) 5, 277–85 (p. 277) for further discussion of the changing definition of the term 'record'.

[2] PRO 1.133. 1872/3. Memorandum on the expediency of separating the Office of Keeper of the Public records from that of Master of the Rolls.

had first raised the subject of the state of the national records before the Commons in February 1800. Out of his motion arose the first of the six Record Commissions appointed between 1800 and 1831. Their brief was an ambitious one: as well as regulating and providing for better preservation of the records, they were charged with the responsibility of publishing calendars, indexes and manuscript editions.[3]

It was not until the appointment of the sixth Commission, however, that any members with apposite historical or antiquarian knowledge were appointed but it was their term of office which, ironically enough, attracted the heaviest criticisms.[4] By 1836 their activities – and more especially their expenditure – had excited a sufficient degree of parliamentary concern for the appointment of a Select Committee of investigation. The Committee produced a lengthy catalogue of misdeeds, accusing successive Commissions of failing to fulfil their brief. The continued inadequacy of the repositories, the damp, decayed and putrefied condition of many irreplaceable records[5] and abuse of the fee system all paled before the Committee's revelations on expenditure and publishing. The six Commissions had squandered an estimated half a million pounds, and the published volumes on which the larger portion of that sum had been spent were often poorly edited and full of errors. There was even evidence to suggest that the Commission had permitted the printing of the same document more than once in different volumes.[6] The Select Committee, not unreasonably, declared that their emphasis on publishing had been further detrimental to the already parlous condition of the records. On the recommendation of the Select Committee the Commission was allowed to expire without further renewal, and in August 1838 the main proposals set out in the Committee's report found their way onto the statute book. As Charles Abbott had done in 1800, they

[3] Abstract of Annual Report of first Record Commission, July 1800.

[4] The 1831 Commission included a number of suitably 'qualified' members: Sir James Mackintosh, M.P. for Knaresborough and author of a life of Sir Thomas More and a *History of England*, both published in 1830 in Lardner's *Cabinet Cyclopaedia* and of a *History of the Revolution in England in 1688*; the Rt Hon. George James Welbore Agar-Ellis, first baron Dover, whose various historical publications were well-known; John Allen, author of *An Inquiry into the Rise and Growth of the Royal Prerogative in England* (1830); Henry Hallam; Henry Hobhouse, Keeper of the State Papers; Edward Vernon Utterson, F.S.A. one of the six clerks in Chancery and an antiquarian author.

[5] The Select Committee reported on the extent of this neglect. 'Your Committee has seen the Public Records deposited at the Tower over a gunpowder magazine, and contiguous to a steam-engine in daily operation [. . .] in dark and humid cellars [. . .] in stables.' Select Committee Report, *PP*, House of Commons, 1836. xvi. 565. p.x.

[6] As part of his evidence before the Commons when urging the appointment of a Select Committee, Charles Buller (M.P. for Liskeard) produced before the House a copy of the *Rotuli Selecti* 'as a specimen of the accuracy of the present Commission's editorship. The work contained a patent roll twice printed by the Commission and other rolls of Henry III, transcripts of which were twice made at the public expense. In this work there were more mistakes than might be expected to occur in proof sheets sent to an author for correction.' Report of a debate in the Commons on Buller's motion for a Select Committee on Public records, 18 February 1836, p. 13.

wanted to see the establishment of a central general repository under a Keeper General alongside the abolition of the fee system.

Under the provisions of the new Act, Henry Bickersteth, Baron Langdale was made custodian of the records. Langdale was Master of the Rolls but there was no inherent legal reason for making the incumbent of that position also Keeper of the Public Records. Langdale had been a record Commissioner and was asked by the Home Secretary to take temporary charge of the business of the Commission after the report of the Select Committee. When the Public Record Office Act became law, Langdale was appointed Keeper rendering *de iure* a *de facto* situation, because he had shown a degree of interest in record affairs and had been a leading mover in getting the 1838 legislation passed. Thus it was not by virtue of his office of Master of the Rolls that the holder of that office became Keeper. The 1912 Royal Commission on the Public Records further made the point that this 'fruit of accident' was enhanced by the proximity of the Record Office and of Rolls House, the official seat of the Master of the Rolls.[7]

The legislation was concerned primarily with rationalising record administration under one person with whom ultimate responsibility would lie for the reception of new records, their repair and preservation, arrangement, calendaring and indexing as well as the general administration of the record establishment. Its main function was 'to allow the free use of the said records, as far as stands with their safety and integrity, and with the public policy of the realm'.[8] The Act was careful to preserve simultaneously the important legal status of the records by laying down that copies of records bearing the stamp or seal of the Office would be received as evidence in courts, tribunals and in both chambers of Parliament.

The Act established in principle the need for a central general repository but no building was undertaken until 1851. The embarrassment occasioned Parliament by the cost of their own new premises was exacerbated by the memory of the extravagances of the earlier Record Commissions. Public interest had to be tempered by economy. Lord Langdale's concerted efforts to persuade government to initiate building plans were, in the first instance, blocked by the Treasury's alternative money-saving schemes.

My Lords entirely concur with Lord Langdale in thinking that one General Record Office under efficient management and responsibility is essential to the introduction of a perfect system. Two plans have been suggested [. . .] the one the erection of a new Building on the Rolls Estate which is recommended by Lord Langdale, the other an adaptation of the Victoria Tower connected with the new Houses of Parliament [. . .] it has been determined by Parliament that the Victoria Tower shall be erected if that

---

[7] *Parliamentary Papers*, House of Commons, 1912–13. xliv. 13. Part I. *First Report of the Royal Commission on Public Records* p. 45.

[8] 1 & 2 Vict. c. 94: An Act for keeping safely the Public Records, 14 August 1838.

Building can be adapted for the safe custody of the Records, the expence [sic] to the Public of a Second Building will be altogether avoided.[9]

Although the plan to use the Victoria Tower was abandoned, little else was done in the early years to effect the implementation of the Act. The Master of the Rolls was still wearily petitioning Parliament in the late 1840s.

The Records [. . .] continue to be exposed to the same risk of destruction from fire and other casualties; and from want of space, and adequate means of arrangement [. . .] the public is still without many of the most important benefits which were justly expected to be secured by the Record Act.[10]

And even after the first phase of building was completed in 1861 the facilities were still inadequate. Langdale's successor, Sir John Romilly, took up the fight. Outlining 'the necessity of immediately commencing another block of the Record Repository',[11] Romilly painted a grim picture of the state of the records a full twenty-three years after the passing of the Public Record Office Act.

The present edifice being totally inadequate to afford proper accommodation for the Muniments and Papers now under my charge, as well as for the Readers and Searchers consulting them [. . .] I have been obliged to deposit a vast collection of important documents in certain Houses in Chancery Lane which are both unsafe and exposed to accidents from Fire [. . .] The roofs continually let in the wet and are perpetually under repair.[12]

He was deliberately inviting comparison with scandal over the chaos left untouched by the Record Commissions.

The contradictions in governmental attitude whereby financial consider-ations took precedence over the proclaimed ideals of public access were evidenced not just by internal office dissatisfaction but by outsiders too. In 1880, seventeen regular searchers brought to the notice of the Master of the Rolls, 'the very great inconvenience, loss of valuable time and injury to the eyesight we are subject to from the want of artificial light in the Search Office'.[13] The introduction of gas for lighting and heating was inhibited as much by fears for the safety of the records as by financial caution.[14]

The most radical feature of the new Act was public access to the records, a feature ushered in even before the new Office was begun. Before 1838, most repositories had operated very restricted opening hours, often charging cripplingly high fees for the minimal services they rendered. It had often been necessary, and always advisable, to ensure in advance that the Keeper of the records would be in attendance and that the documents required would be available for they were frequently mislaid, or housed unofficially at the Keeper's private residence. The Act aimed to make the records more freely available

---

[9] PRO 1.2. Treasury Minute, 8 April 1839.
[10] PRO 1.10. MR to Sir George Grey, 9 November 1846.
[11] PRO 1.25. MR to G. A. Hamilton, Treasury, 6 December 1861.   [12] *ibid.*
[13] PRO 1.45. 7 January 1880.   [14] PRO 2.73. Alfred Kingston to DK, 30 October 1875.

through the reduction and in some instances the abolition of fees, and by imposing a degree of standardisation on the many repositories now under its jurisdiction. Soon after the passing of the Act Langdale, recalling its intentions, had grandly declared that

the Records have justly been called the Muniments of the Kingdom and the People's Evidences; and they ought to be kept and managed under such arrangement as may afford to the public the greatest facility of using them that is consistent with their safety. The public ought to have access to them.[15]

The new administration certainly encouraged increased use of the records and the annual reports of the Keepers reflect some considerable success. 'The facility of access occasions a very great and increasing resort to the records', maintained Thomas Palmer, Assistant Keeper at the Rolls Chapel.[16] His colleagues endorsed his experience of the 'increase in Public business'.[17] Public use continued to rise over the years; the annual reports spoke frequently of a growing number of applications and enquiries. The opening of the public search rooms in 1866 and the earlier decision in 1852 to remit fees for literary searchers meant that many who before might have ignored the records as potential source material were encouraged to make use of them.[18] The gratuitous admission of literary searchers was justified on grounds which suggest a moral hierarchy. It was argued that whereas the legal searcher sought record evidence for the settlement of matters of personal profit, literary applicants were indulging a scholarly principle dissociated from material gain.

The admission of the public necessarily involved a greater degree of wear and tear on state documents and it was not long before the problem of defining a responsible public replaced the blanket ideal of unrestricted access. Both legal and literary applicants had to satisfy the authorities that they were 'sufficiently qualified by age, knowledge and discretion', before being granted access.[19] They had already to be well acquainted with the nature and handling of the materials they required.

No Applicant ought to present himself who is not sufficiently acquainted with the handwriting, abbreviations and language of documents, so as to be able to read and decypher [sic] their contents.[20]

Access thus quickly became limited in an institutional sense to those already in possession of what was, after all, an arcane branch of knowledge. The returns from both the search rooms at the new central Public Record Office and from the individual repositories suggest that there was a small class of regular searchers comprising record agents, antiquarian and historical writers and

---

[15] PRO 8.28. MR to Lord John Russell, 7 January 1839.
[16] PRO 4.1. Report of Proceedings of Assistant Keepers. Vol I. 1840.   [17] *ibid.*
[18] Note the use of the term 'literary' as the equivalent of 'historical'. The view of history as a literary pursuit was still strong in this period.
[19] PRO 1.20. Letter Book, 1856.   [20] PRO 1.22. 5 July 1858.

legal clerks. In 1853, the first year in which fees for literary searchers were remitted, Deputy Keeper Sir Francis Palgrave reported that 'forty five individuals have applied for admission under the Regulations [. . .] [their] attendance [. . .] may be reckoned on the average at ten per week, during the business portion of the year'.²¹ At this early date, there were still comparatively few readers. Within a couple of decades, however, the amount of business had increased markedly. In 1874, 25,830 applications for records were made (the number of applicants is not given) of which 16,310 came from literary searchers; in the period 10 May to 25 September 1871, 117 readers attended whilst the same period in 1885 attracted 189 readers.²²

The Keepers were not always convinced that the degree of public access ushered in by the legislation of 1838 was consonant with the well-being of the papers in their charge. In 1860, Sir John Romilly who had succeeded Langdale as Master of the Rolls in 1851, solicited the opinions of his Assistant Keepers as to the continued expedience of gratuitous admission for literary purposes. H. J. Sharpe doubted whether 'anyone compiling his own pedigree, or that of his friend, adds to the advancement of literature, or that there is any good reason why he should not pay the same fees as another who is compelled to consult the Records for the purpose of ascertaining legal rights to property'. He also felt 'that the persons at present exempt from paying [fees] are generally persons of fortune'.²³ Joseph Hunter was of similar opinion. 'Persons with very slender literature have gained advantages which ought to belong only to persons who have devoted themselves to these enquiries and obtained reputation.'²⁴ Hunter was concerned with the 'unseemliness of standing at the door to ask a shilling or five shillings a week [of] persons who belong to a high order of literature and especially where [. . .] united with the distinction of rank'.²⁵ Sharpe was also contemptuous of those he considered intellectually unworthy of access, citing two examples of their demands on his time.

Mr Meakins on first presenting his card of free admission [. . .] confessed he had no idea of what nature the Records were, but requested that "All the papers relating to a Murder in Ireland be brought to him at once" [. . .] Mr Hammond, an auctioneer in Chancery Lane, wished to ascertain the history of a manor in Yorkshire, but he could not read Latin, nor understand it when it was read to him.²⁶

Unfamiliarity could thus disqualify the enquirer. Sir George Jessel, who became Master of the Rolls in 1873, declared before the House of Lords in 1877 that whereas he 'had no power to restrict the free access of the public [. . .] everybody knows if it is a Foreign Office paper, or a War Office, or Treasury paper; people who want to use them know where they come from.'²⁷

²¹ PRO 35.1. DK to MR, 5 February 1853.   ²² PRO 2.100; 6.1; 6.20.
²³ PRO 1.24. H. J. Sharpe to MR, 13 March 1860.
²⁴ *ibid*. Joseph Hunter to MR, 14 March 1860.   ²⁵ *ibid*.   ²⁶ *ibid*. H. J. Sharpe.
²⁷ PRO 8.30. Select Committee of the House of Lords on the Public Record Office Bill, 1877. Minutes of Evidence.

The degree of public right of access fast became a highly sensitive issue. By an Order in Council of 1852 the records of government departments were brought under the control of the Master of the Rolls and the absorption of the State Paper Office into the Public Record Office in 1854 extended his responsibilities even further. Both the Foreign Office and the Home Office were alarmed at the prospect of access to or publication of some of the materials thus transferred to the Public Record Office. In a letter to the Master of the Rolls soon after the State Paper Calendar series was initiated, the Foreign Office dictated that certain classes of documents be withheld from the public. 'Especial care [. . .] must be taken that no Papers are ever given to Applicants, especially Foreigners, without the previous sanction of this Office.'[28] The Foreign Office was thus able to reserve access to material regarded as sensitive or unsuitable. The Home Office similarly sought to suppress publication in the *Calendars* of correspondence relating to Irish affairs amongst others.

Clashes between Calendar editors and cautious Home Secretaries also occurred although politicians tended to justify their power of embargo on more personal grounds than those of the Foreign Office for whom present security was the chief concern. In a confidential letter to the Master of the Rolls, Sir William Harcourt explained his own position.

I find that Ld Beaconsfield and Cross[29] put a veto upon the publication of a good many of the Irish papers. The period with which the forthcoming volume deals viz, that of the Executive during the American war under Ld North's government is not one that commends itself to frank indiscretions in the way of publication of secret papers, and though I reckon myself a good Whig of the Rockingham period, I don't desire to foul the rest of my predecessors in office even a hundred years ago [. . .] I have seen quite enough [. . .] to be satisfied that there is a great deal in it which ought not to be published [. . .] things which ought never to be revealed whatever may be the lapse of time.[30]

Political considerations overrode the ideals of public access and historical truth. In Harcourt's case, it was not a question of security that prompted his veto but the good name of his political ancestors.

The Royal Commission on Public Records established in the Edwardian period, and following the Victorian example, drew up a complete schedule of 'subjects that have been explicitly or tacitly excluded from the scope of general departmental permits prior to 1903' embracing the Home, Foreign, Colonial and War Offices as well as the Admiralty and the Treasury.[31] A general *caveat* asked record officers to check and censor certain categories of documents, anxious to prevent earlier acts of diplomacy from jeopardising present relations with other countries:

[28] PRO 8.29. E. Hammond, Foreign Office, to MR, 21 January 1858.
[29] Cross was Harcourt's predecessor as Home Secretary under Disraeli.
[30] PRO 1.163. Sir William Harcourt to MR, 25 January 1885.
[31] *Parliamentary Papers*, House of Commons, 1912–13. xliv. 13. *ibid.* Part II. Appendix V.

names of secret service agents or payment of secret service money, references to scalping, and other atrocities in war, reference to individual convicts, passages likely to give offence abroad or to prejudice diplomatic negotiations.[32]

There was thus a sense in which the past was too dangerous simply to be thrown open to the public. The idea of history as a means of political education thus acted as a counsel of suppression. Its importance was seen in terms of its promotion of consensus; an expression of the widely held view that the English past should be seen not in terms of a series of conflicts but, in classic Whig terms, as a natural progression of events tending towards the development of the peaceful, civilised and prosperous society which was the Britain in which they lived. Conversely in 1876, the historian Froude urged Deputy Keeper Thomas Duffus Hardy to proceed with the calendaring of papers from Trinity College Dublin relating to the Irish rebellion of 1641.

The Irish are now taught to believe that the whole story of the massacre was got up to justify the confiscation, and that if there were a massacre at all it was a massacre of Catholics by Protestants [. . .] there is no limit to the mischief which a general conviction of such a kind, if allowed to grow up without some authoritative contradiction will produce in Ireland.[33]

In both cases – suppression and publication – the intention was the same: the promotion of a consensual view of English history. The urge to make accessible the annals of history was rooted very strongly in that tenacious sense of national pride which informed the historical communities at this time.

It would show to the People of this Country, that as their history yields to no other, in ancient or modern times, in the vast importance of the acts which it records, in their variety, their fullness, and their paramount interest, so the chronicles, records and state papers, in which those acts are registered, bear the like impress of the national character.[34]

The *Calendars of State Papers* published by the Public Record Office were eagerly consumed by enthusiastic nationalists. Noel Sainsbury's *Calendar of Colonial State Papers* relating to the East Indies, China and Japan 1574–1660 prompted one reviewer to intone:

It is impossible for anyone to understand the history of Elizabeth's reign who is not familiar with the lives of the famous sailors whose love of adventure and hatred of the Spaniard led to achievements which Englishmen will recall forever with pride [. . .] these men won for England her Queenship of the Seas.[35]

Sainsbury's work evidently excited much jingoistic fervour for the review of it in *The Reader* spoke proudly of the English subjects who had fought their way 'through ice and mist to the other side of the world [. . .] to plant the standard of Protestant Christianity and English civilisation in regions yet unknown'.[36]

[32] *ibid.*   [33] PRO 37.1. J. A. Froude to DK, 26 October 1876.
[34] PRO 1.20. 25 October 1856.
[35] PRO 8.6. Press Cuttings. *Morning Herald and Standard*, 22 January 1863.
[36] *The Reader*, 31 January 1863.

The annual receipt of new records amplified by the ever increasing responsibilities of government created an urgent problem of space exacerbated by the added responsibility which the Public Record Office acquired for the contents of the State Paper Office and of government departments. During the course of building the new Public Record Office, it had been anticipated that the storage rooms would not reach capacity within twenty years. Inaccurate calculation thus led in 1877 to a second and urgent chapter of legislation which posed ethical as well as intellectual questions. This was the Act for the disposal of Valueless Documents of later date than the year 1714.[37]

It is expedient to prevent the Public Record Office from being encumbered with documents of not sufficient public value to justify their preservation.

The controversial issue of deciding which documents – and why – might be deemed valuable was in fact skirted by the wording of the Act which failed even to define in clear terms what characteristics lent a document posthumous value. The final Act stipulated merely that Parliament would investigate any schedule offered by the Record Office of documents whose destruction was proposed. The Master of the Rolls had initially suggested the establishment of a committee, of at least three members, entrusted to decide the fate of records already deemed valueless by record officers within the establishment. He recommended that two should be barristers, one with Chancery experience and the other with Queen's Bench, Common Pleas and Exchequer experience, and the third an officer of the record establishment well versed in 'the historical, topographical and statistical bearing of the different classes of records'.[38] In the event the Act was even more cautious, requiring Parliament itself to endorse any proposed destruction. It further laid down that 'no rule made in pursuance of this section shall provide for the disposal of any document of older date than the year one thousand seven hundred and fifteen'.[39] It was the later records which the Deputy Keeper described dispassionately as 'large masses of legal and Governmental documents which are wholly useless for legal, historical, military, statistical, economical, or official purposes, and of no possible interest to anyone'.[40] An Act of 1898 permitted extension backwards in time in the definition of valueless documents to a date no earlier than 1659. Even before the deluge of departmental records had burdened the office, important documents were seemingly endangered.

The Registrar-General informed me that [. . .] a doubt [. . .] had arisen in his mind whether, inasmuch as all the Statistical facts, figures &c., contained in the books [census enumerators' books] are collected in the Volumes published by authority of Parliament, it is no longer necessary to keep the Documents from which the facts &c., have been collected. In such opinion, I do not coincide. It appears to me that these Books are of great national importance, and fit to be preserved. The particulars which they may furnish as to the identity, residence, occupation, and age, of all the enumerated

---

[37] 40 & 41 Vict. c. 55.   [38] PRO 1.137. 20 November 1875.
[39] 40 & 41 Vict. c. 55.   [40] PRO 1.137. n.d.

inhabitants of the United Kingdom on the Census Day, will hereafter be invaluable for Historical and Legal purposes. I should think that no care ought to be spared for their preservation as a portion of the National Archives.[41]

It was not only the records under the aegis of central government which caused anxiety. When Assistant Keeper William Henry Black was commissioned to report upon the records of the Court of the County Palatine of Chester and the Principality of Wales in 1839, he found their condition even more dilapidated than those in metropolitan repositories. Reporting from the Isle of Man he noted:

Nothing here can be found, and I am assured [. . .] as *no secret*, that anything may be stolen or destroyed by any lawyer [or] clerk on the Island. There are no calendars, nor anything to prove what belongs to the Public.[42]

Thirty years on, similar concern over the state of local and county records was addressed to the Master of the Rolls.

[I] invite your attention to the very unsatisfactory condition of Parish Registers [. . .] and the dangers and inconveniences which result from the system under which they are at present (nominally) preserved [. . .] it is important to bear in mind that the process of destruction, arising from neglect, fraud and violence, from which the registers have for centuries been suffering, is still going on.[43]

Parochial material was not covered by the provisions of the 1838 Act and the almost simultaneous introduction of civil registration had clearly failed to confront the problem of its safekeeping. New forms of local government later in the century had little effect on the condition and keeping of records, for in 1890 scarce improvement seems to have been made.

Mr Phillimore [. . .] is extremely anxious to have introduced into Parliament a Bill providing for the better custody of County records, which are at present scattered in various places, and are more or less under uncertain guardianship.[44]

A tacit acceptance of the precedent claims of metropolitan and national records over and above those of local records meant that central government showed little interest in tackling municipal problems of arrangement and preservation.[45]

By the time that the Royal Commission on the Public Records made its third report in 1919 some, but not sufficient improvements had been effected, but the Commissioners made the point that 'there is not any received uniform standard, nor even an approximation to one' governing the administration of local records.[46] Little *cachet* attached to posts in local record keeping and such

[41] PRO 1.15. DK to MR, 10 July 1851.
[42] PRO 1.121/6. W. H. Black, Memoranda made in my journey to survey and report on the records of the Court of the County Palatine of Chester and the Principality of Wales, September 1839. p. 30.   [43] PRO 1.22. T. P. Taswell-Langmead to MR, 4 April 1870.
[44] PRO 1.55. B. G. Lake to MR, 31 December 1889.
[45] *PP*, House of Commons, 1867–8. lv. 245. DK to MR, 14 October 1867.
[46] *PP*, House of Commons, 1919. xxviii.l. *Third Report of the Royal Commission on Public Records.* p. 24.

repositories were largely in the care of amateurs against whom the staff of the national repository could measure their professional identity and status. The Historical Manuscripts Commission, founded in 1869, went some way towards coping with local records by inviting corporations as well as individuals and families to open their archives to the Commission's Inspectors.

II

Without Calendars and Indexes, the Public Records are as a sealed book, and comparatively useless; for few persons who could spare the time have the skill to search them.[47]

The *Calendars of State Papers*, begun almost simultaneously with the series of *Chronicles and Memorials* in 1856–7 were intended to provide a guide to the manuscripts to be found in the Public Record Office. They were edited by an assortment of full-time employees of the record establishment – Charles Roberts, secretary of the Public Record Office, Deputy Keeper Sir Thomas Duffus Hardy and James Gairdner – and those who worked free-lance on the Calendars and were paid by results. Amongst those most frequently engaged for these projects were the Rev. J. S. Brewer, Mary Ann Everett Green and Joseph Stevenson, formerly a sub-commissioner of the 1830 Record Commission. The task they undertook was an onerous one involving above all a capacity for close arduous work. J. S. Brewer's lengthy account of his problems with the papers of Henry VIII instances the difficulties and labours involved in preparing such papers for the press.

The correspondence of this reign came into my hands in the greatest confusion. It had never been collected into one place; parts of it lay concealed in different depositories; the existence of important portions were till then unknown [. . .] this preliminary task [of arranging the papers for calendaring] alone [. . .] occupied three years of incessant labour [. . .] These difficulties have been greatly augmented by the abstraction of large portions [. . .] transferred to the library of Sir Robert Cotton [. . .] not unfrequently parts of the same letter have got into different places [. . .] The body of the letter, its address or its postscript, are often similarly separated [. . .] Of letters in cipher; the cipher will be in the Record Office; the decipher in the Museum [. . .] as the great majority of the Letters are undated, no arrangement can be made until their chronology is decided; and this cannot be done until the parts and directions of the letters have been brought together [. . .] The mutilated and faded condition of the documents has often made it absolutely indispensable to copy out large portions of them, word for word, in order to arrive at a distinct conception of their meaning [. . .] and though this process may occupy many hours, the whole result may be, and often is, expressed in a very few words, which, to the reader who has not seen the original, convey no adequate notion of the labour which they typify.[48]

Brewer's problems were obviously magnified by the added hindrance that the relevant bundles of state papers were not already collected together in the

[47] *Report of the D.K.* XXIII. 22 February 1862.
[48] PRO 1.24. J. S. Brewer to MR, 9 January 1860.

Record Office. The problems he discusses are nonetheless those to which all the editors were commonly exposed. One of the most prolific and active of them, Mary Ann Everett Green, was wary in her commitments, adamant that her health should not suffer.

I should undertake the task under a distinct proviso that I may do as much or as little as suits my health and convenience. I worked too hard in the early part of last year and suffered in consequence.[49]

The enormous efforts of these editors were, alas, not always productive of a high standard of scholarship. Many of the volumes both at the time of publication and subsequently were heavily criticised. As late as 1912 when the Royal Commission on Public Records reported, it found fault with some of the editors.

Some of them are imperfectly acquainted with the materials with which they have to deal [. . .] Other editors are imperfectly acquainted with the printed materials for the history of the period whose papers they are set to calendar.[50]

The Commission laid the blame for this on the inadvisability of entrusting their appointment and supervision to a single individual. However, tight financial considerations, the speed with which many of the volumes were rushed into print, the paucity of experienced record scholars and the sheer drudgery of much of the workload associated with the venture must to a large extent have helped determine the quality of the issue.

One of the most frequent criticisms aimed at the series was its lack of uniformity, despite Romilly's attempts at standardisation. The *Saturday Review* thought that 'two different styles of editing have been adopted',[51] some editors providing skeletal entries whilst others lingered over minute detail. No limit was placed on the length of the actual calendar, but editor's prefaces were confined to fifty pages, a regulation 'mainly framed with reference to the financial question'.[52] From the inception of the series the Master of the Rolls had laid down a series of *Instructions to Editors* in an attempt to secure some degree of uniformity.

1st. As the most efficient means of making the national archives accessible to all who are interested in historical inquiries; 2nd as the best justification of the liberality and munificence of the Government in throwing open to the public, and providing proper catalogues of their contents at the national expense.[53]

The Calendars were never really seen as a business enterprise and the annual grant of the Office reserved only £1,500 per annum for them.[54]

[49] PRO 1.125. Mary Ann Everett Green to MR, 6 July 1855.
[50] *PP*, House of Commons, 1912–13. xliv. 13. *ibid.* Part II. Appendix VI.
[51] PRO 8.14. Press Cuttings. *Saturday Review*, 3 March 1866.
[52] Soc. Ant. MS. Memorial, 6 April 1876.
[53] PRO 1.179. Calendars: *Instructions to Editors.*   [54] PRO 1.22.

The publication [. . .] of Calendars, Indexes or Catalogues &c., affording the means of consultation to manuscript materials in Government Repositories should not be treated by the Treasury upon or regulated by commercial principles but as a branch of public instruction.[55]

The volumes, each amounting to about 800 pages, were sold to the public for 15/- and the cost of printing them varied between 12/- and 14/-. By 1876, twenty years after the introduction of the series, between one hundred and one hundred and fifty of each volume had been sold.[56] The figure in no way reflects usage. As reference books, these volumes were of undisputed value but they contained little more than listings of the contents of the manuscripts and were thus hardly destined to sell well.[57] They were nonetheless an important step towards greater access. As the Master of the Rolls pointed out in his *Instructions to Editors*:

The greater number of readers who will consult and value these works can have little or no opportunity of visiting the Public Record Office, in which these papers are deposited. The means for consulting the originals must necessarily be limited when readers live at a distance from the metropolis [. . .] Even when such an opportunity does exist, the difficulty of mastering the original hands [. . .] will deter many.

Public opinion was also influential in determining the character and indeed the authorship of the Calendars. In 1859 Romilly had appointed the well-known Scottish antiquary William Turnbull to calendar the foreign state papers from the Reformation to 1688, the period of Britain's severance from the Catholic church and the disorders subsequent upon it.[58] Turnbull, who had been a practising lawyer at the Scottish bar before moving to London in 1856, had seceded to Catholicism in 1842. Some of the more zealous Protestant organisations regarded his appointment as a breach of faith and several memorials arrived on the desk of Lord Palmerston demanding his replacement by an Anglican editor. The Protestant Alliance, the Religious Tract Society and the Scottish Reformation Society were unanimous in their claim that Turnbull was, by virtue of his Catholicism and his championship of Jesuit principles, 'unfit to be intrusted with [. . .] valuable Foreign papers'.[59] The uproar reached the national press and throughout January and February of 1861 the editorials and letter pages of the newspapers and journals took up the case with gusto. The *Daily Telegraph* of 16 February 1861 carried a representative example of Protestant objections to the appointment of Turnbull. Having described him as

[55] PRO 1.125. 17 July 1856.
[56] PRO 37.72.
[57] PRO 1.179. *op. cit.*
[58] William Barclay David Donald Turnbull (1811–63) was an active antiquarian. He had founded the Abbotsford Club in his native city of Edinburgh in 1834 and was a member of many antiquarian societies. He left Edinburgh for London in 1852 and was called to the bar at Lincoln's Inn in 1856. He edited a volume for the Rolls Series in 1858 entitled *The Buik of the Cronicles of Scotland*.
[59] PRO 1.129. Memorial of the Protestant Alliance, n.d.

'a pervert from the Reformed Faith', the writer continued by stating that, 'we know, and it would be the merest audacity to deny, that the Roman Catholic principle of dealing with history is one of systematic falsification'.

Turnbull, unable to withstand the tide of opposition, tendered his resignation. In response, many of the leading intellectuals of the day attached their names to the *Turnbull Memorial* attesting to his intellectual qualities and calling on the Master of the Rolls not to accept his resignation.[60] It was organised by the historian Charles Pearson, Professor of Modern History at the Anglican King's College London, and the barrister Henry Coleman Folkard who was later that decade to publish, appropriately enough, on the law of slander and libel. None but Protestant signatures – Anglican and Nonconformist – were accepted. Amongst the eight hundred signatories were Sir Francis Palgrave (the outgoing Deputy Keeper), Frederick Denison Maurice, E. A. Freeman, J. A. Froude and Benjamin Jowett.[61]

The Master of the Rolls remained adamant that his choice of editor had been a reasonable one. 'Mr Turnbull is the fittest person who could be selected for the purpose for which he is employed.'[62] Palmerston, however, thought differently.

I certainly think that the selection of a bigoted Pervert for the particular duties which Mr Turnbull has had to perform in Connection with a Period of our History the events of which were so much connected with our separation from the Church of Rome, was an unfortunate one, as some other Person equally competent might no doubt have been found.[63]

The controversy finally reached the House of Lords where the Marquis of Normanby petitioned unsuccessfully for a Select Committee to be set up on the issue. Turnbull's resignation had, however, already been accepted by this time. His place was filled by Joseph Stevenson who, ironically enough, was himself to become a Catholic in 1863. Stevenson was more fortunate than the ill-used Turnbull; his conversion earned him the opportunity of transcribing manuscripts in the Vatican archives on behalf of the Record Office and the British government. No hint of this unpleasant occurrence reached the pages of the Deputy Keeper's *Annual Reports* beyond a note to the effect that a new calendarer had been appointed.

Turnbull, for all his anguish, still found time to write generously to his successor.

I congratulate you upon your appointment most cordially. It is a compliment to me that the Treasury has given me such a successor: and I only wish that the place were more worth your acceptance.[64]

[60] Reported in *The Times*, 14 February 1861.
[61] Francis Palgrave was a convert from Judaism. His name had originally been Cohen.
[62] PRO 1.129. MR to Lord Palmerston, 1 November 1856.
[63] PRO 1.129. Palmerston to MR, 13 January 1861.
[64] Society of Jesus, Farm Street, London. MS CB/5, f.423. Corresp. Joseph Stevenson, 1846–93. Turnbull to Stevenson, 28 December 1861.

The other great publishing venture of this era was *The Chronicles and Memorials of Great Britain and Ireland during the Middle Ages* – the Rolls Series. It commenced publication in 1857 with a Treasury grant of £2,000 rising after the first year to £3,000 for the next ten years before dropping back to £2,000.[65] The series was the natural successor to Duffus Hardy's publication in 1848 of a three-volume *Monumenta Historica Britannica* and was intended to make available literary sources for English medieval history. 'They [. . .] consist of general and particular Histories, of Chronicles and Annals, of Contemporary Biographies, of Political Poems, of State Papers and Records, Proceedings of Councils and Synods, private Letters and Charters, and the Public and Parliamentary Records.'[66] Eleven volumes appeared in 1858, all unadorned by translation but accompanied by footnotes designed to compare the different extant manuscript readings.

The editors were largely well-known antiquarian and record scholars; some well-known figures were invited to contribute to the series whilst others took the initiative themselves. Amongst those who volunteered their skills was William Stubbs, whom the Deputy Keeper was at first disinclined to employ.

This is the third application Mr Stubbs has made for employment under the Master of the Rolls. He has not as yet done anything to show that he is competent to edit such works as he has proposed, but it does not follow that he is incompetent.[67]

Stubbs clearly felt his exclusion sharply, for he was highly critical of the efforts of the Master of the Rolls. Writing to Freeman he commented

If you review the New Chronicles, mind you praise the Master of the Rolls not for his choice either of Books or of Editors – for he seems to have chosen the Editors from knowing their names or other writings [. . .] and to have chosen the Books because the Elect Editors proposed them [. . .][68]

The appointment of reliable and competent editors was no easy task. In the first instance, the need to avoid controversy was of great concern to the Master of the Rolls, particularly in the wake of the Turnbull incident. He rejected R. B. Knowles' application to edit for the series in frank, if painful terms.

I am unfortunately obliged to be explicit with you and to state that [. . .] I do not feel myself justified in recommending any work to be edited by a Gentlemen of the Roman Catholic persuasion.[69]

Similarly delicate reasons led him to reject Shirley's plan to edit four of John Wycliffe's works.

---

[65] David Knowles in his piece on the Rolls Series in his *Great Historical Enterprises. Problems in Monastic History* (London, 1963) maintains that the grant was £3,000.
[66] PRO 37.12.   [67] PRO 37.61.
[68] Bodl. MS. Eng. misc. e. 148, ff. 23–4. Letters of William Stubbs to E. A. Freeman, 22 November, n.d. (1858?).   [69] PRO 37.73. MR to R. B. Knowles, 2 December 1861.

They must necessarily, from their character, provoke religious controversy which is a matter, which, if I am able, I am peculiarly anxious to avoid in the publication of these works under the Grant at present sanctioned by the Government.[70]

Choice of material as of editor was also governed by factors beyond the purely intellectual. Stubbs regarded the *Lives of Edward the Confessor* published in 1858 as overly biased towards philological interests.

I am sorry to see that the philological side of things is to be kept so exclusively in view in these publications. For interesting and important as it is, it is not History – but Thomas Duffus Hardy tells me nothing but the Philological will go down and the books must be made to sell.[71]

Even when the Master of the Rolls had ensured that a safe choice of texts would not jeopardise its grant, he still faced the innumerable difficulties posed by inefficient and unreliable editors. Romilly was as vigilant a reader as he could be under the circumstances yet poor scholarship did slip through. On occasion he felt obliged to hold up publication, as with Benjamin Thorpe's proposed new edition of the *Anglo-Saxon Chronicles*. Thorpe had undertaken to collate all the extant manuscript versions of the *Chronicles* but Romilly was horrified to discover that Thorpe had not only failed to fulfil that promise but that his text was riddled with errors. He instigated an enquiry.

The Master of the Rolls [. . .] thought it necessary to compare Mr Thorpe's text with the facsimile in the *Monumenta* [*Historica Britannica*] and having found so many variations between the facsimile and Mr Thorpe's text, he then compared them with those that had been expressly executed for Mr Thorpe and having found a still greater number of variations between the two he considered it necessary to give directions to the Queen's Printers to suspend the printing of the text of the *Anglo-Saxon Manuscripts*.[72]

Thorpe protested that inflammation of the eyes and head had prevented him from pursuing his task more thoroughly but his failure was a costly one: 208 printed pages had to be cancelled and the ten months' work on those pages to be paid for. In the case of the Rev. F. C. Hingeston, the Master of the Rolls found both his translations and his orthography so questionable that he declared to the editor: 'If I were to consult my own feelings, I should cancel the whole volume. I regret also to say that the letters selected appear to me to be in a great many instances devoid of interest.'[73]

Shoddy editing was not the only setback with which the series had to contend. Another major problem was actually getting editors to complete their editions within a reasonable period, a problem exacerbated by their frequent reliance on the scholarship of amateurs. One of the most notorious examples of delay was Frederick J. Furnivall's *Robert de Brunne*. It had been authorised on

[70] PRO 37.12. MR to W. W. Shirley, 11 February 1859.
[71] Quoted in W. H. Hutton, *Letters of William Stubbs, Bishop of Oxford, 1825–1901* (London, 1904) p. 44. Stubbs to Freeman, 22 May 1858.
[72] PRO 37.13. Memo to G. A. Hamilton, Treasury, 13 March 1861.
[73] *ibid.* MR to F. C. Hingeston, 15 December 1864.

March 31 1865 but did not appear until 1887. Lengthy delays such as this caused problems not just for the Office but also for the printers who were generally paid only on completion of a work. Their approach to the Deputy Keeper in 1881 is typical of the dilemma they faced all too frequently. 'Although our outlay commenced so long ago, no payment has yet been made to us because each book is nominally still in progress; and we are further burdened with the expense and risk of storage.'[74] Neither the pleas of the printers nor the ultimatums issued periodically by direction of the Master of the Rolls had any effect on Furnivall's conscience however. In July 1886, the Deputy Keeper wrote to him.

Being reluctant to cast such a slur upon a well-known scholar, I now write to say that I shall be happy to receive your Preface [. . .] in the course of the present month [. . .] If however, the Preface, or at any rate the greater part of it is not in my hands by the morning of 2nd August next I shall immediately and without further notice, take such steps as may be necessary to ensure the publication of the work at an early date.[75]

And yet four months later, Furnivall could write cheerfully and without remorse to the Deputy Keeper explaining yet again why he had still not completed his twenty-one year old obligation.

I took all my books to Yorkshire but never opened them. Lawn tennis, cricket, walks, picnics, getting up a Concert and Dances, occupied all the holiday. Then since my return, there's been the practice for our Sculling Four Race next Saturday.[76]

Furnivall's cavalier attitude was matched by the editors of the *Icelandic Sagas*, G. W. Dasent and G. Vigfusson, who were first commissioned in 1859 and whose volumes finally appeared between 1887 and 1894.

In general, the reception given to the Rolls Series was an enthusiastic one. Bad editing did not go unnoticed, but the principle behind the series was much applauded. 'When five or six foolish, blundering books have been removed from the number, [the Series] must be spoken of in terms of highest praise, and used with hearty thankfulness by every student of medieval history.'[77] Many of the problems arose simply from the meagre finances granted the publications. The small and fixed Treasury grant compelled the Master of the Rolls to limit editors to producing only one volume per annum and to receiving payment on the same basis in order not to exceed the funds available. Many prospective editors and projects were thus put off from year to year as the lists quickly became full. In 1859 soon after the series had commenced publication, the Master of the Rolls was explaining to would-be contributors: 'I have already been compelled on several occasions [. . .] to decline the offers of service of gentlemen of great

[74] PRO 37.14. H. M. Printers to DK, 7 December 1881.
[75] PRO 37.16A. DK to F. J. Furnivall, 8 July 1886.
[76] *ibid.* Furnivall to DK, 15 November 1886.   [77] PRO 8.6. *The Reader,* 21 March 1865.

knowledge and capacity who have been desirous of editing manuscripts of great interest and value.'[78]

The most frequent criticism levelled at the series was the same as that at the Calendars, lack of uniformity.[79] The Master of the Rolls issued a set of *General Directions for the Guidance of Editors* resembling those directed at Calendar editors. They dealt largely, though not exclusively, with matters of orthography – spelling of classical names, use of the diphthong, abbreviations and the like, but it was economy which continued to dictate. 'No volume is to exceed 500 pages, including prefatory matter, index and glossary.'[80]

The standard of scholarship varied considerably throughout the period. As late as 1897, the historian F. W. Maitland criticised the notes, the absence of manuscript collation and the inaccuracy of the introduction in one volume on which he had been asked to comment.

I do decidedly think that among scholars it will add to the curses of regret that in the past the Rolls Series was not subjected to central and official supervision and I do decidedly think that critics who know their business will speak evil of the book.[81]

Despite the concerted efforts of the Master of the Rolls and the Deputy Keeper to impose some degree of uniformity 'no level standard of competence, not even a low standard, was maintained. Some volumes, *e.g.* those of Luard, Stubbs and Maitland are admirable; many are more or less competent; some are wholly inadequate'.[82]

The project was an ambitious one, and coming under the aegis of the Record Office, few there could devote wholesale attention to its success particularly since the instigation of the series had coincided with the first period of major record re-organisation after the opening of the new buildings. Under the Deputy Keepership of Sir Henry Maxwell-Lyte[83] towards the close of the century, the series was wound down, the final volume of the *Year Books of the reign of King Edward III* appearing in 1911.

In addition to the Rolls Series and the *Calendars*, the Office was also involved in 1861 in a short-lived attempt to produce volumes of photozincographic facsimiles including that of the *Domesday Book* and other manuscripts deemed to be of particular national significance. Costlier than the Rolls Series at 16/- per volume as opposed to 10/- they sold badly, and by the end of 1876 the first volume of the facsimile *National Manuscripts of England* had sold a mere seventy copies out of a print run of five hundred.[84]

---

[78] PRO 37.12. MR to Rev Octavius Freire Owen, 1 January 1859.
[79] V. H. Galbraith, *An Introduction to the Use of the Public Records* (Oxford, 1934) p. 71.
[80] PRO 37.72.   [81] PRO 37.52. F. W. Maitland to DK, 15 March 1897.
[82] Galbraith, *op. cit.* p. 72.
[83] Maxwell-Lyte succeeded to the post of DK in 1886 taking over from William Hardy, brother of Thomas Duffus who had himself gained the post on his brother's death in 1878.
[84] PRO 37.72.

Despite the dubious quality of some of the editions, the idea of cheap freely available editions[85] of primarily medieval manuscripts, accompanied by thorough footnoting (in theory, at least) and far more legible than the manuscripts themselves was a major advance, as were the *Calendars* in opening the national archives to a wider public.[86] In his *Instructions for Editors* of Calendars the Master of the Rolls urged that 'the entries should be so minute as to enable the reader to discover not only the general contents of the originals, but also what *they do not* contain'.

III

The Historical Manuscripts Commission, first appointed in 1869, was founded with similar intention. Its function was to establish a systematic investigation of the manuscript sources known to exist in private hands. This tentative extension of record accessibility into the field of private property was fraught with political sensitivities.

In these days, when 'Compulsory Purchase' [. . .] has [. . .] openly declared itself as one of the most active motive forces of the State – there may be a particular significance in the portentous eyes of a Royal Commission specially directed to that class of private property which exists in the form of ancient manuscripts. Something it is, indeed, under the present aspect of the political atmosphere, that the Noblemen and Gentlemen of England are asked voluntarily to produce their most precious heirlooms, and often the most costly of their moveable property [. . .] to be examined and inventoried by the agents of a Government deeply pledged to the principle of expediency – confiscation: – to place them indeed under the surveillance of the central power of the State.[87]

The ever-critical Sir Thomas Phillipps regarded the Commission with a similarly suspicious eye. He told Thomas Duffus Hardy that its establishment was 'an arbitrary interference with the Rights of Private Property set on foot by the contrivance of the Jesuits'.[88] The Commissioners, however, were anxious to make clear that the co-operation of owners of manuscripts would be strictly voluntary and their rights respected by a guaranteed exclusion from publication or public mention of any findings 'of a private character, or relating to the title of existing owners'.[89] In fact the Commission experienced very little concrete opposition. Owners of manuscripts were generally happy to take

---

[85] There is an interesting comparison here with the phenomenon of the printing clubs whose aims were very similar. They were, of course, often curtailed in their intentions by lack of money. Their subscription publishing schemes necessarily meant that their editions were not freely available in the same way as were the Rolls Series. It was not uncommon for the private printing clubs to see themselves as fulfilling a rôle which they felt government *ought* to undertake but had failed to do so.   [86] See p. 111.

[87] HMC 1.7. *Kerslake's Catalogue of Books*, January 1871.

[88] A. N. L. Munby, *Phillipps Studies* IV (Cambridge, 1956) 156.

[89] Royal Commission on Historical Manuscripts, 2 April 1869.

advantage of the gratuitous cataloguing, cleaning and repairs offered by the Commission's Inspectors.

It is very gratifying [. . .] to state that your Majesty's Commission has been fully appreciated and favourably received. Many collections, the existence of which was [sic] unknown, have been brought to light and submitted to the Inspection of the Commissioners [. . .] No less than 180 persons and heads of institutions expressed their willingness either to co-operate with the Commissioners or to request their aid in making known the contents of their collections.[90]

The idea for a commission of this sort was no novelty in 1869. George Harris, a barrister from Rugby, had made a similar proposal in 1857 to the National Association for the Promotion of Social Science. A memorial based on Harris's paper was delivered to the Treasury in July 1859 urging the appointment of 'competent and trustworthy persons' to effect an investigation of the 'great number of ancient and other original manuscripts and documents'[91] in private collections. Its signatories included Gladstone, Maurice, Froude, Kingsley, Grote, Hallam, Carlyle, Creasy, Henry Vaughan and Agnes Strickland as well as the publishers Thomas Longman and Henry Bohn. There were those who refused to add their names: Buckle – opposed on principle to any government interference in the literary sphere, J. H. Parker and Lord Stanhope.[92] Opposition too came from the new Historical Society (later to become the Royal Historical Society) who discussed the proposals as they went to the Treasury; Lord Bateman interpreted the intention as an attempt to 'pry into titles to estates'.[93]

The plan was rejected officially by the Home Office in October 1860, largely on grounds of economy; the expensive mistake of the Record Commissions, the building of the new Record Office and the recently instituted publishing projects left little cash spare for such purposes. The scheme that was finally realised was one proposed by Sir John Romilly.[94] It was, from the start, closely tied to the new record establishment, administered by its employees and numbering both the Master of the Rolls and the Deputy Keeper amongst the original Commissioners. Romilly had estimated that it would cost a mere £500 annually but this was a cautious and unrealistic figure.[95] The Commission was awarded an annual grant of £1,200 per annum plus a further sum of £500 specifically earmarked for the arrangement and calendaring of the papers of the House of Lords.

---

[90] First Report of the Commissioners, 1870.   [91] HMC 1.362. Memorial, 9 July 1859.
[92] Paul Morgan, 'George Harris of Rugby and the Prehistory of the Historical Manuscripts Commission', *Trans. Birmingham Archaeological Society* 82 (1967) 28–37 (p. 32).
[93] *ibid.* p. 32.
[94] Roger Ellis suggests that Romilly used the excuse of official economy to dispose of Harris. He reasons that Romilly's idea was first, to secure that no money was diverted from the funds for the building works on the Office and second, to promote his own scheme for a similar commission under the aegis of his establishment. Soon after the rejection of Harris's scheme, he submitted a very similar plan. 'A short history and explanation', *Manuscripts and Men: the Royal Commission on Historical Manuscripts 1869–1969, An Exhibition*, 1–36.   [95] *ibid.*

Inspectors of manuscripts were employed by the Commission on specified and limited inspections at a rate of two guineas per day but the Commissioners were unpaid. The original members included a number of appropriately qualified men; in addition to Romilly and Duffus Hardy, Earl Stanhope and G. W. Dasent were amongst the early Commissioners. The second Commission appointed in 1882 brought both Lord Talbot de Malahide and Lord Acton into its fold. Similarly most of those employed as Inspectors were experienced record clerks – the Scots and Irish inspectors were respectively employees of the Register House Edinburgh and the Public Record Office Dublin – requested to undertake the work either by the Commissioners (although initially promoting themselves) or by the actual owners of manuscripts. Joseph Stevenson was often favoured in this way by Catholic manuscript-owners.

The Commissioners were generally influenced in their appointment of Inspectors more by proof of practical record experience than by any vague notion of literary aptitude. Charles Kent solicited the Commission for work in 1882 and was rejected on these grounds.

It has not hitherto [. . .] been the practice of the Commissioners to engage any Gentleman temporarily who has not some special qualifications in the way of experience of Records and State papers – experience which as a rule can only be acquired by work among early manuscripts in the Public Record Office and the manuscript department of the British Museum – qualifications which are entirely distinct from the literary and legal ones which the Master of the Rolls is fully satisfied you possess.[96]

The paucity of monies available limited the number of Inspectors who might be employed at any one time; the Commission permitted one Inspector each for Scotland and Ireland and two for England. There was no guarantee moreover that one labour having been completed, the Inspectors would find more work with the Commission. When Catholic manuscript owners requested that Stevenson be engaged to inspect their collections, Duffus Hardy pointed out that he could not be employed under the terms of the Commission 'until one of the other Inspectors has made his report'.[97]

John Cordy Jeaffreson's recollections of his duties as an Inspector under the Commission describe them as often 'rough and dirty [. . .] but the employment proved much less monotonous than [I] expected to find it'. Often the work was enlivened when curious spectators came to watch. Jeaffreson was at work on the Chester municipal archives in 1878 and was much bothered by interruptions.

To see what the documents were like, and what the gentleman from London was doing with them, the idlers of both sexes and of all the social degrees above the order of mere

---

[96] HMC 1.344. J. J. Cartwright to Charles Kent, March 1882.
[97] HMC 1.57. 13 September 1869.

labourers came day after day to the lecture-room in such numbers that I was constrained to beg the chief caretaker of the Town Hall to allow no one but [. . .] personages of superior municipal quality to enter.[98]

IV

The middle years of the century thus saw an unprecedented flurry of governmental activity in the field of record and manuscript administration.[99] During the 1850s and 1860s, the central record repository was finally built and opened to the public, major publishing projects were introduced and private manuscript collections brought tentatively into the public sphere. A similar rationalisation was also occurring at related institutions like the British Museum where in the 1860s the Department of Antiquities was subject to major re-organisation. On the retirement of the Keeper, Edward Hawkins, in 1860 it was split into three new departments: Greek and Roman, Egyptian and Oriental, and Coins and Medals. Antiquities not catered for under those headings became the separate responsibility of Samuel Birch who headed the Egyptian section. It was not until 1866 that a Department of British and Medieval Antiquities and Ethnography was formed under the Keepership of Wollaston Franks. These various schemes were all part of a single development aimed at providing greater accessibility and better preservation of documents and artifacts deemed to be of national significance. In one sense they were all part of a general governmental trend towards a rationalisation of state administration, but the record schemes in particular deserve separate attention, for governmental intervention in the preservation and organisation of historical documentation was fundamental in establishing the structure of the emergent historical discipline, still tied at this juncture to a nationalist sense of English pride.

Between the growing mountain of publications issued by the Master of the Rolls and the Record Office, and the spreading inquiries of the Historical Manuscripts Commission [. . .] the means will be at hand, as they never were before, for the GIBBON of the future, when he emerges, to make his general survey and rear his abiding monument of English history.[100]

The reluctance of Parliament to grant adequate financial aid to record administration sits curiously with its celebratory view of English history and its declaration of the rights of public access. The difficulties faced by Lord Langdale and his successors in persuading the Treasury to provide sufficient resources for building and equipping the new repository, the paltry funds provided for the various publications and for the Commission of 1869 suggest that discomfiture over the wasteful expenditure of the Record Commissions was slow to disappear.

[98] J. C. Jeaffreson, *A Book of Recollections* ii (London, 1894) 135.
[99] Similar pressure had been put on government in the late 1820s to increase the level of patronage afforded to science and its devotees. See Morrell & Thackray, *Gentlemen of Science. op. cit.* p. 41.
[100] HMC 1.7. *The Times,* 30 August 1882.

Government was willing to espouse the cause but was nonetheless anxious to do so as economically as possible. Funding of the Public Record Office remained almost static throughout the nineteenth century: the grant for 1879–80 was £24,377 and in 1887–8 it had only risen to £27,038.[101] The British Museum was little different. There a reluctance to spend money typified the approach of the Museum's Trustees; Layard's frequent and bitter complaints to Henry Ellis about the lack of financial aid offered him by the Museum in the 1840s was typical. Thomas Kendrick maintains that it was British antiquities in particular which suffered from this financial stringency. In the 1830s, the Trustees spent no more than £30–40 a year on minor antiquities and caused a major uproar in the antiquarian world in the mid 1850s by refusing to purchase the Faussett Collection of Kent antiquities. The national antiquarian bodies protested in vain at the decision.[102] Governmental acceptance of responsibility for historical monuments took even longer to achieve than did recognition of the need to preserve historical records. Attempts to protect physical monuments ran aground on the same rock of the sanctity of private property as had the earlier Historical Manuscripts Commission. Sir John Lubbock, author of *Prehistoric Times*, made frequent attempts to introduce a private member's bill on the subject beginning in 1870. Much modified, his proposals finally reached the statute book in 1882 but as a wholly permissive act of legislation the Act had no effective power over proprietors of ancient monuments. They could offer their properties into state care if they desired but were under no compulsion to do so. Anyone found defacing or damaging a monument named in the Act's Schedule, excepting its owner, was liable to a fine of £5 or one month's imprisonment. The sixty-eight scheduled monuments were primarily pre-historic, and ecclesiastical buildings still in use were specifically excluded from the provisions of the Act. It was 1900 before its terms were widened to include monuments not specifically named in the Schedule and embracing unoccupied medieval buildings and 1913 before compulsory powers were introduced via preservation orders.[103] The first Inspector appointed under the Act of 1882 was the archaeologist and close friend of Lubbock, Pitt Rivers, who drew a salary of £250 per annum.[104]

V

The most important outcome of nineteenth-century record reform by Government was without doubt the creation of a nascent class of professional record

---

[101] *PP*, House of Commons, 1912–13. xliv. 13. *op. cit.* Part I. Appendix III.
[102] T. Kendrick, 'The British Museum and British Antiquities', *Antiquity* III (September 1954) 132–43 (pp. 135–7).
[103] N. Bolting, 'The law's delays: conservationist legislation in the British Isles', in ed. J. Fawcett, *The Future of the Past. Attitudes to Conservation, 1174–1974* (London, 1976) pp. 9–33.
[104] G. Clark, 'Archaeology and the State', *Antiquity* VIII (1934) 32, pp. 414–28; M. W. Thompson, *General Pitt-Rivers. Evolution and Archaeology in the Nineteenth Century* (Wiltshire, 1977).

scholars amongst the full-time employees of the Public Record Office. From the first days of the Public Record Office Act in 1838 Sir Francis Palgrave had been insistent about the need to create a professional corps of archivists.

The Records service, requiring as it does a knowledge of law, of Languages, and of General History, must if it is to be rendered efficient be treated as a distinct profession [and] the Establishment so constructed as to train up and educate within it a supply of qualified persons.[105]

Defining the 'professional' or a 'profession' is a complex task. The nineteenth century saw the emergence of many new middle-class occupations as well as an expansion in the three traditional professions of the bar, the altar and medicine, all of which began to formulate practices and regulations designed to exclude the unsuitable and above all the unqualified from their ranks. It is perhaps more accurate therefore to concentrate attention on the dynamic of professionalisation as characteristic of events in this period.[106]

Both the Civil Service and the army were subject to major reform in this period. In 1849 an oral examination for the award of an army commission had replaced the old system of purchase. The Civil Service Commission of 1855 established after the Northcote-Trevelyan report did not abolish or even reduce patronage, but it did at least require a patron's nominees to pass competitive examinations in various subjects before entry to the service could be guaranteed. In 1857 open competition for entry into the army was introduced and finally in 1870 by an Order in Council designed to circumvent opposition, the Civil Service followed suit.[107] In this context, Talcott Parsons' point about the synonymity of professionalisation and rationalisation has distinct resonances.[108]

As a government department, the Record Office was subject to this general process of rationalisation and reform. In many respects, however, its work and functions set it apart from other departments. Despite the general Civil Service principle of positively discouraging special qualification prior to general entry, the instruction dictated by the specialised duties demanded of Public Record Office clerks certainly equipped young Record Office trainees with unusual attributes which they themselves recognised as a symbol of their uniqueness within the service.

Any noodle fresh from a "High School" with his flowing commercial hand, and without his aspirates, or with a superabundance of them, with his mean ideas and low view of life, can "tot up" and even do sums in what he is pleased to call his "mind". But he would

---

[105] PRO 36.54. Sir Francis Palgrave's Observations on the Plan of Management of the Public Records, 23 October 1838, pp. 13–14.

[106] H. M. Vollmer & D. L. Mills, *Professionalisation* (New Jersey, 1966) p. vii.

[107] W. J. Reader, *Professional Men: The Rise of the Professional Classes in Nineteenth Century England* (London, 1966) pp. 79–97.

[108] Talcott Parsons, 'Professions', ed. D. L. Sills, *International Encyclopaedia of the Social Sciences* 12 (New York, 1968) 536–47 (p. 545).

not be quite up to the work – even the easiest work of the Public Record Office. And further, an appeal to the "open market" for gentlemen [. . .] is simply "fudge" – because the market to begin with is not open.[109]

The training to which new record clerks were subjected was a stringent test of capabilities. Romilly described their initiation in a long letter to the Treasury.

The Clerks in the Record Service are required to possess a very unusual amount of intellectual qualification [. . .] Every clerk on his appointment, in addition to the usual course of examination before the Civil Service Commissioners [. . .] is required to qualify himself for a variety of arduous official duties. He must understand ancient French and medieval Latin. He must be able to decipher every form of handwriting from the earliest to the latest period, an acquirement not easily gained. He must make himself perfectly acquainted with obsolete Law terms and with the usages existing in the management of Public business. He must understand the ancient method of dating documents, their proper titles and descriptions and a variety of technical details not to be mastered without much labour and reference to expensive works. This variety of acquirement is as indispensable for his advancement in this service as reading and writing English is in other departments.[110]

With the establishment of the Civil Service Commission in 1855, the question of the qualification and training of record officers received specific attention, and the introduction of competitive examination gave the Record Office an opportunity to establish its specific and unusual requirements. Even before then some form of selection had operated but in December 1857 the Civil Service Commission agreed that clerks intended for the Public Record Office would be required to sit papers in a choice of eight subjects: handwriting and orthography, arithmetic, book-keeping by single entry, geography, the history of England, translation from the Latin, translation from the French and précis.[111] In 1868 book-keeping was abandoned but Romilly's attempts to have it replaced by an examination on Blackstone's *Commentaries* met with resistance: 'if this condition were enforced no one of the selected Candidates might be found capable of satisfying it, and [. . .] the result might be to postpone indefinitely the filling up of the existing vacancies'.[112] It was with the introduction of a two-grade open examination in 1872 in which candidates for the Record Office were classified in the higher grade that Blackstone was finally included, although only in the final and not in the preliminary test. Although the general principle of encouraging entrants with a good general education rather than specialists was a tenacious ideal in the Civil Service, there were many instances in which the Commissioners did admit of the necessity for specialist examining, although principally in the more technical departments such as surveying.[113] And at the British Museum, they had also agreed to

[109] PRO 1.140. F. S. Haydon to DK, 3 January 1887.
[110] PRO 1.24. MR to G. A. Hamilton, Treasury, 3 February 1860.
[111] Public Record Office, CSC 2.29. Civil Service Commission to DK, 7 December 1857.
[112] *ibid.* Commission to Secretary, 19 December 1871.
[113] K. M. Reader, *The Civil Service Commission, 1855–1975* (London, 1981) p. 18.

examine prospective candidates in the subjects considered essential by the Museum's authorities.

These entrance requirements were, however, little more than a preliminary sifting of potential records officers and as such not always effective. The original structure of the general Civil Service examination, based upon winning as many points as possible regardless of the relevance of the topic, resulted on occasion in unsuitable appointments being made. In at least two recorded instances in the 1860s, vacant clerkships in the Record Office were filled by the candidate with the highest overall score who was subsequently found to lack the requisite proficiency in French and Latin.[114] It was not unknown for high scoring candidates to have failed altogether in one subject but to have tempered that with high scores in others. It was such incidents which prompted the implementation of more specific requirements for these specialised clerkships. The net result of these developments was to ensure that from the 1870s on, men entering the Public Record Office were almost exclusively university graduates. Luke Owen Pike, a junior clerk in the Office, gave evidence before Lyon Playfair's Civil Service Inquiry Commission in 1875. Himself a graduate of Brasenose College Oxford, Pike was asked by the Commissioners whether all the junior clerks were 'men of education'.

I should say most decidedly so. A great many of them have been either called to the Bar, or have entered an Inn of Court with the intention of being called to the Bar.[115]

Whereas the first generation of record keepers had been men whose skill and experience was acquired almost exclusively through apprenticeship in record establishments, later recruits to the Office boasted a university career. Of the earliest staff of the Record Office in 1838, most had transferred from positions in the smaller record offices or from the Record Commissions. Applauding the introduction of competitive selection, James Gairdner who had entered the Public Record Office in 1846 and retired in 1893, told the 1910 Royal Commission that 'we had not all of us received a first-rate education [. . .] and there were really no means of proper training for those duties for which we ought to have qualified ourselves'.[116] Investigating the pedigree of the clerical establishment at the start of the twentieth century, the Commissioners found that most applicants for the Record Office 'have a good classical (and occasionally mathematical) training [. . .] and have obtained high (but not usually the highest) honours in the examinations.'[117] Thus by the end of the century the Office was staffed largely by graduates anxious to maintain the division proposed by Northcote and Trevelyan in the 1850s between

---

[114] CSC 2.29. MR to Commission, 4 July 1868. He also gives details of an incident, 5 March 1867.
[115] *PP*, House of Commons, 1875. xxiii. 451. *Second Report of the Civil Service Inquiry Commission* 12 March 1875.
[116] *PP*, House of Commons, 1912–13. xliv. 247. *op. cit.* Part III.   [117] *ibid.* Part VIII.

intellectual and mechanical labour.[118] Assistant Keeper John James Bond told the Civil Service Commission of Inquiry in 1875 that the work of the clerk was 'all intellectual work'.[119] His comments are reminiscent of the description of the new grade of Class I clerks offered by the Civil Service Inquiry Commission who described them as 'drawn from the best class of university men, and [. . .] intended to form the superior class in those offices which need high social and educational acquirements'.[120] Despite the protestations of Henry Maxwell-Lyte who had succeeded William Hardy as Deputy Keeper in 1886, that 'we prefer to have a man whose first wish is to be in the civil service', a sense of the specialised nature of the skills attached to Record Office work fostered a strong sense of corporate pride.[121] The small and highly skilled staff of the Record Office were the sole bearers of a special and singular knowledge unique in – and to – the Civil Service through which they could identify their status and authority.

Their sense of a professional unity was further consolidated by the many ambitious projects associated increasingly with the Public Record Office which had come to dominate the archival and historical scene by the middle years of the century. An important element in maintaining that internal sense of professional unity was derived from social stratification, the sectioning off of gentlemanly from manual skills as recommended by the first report on the Civil Service in 1854. Sir Francis Palgrave had always been convinced of the need for this distinction to be understood long before the Northcote-Trevelyan Report recommended such a division of labour. In his suggestions for the management of the proposed Office in 1838 he noted

it is exceedingly important to effect a proper division of labour amongst the clerks and other persons composing the Record Establishment [. . .] so as to use each of your Tools for its proper work. If you place a Man of literary requirements in a situation where his time is constantly broken up by attending to the *Customers* of the office; if you employ a Clerk who is qualified to calendar Records upon the task of paging and numbering them it is obvious that you are frittering away your powers.[122]

The demarcation between manual and non-manual tasks was as stringently upheld in the Record Office as in other Civil Service departments, through devices such as mode of remuneration, restrictions on movement and entitlement to privileges.

It is considered that it will possibly be expedient that no Workman should enter a Record Room, except accompanied by a Superior Officer, for though argumentatively it may be assumed that all the Workmen are trusty, yet no distrust is implied by adopting every practical safeguard [. . .] Provision should be made for the strict superintendence of the Workmen; and that there should be a Superior Officer of the rank of Gentlemen, in addition to the Foreman.[123]

[118] R. A. Chapman & J. R. Greenaway, *The Dynamics of Administrative Reform* (London, 1981) pp. 27–9.   [119] *PP*, House of Commons, 1875. *op. cit.* Appendix A.   [120] *ibid.* p. 6.
[121] *PP*, House of Commons, 1912–13. *op. cit.*
[122] PRO 36.53. Suggestions of Sir Francis Palgrave as to the Plan of Management, 14 June 1838. p. 2.   [123] PRO 1.18. 1 February 1854.

Highly skilled crafts such as repairing and binding as well as fetching and carrying were the province of a separate class of workmen, paid generally on a weekly basis unlike the clerical staff who drew annual salaries. In 1872, the seven First Class Assistant Keepers earned salaries ranging from £500 to £800 and the twenty-five clerks in the Office earned salaries ranging from £100 to £400 depending on seniority. The forty-nine workmen employed earned between £52 and £83-4s a year, a reasonably high wage perhaps for a working-class man but significantly less than the earnings of the most junior of the clerks. Only their superintendent exceeded clerical earnings with his wage of £124-16s. Five female charwomen also figure on the payroll for that year and their earnings were a mere £26 a year.[124] The holiday entitlement of manual staff was one week per annum compared with the lowest of the non-manual grades who were allowed five weeks. They were granted only one day of sick leave without a medical certificate compared with the three days allowed for the higher grades. In addition they were subject to various disciplinary procedures not applied to the permanent staff, including the imposition of fines for offences such as tardiness, untidiness in the workrooms and damage to tools. Their conditions were significantly improved when Sir Thomas Duffus Hardy succeeded his long-standing enemy Sir Francis Palgrave as Deputy Keeper in July 1861.[125] His first edict was to abolish wage deductions for absence arising from sickness, holidays, births, deaths and burials, and to regularise both hours and pay for the manual workforce thereby creating a more stable environment.[126] In the wake of the first Civil Service reforms there was some discussion too of the entrance qualifications relevant to the technical establishment of the Office. Romilly, whilst recognising their important rôle as craftsmen, saw no reason for examining them in an academic context. 'I think that for men of this class the examination should proceed no further than "Handwriting, orthography and Elementary Arithmetic."'[127] The strict class division of labour remained crucial to the maintenance of professional status. And yet, by contemporary standards, the workmen of the Public Record Office were a fortunate élite. At the British Museum where employment was broadly comparable, conditions were even more restrictive.

The Workmen and the Attendants are paid by the day, receive only their pay for the days when they have actually come to their work. No allowance is made for absence caused by illness nor for holidays, not even for Ash Wednesday, Good Friday and Christmas Day when the Museum is closed.[128]

[124] *PP*, House of Commons, 1872. xxxvi. 437. Return of All Persons Employed in the Public Record Office, England.

[125] Thomas Duffus Hardy (1804–78) began his career in the records service as a junior clerk at the Tower of London, aged fifteen. His mentor was the Keeper at the Tower, Henry Petrie, whose projected *Monumenta Britannica* was issued posthumously by Hardy in 1848. John Cantwell gives a succinct account of his disagreement with his predecessor in office, Palgrave, in his article, *loc. cit.* pp. 282–3.   [126] PRO 1.125. 18 July 1861.

[127] CSC 2.29. MR to Commission, 15 July 1870.

[128] PRO 8.28. DK to Charles Roberts, 15 January 1851.

Among the officers, distinctions in rank and status were no less essential. The annual salary increments of the clerical staff rested upon testimonies from their superior officers. The Treasury had laid down that

no periodical increases of salary should be granted excepting after careful enquiry, and on the written certificate of the Deputy Keeper and Assistant Keeper under whom the several Clerks are placed, that they are deserving of such increase by reason of their regular attendance, their diligent performance of their duties and their general good conduct.[129]

Moreover, an emphasis on productivity made demands not just on their conduct but also on their time.

Every Officer below the rank of Assistant Keeper wholly or partially employed on Calendaring or Indexing should state how many abstracts of Documents he has made each day, and from what date to what date they have been made, and he is also to state how he has been otherwise employed.[130]

The distinction between clerks and keepers was thus as essential to the maintenance of the hierarchy as was that between manual and non-manual staff. Although the rank of Assistant Keeper carried with it a distinct social position and the conditions of employment were adjusted accordingly, the Treasury still required Assistant Keepers to record both their own and their subordinate's attendance. No fixed regulation governed the number of hours worked daily. In practice, most Assistant Keepers worked long if not always regular hours. W. H. Black's private journal, kept during his tenure as Keeper at the Rolls House, cantankerously recalls his labours.

[1844] Saturday January 6: God's Holy Sabbath. I have a right to be absent; and I pay dearly for the privilege too: but I don't refuse (when needful) to work on the idolatrous and superstitious [. . .] January 7: Busy all day at house, on material for my year's Report; while others are keeping the traditional holiday.[131]

The journal shows variations in his working day from as little as three to as much as eleven hours.

One problem which did arise in the officer class was that of the limited prospects of promotion. In 1877 the Office considered means of reducing staffing numbers by enforcing a retirement age in response to governmental economies, whilst at the same time not filling the vacancies thus created. In an environment already so small and specialised, this created inevitable dissatisfaction by blocking the only avenues of promotion for more junior officers trained in the expectation of such rewards.[132] The size of the Record Office remained stable throughout the century with only minor changes to the numbers in the establishment. In general, such alterations as were effected left

---

[129] PRO 1.20. Treasury minute, 11 May 1855.
[130] PRO 8.29. Instructions, 11 January 1856.
[131] Chetham's Library, Manchester. Mun.A.2.111. Private Journal of W. H. Black, 1844–6.
[132] PRO 1.140. Private Reports from Officers as to the best means of promoting efficiency and economy, in connexion with enquiry from the Civil Establishments Commission, 1887.

the overall size of the staff unaltered, thereby limiting the prospects of promotion, an extremely slow process in any case. It was only with the amalgamation of the State Paper Office that a slight rise in numbers occurred, bringing the officer class to a total of thirty-five. It remained at around that figure throughout the period. The Assistant Keeper Class II position was abolished in 1860 in favour of a division between Senior and Junior Clerks, and in 1862 a new class of Transcribers – initially of six, rising to eight in 1867 – was introduced below the rank of junior clerk and engaged on non-specialist copying. They were the equivalent of the copyist class used elsewhere in the Civil Service, and their pay was duly lower than that of the junior clerks.

There always remained a tension between the hard-headed economies imposed by a cash-conscious Treasury and the gentlemanly ideal of honourable and trustworthy agreements, and the relationship between the record administration and the editors of *Calendars* and Rolls Series volumes often foundered on this ambiguity. Those who were, in addition to their editorial duties, already on the staff of the establishment were only permitted to undertake editorial work on the strict condition that it would be done outside office hours and not impinge upon their daily duties. Treasury permission to undertake editing was a preliminary requirement of employment. Non-staff editors, however, were employed to work on specific commissions in the same way as the Inspectors of the Historical Manuscripts Commission. Unlike the Commission's employees, however, their mode of remuneration was not standard. A few received the equivalent of an annual salary. J. S. Brewer who was engaged on the gargantuan task of calendaring the Henry VIII papers and Rawdon Brown, transcribing materials for English history abroad, were employed in this way. Most, however, were paid by result, generally at a rate of eight guineas per completed printed 'sheet'. The necessarily sporadic nature of the payments in the latter instance, although alleviated by advances, hardly afforded their recipients any financial security. It was common for editors to excuse their own delays by reference to other more pressing engagements.

It was quite my hope and intention that Robert of Gloucester should have gone to press last year, but the Universities Commissioners deprived me of the slight amount of leisure I can command and the preparation of the returns which I had to make to them as Bursar of the College [Trinity College, Cambridge] prevented me from being so forward as I could wish with the work for the Master of the Rolls.[133]

A shrewd understanding of market conditions overrode gentlemanly honour in the matter of large sums of money. The process of rationalisation was written very distinctly in economic terms. Although the publications themselves could be regarded non-commercially as a form of public instruction, the relationship between the government as employer and the editor as employee was in

[133] PRO 37.1. William Aldis Wright to DK, 30 March 1874.

essence seen no differently than any other productive agreement. In the case of the editors, payment by result was thus the normal mode. The Secretary of the Office discussed J. S. Brewer's remuneration for work on the Henry VIII Calendars in distinctly commercial terms.

The Revd J. S. Brewer [. . .] has been paid the full £200, as well as £14-8-10 on account for the sixth volume, and if the quarterly payment of £50 [. . .] be made to him [. . .] will then have received £64-8-10 for another volume (the sixth) before he has finished one half of the fifth volume, for which [. . .] he has been paid in full [. . .] supposing (to avoid any offensive insinuation) that Mr Brewer should die before the work was completed? How would the Treasury recover the money paid in advance? Or who would finish the work gratis, that Mr Brewer ought to have finished and had been paid for?[134]

Under these circumstances, there was little incentive for the editors to form a distinct and self-conscious group, aside from their existing standing in the wider antiquarian comunity. For the full-time staff of the Record Office recognition of their single purpose and shared special knowledge was, however, far easier. Moreover the continuity in staffing between the pre-1838 system and the new Record Office deliberately encouraged by the Government, further consolidated their sense of collective identity. Five of the eight Assistant Keepers and many of the clerks on the establishment in 1840 had transferred from the existing Record Offices. The other three Assistant Keepers had been on the staff of the Record Commission. Palgrave had been Keeper at the Chapter House, Thomas Duffus Hardy was Chief Clerk at the Tower Record Office. Hardy's colleagues from that period, Charles Roberts and H. J. Sharpe, transferred with him as did many of Palgrave's subordinates.[135] Although there was no attempt to form what Millerson has called a 'qualifying association', regulating entry to a profession and organised from within, they clearly regarded themselves as a unified group.[136]

Nonetheless, the virtue and gentlemanliness attached to their calling did not detract from their more material concerns. Not unnaturally when Palgrave was offered the office of Deputy Keeper of the Public Records – a high honour – in 1838, he felt that the consequent drop in income was not consonant with his dignity as a senior public official.

I should at once thankfully declare my unconditional acceptance [. . .] were it not that the immediate salary proposed by the Government, is less than the sum which I am entitled to claim as compensation for the losses which I sustain by the passing of the act in question [. . .] and if I should live until the [. . .] proposed salary would be raised to £800, I should then, after 26 years continuous and laborious employment as a public servant, be placed upon a lower scale of remuneration than I now receive.[137]

---

[134] PRO 1.35. John Edwards, 10 December 1870.
[135] *PP*, House of Commons, 1912–13. xliv. 13. *op. cit.* p. 106; PRO R3*. *Miscellaneous Printed Papers Relating to Records* p. 875.
[136] G. Millerson, *The Qualifying Associations. A Study in Professionalisation* (London, 1964).
[137] Section XVIII of 1 & 2 Vict. c. 94. allowed compensation for loss of emoluments and fees by Keepers as a result of the new legislation; PRO 1.1 DK to MR, 31 October 1838.

For the exacting duties which as Deputy Keeper would be required of him, Palgrave was not unreasonable in his demands. The problem was solved eventually when Palgrave accepted the Treasury's scheme of taking into account his many years of service when considering increments to his salary.

The question of salary was of no small consequence. Salaries in the Public Record Office did not, at any stage in the nineteenth century, compare favourably with the larger and more prestigious branches of Civil Service employment. Clerks in the Treasury or the Home Office were often considerably better paid. The equivalent ranked posts in the Treasury, Home Office and Exchequer were earning as much as £300 more than their archival contemporaries in 1880.[138] 'The Public Record Office, although from the nature of its duties placed in class I still retains a scale of pay lower than that of almost any other office in the Civil Service.'[139] In 1862 the Record Office pointed out to its paymasters at the Treasury that similarly ranked senior officers in other departments enjoyed substantially higher material rewards than those in the Public Record Office. Despite the notions of comparability which normally governed the Treasury's approach to questions of salary, the pleas of the record officers met with little sympathy. 'It is not a class of work which puts them on a par with the superior officers of the Secretaries of State Departments, or one of the Revenue Boards.'[140]

Secure from the vicissitudes of temporary engagements, subject to a minute and thorough training in a closed field and yet not having to acquire those skills prior to appointment, the officers of the Public Record Office represent the earliest move towards professionalisation in the field of history. With the advantage and security of powerful institutional backing, for the university system was yet in its infancy and could offer few employment, these men could boast an expertise akin to that of the ancient professions. They saw themselves as servicing a public cause, raising them above the level of mere business employees. The acquisition of an institutional structure around which a professional career in a historical field could begin to grow did not herald any immediate or sudden change. The historical and antiquarian communities remained largely amateur until late in the century. There were always, of course, free-lance writers, some earning a substantial living from their books and journal contributions. Some held lectureships or professorships as well, but such occupations rarely involved full-time commitment before the 1880s or even later. When Brewer undertook the calendaring of the Henry VIII papers in the late 1850s, he wrote to the Master of the Rolls, 'I could place at your

---

[138] *PP*, House of Commons, 1878–9. xlviii. 1. Estimates for Civil and Revenue Departments for the year ending 31 March 1880.
[139] *PP*, House of Commons, 1875. *op. cit.* Appendix B.
[140] M. Wright, *Treasury Control of the Civil Service 1854–1874* (Oxford, 1969) pp. 246–7.

disposal six hours every day [. . .] with the exception of two hours four days in the week [. . .] during term time at King's College',[141] his professorial teaching duties thus amounting to eight hours a week.

Even the successful peripatetics like Brewer did not form a group of self-conscious stature. It was the Assistant Keepers with their specific and specialised knowledge and their relative security who formed a more identifiable group. Unlike the temporarily engaged editors and inspectors of manuscripts who boasted a roughly similar expertise, the Keepers benefited from the legitimising function of their full-time attachment to an established and permanent institution. Whereas the Historical Manuscripts Commission confidently if mistakenly anticipated that their work would be completed in the foreseeable future, and the *Calendars* and Rolls Series editors worked on short-term commissions, the work of the Keepers could not be contained in such ways. In 1888, their establishment was described as follows.

There is hardly a clerk in the office who does not take an active and intelligent interest in some class of records, and who has not contributed something to their history. In fact, the present and past staff may be said to be teachers of a record school or university, to the very great advantage of the amateur students.[142]

A specific profession of record administration was in process of formation, closely related to but separate from the pursuits of historical and antiquarian enthusiasts. The group in whom the first glimmerings of a historical profession may be recognised had identified their own concerns, and created within a well-delineated institutional form the necessary conditions for their own organisation as a profession.

It has been a common assumption that the professionalisation of history is associated primarily with the changes in university teaching and structure of the later nineteenth century. It would, however, be more accurate to see university expansion as formative for the creation of the academic profession more generally. The distinction between a university training and employment within the university is straightforward enough; it is the former which influences the emergence of the early historical profession more specifically. The Record Office in the latter half of the nineteenth century, with its newly acquired prestige, gathered to itself men of graduate status, few of them the products of the infant schools of history in the universities, to whom it proceeded to impart highly specialised historical knowledge. The growing status of the record officials within the historical and antiquarian community – no longer identified with extortionate fees and a reluctant mien – lends weight to the claim that they, and not the first ill-organised and unrecognised university historians, were the nascent professionals in the historical field. They combined many of the characteristics readily associated with the

---

[141] PRO 37.24. 22 October 1856.   [142] W. Rye, *op. cit.* p. 103.

dynamic of professionalisation; they were motivated in large part by an ideal of honourable altruistic service, offering knowledge virtually unobtainable elsewhere and which they had acquired through long and arduous training. Their attention to status and rank had much to do with professional pride, not merely as civil servants but more specifically as officers of a professional record establishment.

Parliament had created the institutional means whereby such a group could thrive, and from that time on the confidence and self-esteem of this nascent profession was irresistible. A post in the Record Office may have been near-chance for a young Civil Service trainee after 1870, but once part of that establishment the scheme of training ensured the creation of a skilled and knowledgeable professional records expert. By 1886 Sir Francis Palgrave's oft-repeated contention that 'record employment in its higher branches is a *Profession* and requiring previous preparation and long practice and experience' had become a commonplace for those thus employed.[143]

[143] PRO 36.53.

6

∽∽∽

The contribution of the universities

> Facts without philosophy may place a man high, but sham philosophy
> without facts will be quite sure to break down.
>
> (Montague Burrows, Pass and Class)

I

It was during the nineteenth century that the institution of the university began to acquire prominence in a national context. Both through the increasingly dominant idea that such bodies could serve as training grounds for future generations of decision makers and the part they thus came to play in the *rites de passage* which controlled the adolescence of the country's political élite, and through the corresponding growth of confidence in academic disciplines, new and old, the universities experienced a shift in status. The idea of the university as a national institution of moral and political as well as cultural significance became a central axiom of later nineteenth-century English society. In the first instance, these sentiments were directed largely to the ancient universities of Oxford and Cambridge as the oldest and most prestigious of such bodies. The first of the new universities of the nineteenth century – in Durham and in London – offered a more elementary education, often regarded as a preliminary for entrance to the two major bodies.

Oxford and Cambridge were thus the central representatives of this changing rôle of the universities and the Royal Commissions first appointed in 1850 to inquire into their workings signalled a new era in their declaration of the principles of state intervention and state responsibility. The two Commissions voiced crucial questions concerning the overall significance of the university as an institution and of the academic community within it.

Such an Institution cannot be regarded as a mere aggregation of private interests, it is eminently national. It would seem, therefore, to be a matter of public policy that inquiry should be made, from time to time, in order to ascertain whether the purposes of its existence are fulfilled; and that such measures should be taken to raise its efficiency to the highest point, and to diffuse its benefits most widely.[1]

---

[1] Report of H. M. Commissioners appointed to Inquire into the State, Discipline, Studies and Revenues of the University and Colleges of Oxford (London, 1852) p. 3.

135

Simultaneous with this Parliamentary interest, both universities had begun to extend the academic choices open to their students under pressure from the advocates of a more pluralist educational philosophy. The primarily classical curriculum at Oxford and the mathematical emphasis adopted by Cambridge were supplemented, though by no means usurped, by the introduction of new subjects, amongst them history. In 1848 a Natural Sciences Tripos and a Moral Sciences Tripos were introduced at Cambridge, with the latter embracing political economy, jurisprudence, English law and modern history besides moral philosophy. In 1867, both jurisprudence and history were ejected from the Tripos and formed their own short-lived Law and History Tripos from 1870–2 before the final establishment in 1873 of a separate History Tripos. A similarly chequered career followed history's reception at the sister university where it travelled from an association with the cognate sciences to a much-contested marriage with jurisprudence before a School of History was finally inaugurated in 1871. A proposal to include English Literature within the remit of this new School was put forward in the 1870s, only to be firmly rejected by the Professor, William Stubbs.[2] One interesting difference between the two schools that was to emerge was that at Oxford, where Stubbs had so commanding an authority, his stamp was obvious in the concentration there on political history, more particularly medieval, whilst at Cambridge, the force of a single personality had had a less obvious effect on the curriculum. The Cambridge school was less distinctly the creation of so unitary or consensual a notion of the substance of historical study.[3]

The newer universities founded during this period were all alike in relegating history to a subordinate status. The London colleges, University College and the Anglican King's College, the non-denominational Owen's College Manchester and the primarily theological Durham University all laid stress on a traditional curriculum in which biblical or classical knowledge featured heavily. Like Oxford and Cambridge, they all boasted professorships in history from an early date but were careless as to by whom, or whether, such posts were filled.

The acceptance of history as a curricular subject worthy of separate academic attention was attended by a good deal of hostility. From its first tentative recognition in the 1850s a pamphlet war ensued as to its suitability for serious academic consumption and until the early 1870s it was not deemed a sufficient subject for exclusive study. It thus formed one element of a joint course with at least one other subject, a tendency which itself proved a major irritant. Having dismissed Oxford's early attempts to link history and the cognate sciences as a 'refuge for the destitute', Freeman went on to condemn

---

[2] C. E. Mallett, *A History of the University of Oxford* III (London, 1927), 453.
[3] Doris S. Goldstein, 'The Professionalisation of History in Britain in the later nineteenth and early twentieth century', *Storia della Storiografia* (1983) 3, pp. 3–26 (p. 18).

the later association of his subject with that of law. 'As things now stand an examination in 'Law and Modern History' is about as much an harmonious whole as would be an examination in Law and Hydrostatics, or in Phlebotomy and Modern History.'[4] The combination of history and law proved fortunate for neither subject, differing as they did in intellectual intention and methodology. Moreover, the vocational nature of the law syllabus stood in stark contrast to the slender career opportunities which awaited the hopeful student of modern history. Their coupling owed much to the dual association of records as both legal and historical documents, as well as to the more obviously historical stature of precedent law.

The major weapon in the armoury of those who opposed the introduction of history into the universities turned on the question of academic rigour. 'Is the study of Modern History as good an exercise of the mind, with a view to the cultivation and improvement of its powers, as the existing and usual studies of this place?'[5]

One of the factors which held back the development of history was the legacy it inherited from the more established teaching of ancient history within the classical curriculum. Richard Jenkyns' point about the 'habit of discipleship',[6] which served to direct the student's attention towards authors regarded as great tended to create the conditions for a kind of bibliographic hagiography. Charles Oman, recollecting his undergraduate years at Oxford in the 1880s, remembered this phenomenon as commonplace in the Modern History School.

I set myself to the mastery of Stubbs, Hallam and Erskine May – the only text books that were available [for constitutional history] in 1882. Stubbs' *Constitutional History* had only come out two years before and was in the full flush of its glory [. . .] His very tough collection of *Charters* in the original Latin or Norman French [. . .] had already become a sort of bible, from which a candidate was expected to identify any paragraph without its context being given [. . .] I was helped in mastering it by the [. . .] series of lectures [. . .] the 'Steps to Stubbs' as they were called.[7]

And yet at the same time, considerable doubt was expressed over the difficulty of providing adequate authoritative texts as was the practice in the classical syllabus.

Where is the standard author, like Thucydides, Xenophon, Herodotus or Livy? And if there be none, and the Examiner and Candidate have studied different Historians, as well they may, the acquirements of the Candidates can be most praiseworthy and yet be wholly inappreciable by the Examiner.[8]

This emphasis on literary texts was fundamental to the teaching current at both Oxford and Cambridge, and the historian Montagu Burrows was insistent

[4] E. A. Freeman, 'Historical Study at Oxford', *Bentley's Quarterly Review* I (March 1859) 1, pp. 282–300 (p. 291).   [5] *The Fourth School*, anon. pamphlet, n.d. (Oxford).
[6] R. Jenkyns, *The Victorians and Ancient Greece* (Oxford, 1980) p. 80.
[7] C. Oman, *Memories of Victorian Oxford* (London, 1941) pp. 104–5.
[8] *op. cit.*, *The Fourth School*.

that it should remain paramount. 'The old Oxford boast of exacting for her highest honours a most perfect and enlightened knowledge of particular books is certainly no less a reality than ever.'[9] The reverence extended to the classical curriculum and the common belief in its superior educative value guaranteed the tenacious ascendancy of this literary emphasis.

The provision of recommended texts thus proved a contentious issue. Freeman had deplored the use of Hume's inaccurate historical work on England as a standard text, but he was also aware of the opposition the examiners had faced from the Protestant Alliance when attempting to replace it with the more reliable work of the English Catholic, John Lingard.[10] Hume was finally dropped in favour of Freeman's own works along with those of Stubbs, Bryce, Stanhope and other major contemporary commentators.

It was a painful necessity to recognise Gibbon with all his avowed infidelity and the ribaldry of his notes, as the Oxford textbook; yet where were they to turn for a substitute? It was far from desirable that English History should be taught [. . .] by a Roman Catholic; yet Hume had been exploded and no-one but Lingard appeared as a competitor. If the great works of Mr Hallam combined learning with power, and freedom with reverence, there was no denying that the dryness and difficulties of summaries so condensed required some relief.[11]

History, argued its detractors, would lure good candidates away from the more demanding disciplines imposed by classical study.

Many young men of the greatest promise will find their desire of distinction more readily gratified here than elsewhere, and be tempted therefore to neglect the distinctions awarded to the more appropriate studies of the University.[12]

Even the great Oxford doyens of history, Edward Freeman and Bishop Stubbs, added their voices to this chorus of doubt. Freeman, giving evidence before the Commission of 1850, 'briefly recapitulated the grounds on which we considered Modern History to be an inappropriate subject for University Examination',[13] whilst his friend Stubbs confided to a lecture audience in 1876 that

I, for my part, have no desire that, as an educational instrument, the History training should take the place of the classical and mathematical training which must always form the chief part of the school education, and the strongest and favourite work of the University career.[14]

It was Goldwin Smith, Stubbs' predecessor in the Regius Professorship at Oxford, who declared in 1868 that 'the Classics [. . .] are still perhaps the best manual of Humanity'.[15]

---

[9] M. Burrows, *Is Education Reform required in Oxford, And What?* (Oxford, 1859) p. 48. Published anonymously.   [10] E. A. Freeman, *loc. cit.* pp. 298–9.

[11] M. Burrows, *Inaugural Lecture* (printed for private circulation, n.d.) 1862, p. 19.

[12] *op. cit., The Fourth School.*   [13] *op. cit.* Report of H. M. Commissioners. Part I. Evidence.

[14] W. Stubbs, *Two Lectures on the Present State and Prospects of Historical Study* (not published, 1876) p. 11.

[15] G. Smith, *The Reorganisation of the University of Oxford* (Oxford & London, 1868) p. 31.

One manifestation of this was the division which grew up between 'ancient' and 'modern' history. Many modern historians were anxious to restore what they saw as the essential unity and continuity of history, more so because classical studies remained so central. Freeman dismissed the division as a 'vulgar calumny', 'a middle wall of partition that is against us'.[16] He took his cue from the much-revered Thomas Arnold whose inaugural lecture as Regius Professor at Oxford in 1841 had become a by-word for those intent upon restoring an intellectual partnership they regarded as artificially severed for the convenience of university administration.

It was from Arnold that I first learned the truth which ought to be the centre and life of all our historic studies, the truth of the Unity of History [. . .] so-called 'ancient' history without 'modern' is a superstructure ready to fall for lack of a foundation.[17]

Freeman's view was shared by many historians who felt that the importance of ancient history could not be over-estimated.

The historical value of the career of a state is not to be estimated by centuries and square miles, but by its permanent influence on mankind; and thus regarded the brief Olympiads of Hellas are more precious to posterity than the accumulated ages of all the barbaric dynasties whose thrones have ever cumbered the earth.[18]

Comparison with the long tradition of classical studies coupled with the problems invited by history's early and enforced coupling with other often barely related disciplines inevitably led to frequent criticisms as to the academic rigour demanded of its students. A. W. Ward complained that candidates in the Law and History Tripos at Cambridge were 'required to know not quite as much of our National History as should be familiar to every decently educated Englishman; and to dig not very deep in a small oasis of later European history.[19] Henry Luards thought that the new Tripos had been established with a view to providing for the less able candidates; 'the large number of students who not being capable of success in classical or mathematical studies were expected to pass into this tripos'.[20] Montagu Burrows had praised the classical curriculum at his own *alma mater* Oxford for 'providing that well balanced character, religiously, morally and intellectually, that richness of mental culture, that capacity for the highest attainments, which are the true objects of education'.[21] The function of the university was increasingly regarded as the provision of a general education aimed more at training and disciplining the mental faculties than at producing experts in specific fields. These values were applied as much to the new discipline of history as they had traditionally been to classical knowledge. William Stubbs, speaking in 1884, still clung to that

[16] E. A. Freeman, *loc. cit.* p. 288; *The Office of the Historical Professor: An Inaugural Lecture read in the Museum at Oxford* (London, 1884) p. 11.   [17] *ibid.* pp. 9; 11.

[18] E. S. Creasy, *The Spirit of Historical Study: an inaugural lecture delivered at University College London* (London, 1840) p. 10.

[19] A. W. Ward, *Suggestions towards the establishment of a History Tripos* (Cambridge, 1872) p. 7.

[20] H. R. Luards, *Suggestions on the Establishment of A Historical Tripos* (Cambridge, 1872) p. 7.

[21] M. Burrows, *op. cit.* (1859) p. 49.

position. 'I still think that the aim of Historical teaching is the training of the judgment to be exercised in the moral, social and political work of life.'[22]

His view was reflected in the breadth of historical knowledge which the undergraduate historian was expected to imbibe. Even before the introduction of history as a subject of examinable status, the university historian as represented by the Regius Professors of Modern History had ranged promiscuously over the whole history of the post-Christian world. Edward Nares, Oxford's Regius Professor from 1813 to 1841, delivered a course of twenty-two lectures in 1816 narrating a chronology of historical events from the fall of the Roman Empire to the Peace of Paris in 1763. Almost half a century later, Montagu Burrows' handbook *Pass and Class* informed the intending Oxford historian that the choice was between 'the ten medieval or the first two post-Reformation centuries'.[23]

The nature of the syllabus, reading and examination papers in history at this time prompted the criticisms of Continental observer Paul Fredericq as to the organisation of English undergraduate history. 'The strain on memory implied by the number of books prescribed and the questions given is appalling [. . .] but are they [the students] sufficiently familiar with sources of history and original documents? I think not.'[24] The Cambridge Tripos papers for this period uphold his remarks. Most began with a command: 'describe', 'state', 'write the history of'. Of the twelve questions on the English History paper of December 1876, only two did not imply a purely narrative response. The other ten are all of the same ilk.

Question 2. Narrate the principal events which occurred in England between King John's surrender of the crown and the final departure of Lewis from England.
Question 6. Write a brief history of events in Scotland from the beginning of Elizabeth's reign to the flight of Queen Mary into England.
Question 10. Give the history of Ireland from 1782 to 1798.
Question 12. Trace the course of Canning as a party politician.

The more specialised papers were no different. The Cambridge paper on *The Emperors of the House of Hohenstaufen, 1152–1250*, also set in December 1876, asked questions in the same vein.

Question 1. Enumerate the principal duchies and marks of the Empire at the succession of Frederick I [. . .]
Question 4. Write a history of the origin and composition of the first Lombard League.[25]

It was 1885 before the Board of History at Cambridge took steps to remedy the catechetical methodology implied by the negligence of the study of original

---

[22] W. Stubbs, *An Address delivered by way of a Last Statutory Public lecture* (Oxford, 1884) p. 2.
[23] M. Burrows, *Pass and Class: An Oxford Guide Book through the courses of Literae Humaniores, Mathematics, Natural Science and Law and Modern History* (Oxford & London, 1860) p. 205.
[24] Paul Fredericq, 'The Study of History in England and Scotland', *Johns Hopkins University Studies in Historical and Political Science*, 5th series, x (Baltimore, 1887) p. 51.
[25] *University of Cambridge General Almanack and Register for 1878*, pp. 175–6.

source material. The introduction of two compulsory special subjects, chosen from among the four period B.C.31–A.D.800, A.D.800–1453, 1453–1688 and 1688–1851 was designed as a corrective to this over-emphasis on secondary authorities.

Students at institutions other than the ancient universities fared little better. The examinations set at the London colleges were certainly more elementary but nonetheless reveal identical assumptions about the historical knowledge expected of the student. The Faculty of Arts examination in General Modern History at University College in 1853–4 asked candidates to draw a map of Charlemagne's dominions, name 'the four greatest events in the History of the World between 1450 and 1550' and date and name the protagonists of thirteen famous battles.[26] The Junior Classical Scholarship at King's College in 1851–2 included a paper on the Plantagenets: 'Give the date of the Battle of Bannockburn. What were the consequences of it?' and 'Give some account of the Civil War in the reign of Henry III.'[27] As late as 1880, the character of these examinations remained unchanged. When E.S. Beesly set the paper on English History 1066–1216 at University College in that year, the questions were hardly distinguishable from those that had appeared thirty years previously. 'Question 11. Make as complete a list as you can of the Archbishops of Canterbury during this period.'[28] At King's College London, the Junior Classical Scholarship in 1851–2 required candidates to sit examinations in five subjects: Livy, Homer, Latin Elegiacs, Prose Translation and the Plantagenets. This curious intrusion of a single Modern History paper occurred also in the Senior Classical Scholarship. The literary bias remained nonetheless dominant; the ten questions on the Plantaganets included two soliciting Shakespeare's views on the character of various monarchs. And at Owen's College Manchester the examination questions were such as to prompt one of its most famous teachers to comment that the papers gave students the opportunity 'of showing both the breadth and the minuteness of their lore'.[29]

One reflection of this weakness with ramifications in both methodological and practical terms was the inclusion – specific to Cambridge – of archaeology as an element of the Historical Tripos. The Faculty Board established after the demise of the Board of Legal and Historical Studies was responsible for both history and archaeology although, or perhaps precisely because, the latter was regarded as scarcely a subject of academic concern at this stage. The Board rightly felt that both subjects suffered by their enforced coupling which took no cognisance of their increasingly variant practices.

---

[26] *University College London Calendar, 1853–4*, p. 117.
[27] *King's College London Calendar, 1851–2*, pp. 314–15.
[28] *University College London Calendar, 1880–1*.
[29] T. F. Tout, 'The School of History', *Collected Papers of Thomas Frederick Tout* I (Manchester, 1932) 62.

The Board admits that Archaeology may be considered as closely connected with
history, but the special Boards of Studies have not been formed upon any theoretical idea
of the connection of studies with each other, but with a view to the practical conduct of
the studies and examinations of the University [. . .] The Cambridge Historical School
[. . .] has but a slight connection with Archaeology [. . .] The archaeological studies of
the University [. . .] have reference principally to Classical Archaeology and are directed
with a view to [. . .] the Classical Tripos.[30]

The attempt to sever the administrative connection between the two disciplines
initiated by Oscar Browning of King's College was rejected by the General Board
of the Faculties in 1884. A further application in 1886 was similarly rejected.
No archaeology options were available to students doing the Historical Tripos
and the subject continued thereafter to be taught as a primarily classical
subject, concerned largely with an appreciation of classical art.[31]

Nonetheless history as an academic entity was establishing itself as a
prominent and important discipline within the universities. One manifestation
of this was the development of prizes at both undergraduate and graduate level
for work in the subject. Historical prizes for students were introduced at
Cambridge in 1885 – the Prince Consort and Thirlwall prizes. In Oxford the
Arnold Prize, though restricted to graduates, had been established far earlier, in
1850, and was followed by the Stanhope undergraduate prize in 1855.[32] The
Arnold was judged by the three historical professors – the Regius Professors of
Modern History and Ecclesiastical History and the Camden Professor of Ancient
History. It carried an award of £42, alternating its subject matter between
Ancient and Modern History each year. Amongst its recipients were future
historical scholars Albert Dicey who won it in 1860 with an essay on 'The Privy
Council', and James Bryce whose composition on 'The Holy Roman Empire'
won him the prize in 1863. The Stanhope Prize – named after its aristocratic
and literary minded benefactor – was intended to promote 'Historical Studies in
the early part of the Academical career' and awarded books rather than cash as
its prize. Stanhope saw its function additionally as 'conducive to another most
important object in any system of English education – the early and careful
practice of English composition in prose'.[33] Doris Goldstein has pointed out that
these awards acted as an early means of recruiting potential historians from
amongst the student body, drawing her evidence from the marked correlation
between later academic success and the award of these new historical prizes.[34]

[30] University of Cambridge, Seeley Library. MS. Minutes of Board of History and Archaeology, 13
February 1883.
[31] Archaeology was not to achieve university status until well into the twentieth century. The
Disney Professorship at Cambridge was filled by amateurs throughout the nineteenth century.
The Yates chair at University College London was a more serious post but was concerned wholly
with classical archaeology. See Chapter 4.
[32] J. O. McLachlan, 'The Origin and Early Development of the Cambridge Historical Tripos',
Cambridge Historical Journal IX (1947) i, 78–105 (p. 89).
[33] Bodl. Lib. Univ. Arch. W. P. β 11/8, f. 2. Stanhope to Vice Chancellor, 16 June 1855.
[34] Doris Goldstein, *loc. cit.* pp. 13–14.

Stanhope's intentions do also suggest, however, the tenacity of liberal educational values with their emphasis on style as much as on content. At Manchester, the endowment in 1871 of the first prize in history, the Bradford History Scholarship, led many of its holders into further degree-level study at Oxford though it produced few historians of significance.[35]

These competitions rarely attracted more than a handful of participants; nineteenth-century students, like their latter-day counterparts, showed scant interest in topics unrelated to their examinations. Thus did Stubbs sadly remark, 'I have sometimes felt a little hurt that, after preparing and advertising a good course of lectures [. . .] I have had to deliver them to two or three listless men.'[36] Sir John Seeley in his inaugural lecture at Cambridge confessed a similar lack of interest in his student days. He recollected the motley audience who attended Sir James Stephen's professorial lectures at Cambridge in the 1850s. 'Most were there by compulsion; few of them were what we called 'reading men'; I myself only went because I was ill and had been recommended not to study too hard. It was – and I think the Professor felt it – a painful waste of power.'[37] Seeley thus warned the young George Prothero in his turn, and with personal experience, of the fate awaiting lectures irrelevant to Tripos examinations. 'The objection that strikes me to the subjects you propose for lectures is that they have not been set for the Tripos and for that reason I doubt whether men would come to them.'[38] And E. G. W. Bill, in his study of Henry Halford Vaughan, Regius Professor of Modern History at Oxford from 1848 to 1858, noted that many of those attending Vaughan's popular lectures were not candidates in the History school. These annual and traditional lectures 'were a luxury the student anxious for a good class could ill afford'.[39]

The slender likelihood of the history graduate finding direct employment in the field was a further disincentive to disciplined study. The prospects of academic preferment in the subject were meagre in comparison with those offered in more established areas of study. The restrictive nature of Oxford and Cambridge fellowships was not tackled until the abolition of the requirement to take Holy Orders in the 1880s. In consequence few colleges had openings in history before this time, and such jobs as did exist were concentrated either at the professorial level or in the rather more tenuous tutorial capacity. Henry Jackson wrote to George Prothero from Trinity College Cambridge, the first college to establish a lectureship in history, about his prospects of securing a post in the subject at Cambridge.

I wrote a letter to you some days ago but suppressed it on finding that Sidgwick took a less sanguine view of the future of historical study and teaching than I had done – I

[35] T. F. Tout, *op. cit.* p. 72.   [36] Stubbs, *Two Lectures*, p. 7.
[37] J. R. Seeley, 'The Teaching of Politics: an inaugural lecture delivered at Cambridge', *Lectures and Essays* (London, 1870) p. 290.
[38] RHS, UCL Lib. Prothero papers, PP 2/1. Seeley to Prothero, 12 January (?).
[39] E. G. W. Bill, *University Reform in Nineteenth Century Oxford: A Study of Henry Halford Vaughan, 1811–85* (Oxford, 1973) p. 188.

gather that he would advise you distinctly not to come here, whilst I think that you would be making a venture but not a desperate one [. . .] the candidates will not be men of great calibre [. . .] though there will be some work to be done there will not be much. The subject being virtually a new one, it is likely that any one who establishes himself here as a student in the subject would secure such teaching as there is to be had. The teaching would be however elementary.[40]

Jackson's pessimism, whilst understandable, proved unfounded as history rose steadily in popularity. The Oxford and Cambridge examination lists both show a steady albeit gradual increase in the number of Modern History candidates over the years. The first Modern History and Jurisprudence examination in 1853 attracted eight candidates. Before its demise, the School had had at its peak forty-three candidates in the Michaelmas Term of 1867. By 1886, the single honours Modern History school was examining ninety-six candidates. At Cambridge, the Law and Modern History Tripos maintained fairly high numbers: from twenty-four candidates in 1870 it rose to thirty-six candidates in 1874, the last year in which the Tripos was examined. The new exclusively historical Tripos brought an immediate drop in numbers; its first intake numbered ten and it rose only slowly back to the numbers achieved by the earlier combination.[41] It was 1884 before the numbers rose above twenty students again.[42] From then on, there were rarely less than thirty students sitting the Tripos each year, a figure with which the Board of Studies displayed a qualified satisfaction. Their interpretation of the initially modest reception of the new Tripos rested on the problems of career which young enthusiasts would face at a time when expansion was not large enough to accommodate a steady flow of highly qualified entrants. 'Though many men find the study attractive, it is a study which as yet has no prizes and which hardly even offers the prospect of a livelihood.'[43]

At the two London colleges, history was of even less consequence than at either of the two older establishments. University College, having dispensed with religious instruction, laid particular stress on its vocational legal and medical departments. History was a minor subject in the curriculum followed at the college, appearing only as an option for fourth year students. Nonetheless under the direction of Edward Creasy who held the chair there from 1840, the number of students attending his history classes rose

[40] RHS, UCL Lib. Prothero Papers. Henry Jackson to Prothero, 5 February 1873.
[41] The *Cambridge Historical Register* gives the number of candidates as ten, including one aegrotat. In his 'A Hundred Years of the Teaching of History at Cambridge, 1873–1973', *Historical Journal* xvi (1973) 3, pp. 535–53 (p. 536) G. Kitson Clark says that there were nine candidates. The manuscript minutes of the faculty board concur with him but it is possible that neither are counting the award of the aegrotat.
[42] Kitson Clark maintains that there were always less than thirteen candidates before 1883 but the figures suggest otherwise. The *Historical Register* has nineteen candidates sitting the Tripos in 1878.
[43] University of Cambridge, Seeley Library. MS. Minutes of Board of History and Archaeology.

dramatically; with the exception of the academic year 1844–5 when there were only seven students, Creasy's numbers never fell below fourteen and in 1847–8 he had a class of nineteen.[44]

King's College was a specifically Anglican establishment, set up in angry response to the non-denominational constitution of University College. Theology and scriptural teaching were thus central to its curriculum and chapel attendance was often the key to academic success.[45] The department of General Literature and Science offered students a choice of two options, a Classical or a Modern Division. The Classical was intended, in its early days at least, 'to prepare students for the Universities, for Holy Orders, for the Bar and other professions and for competition for appointments in the Civil Service', and its course of study comprised religious instruction, Greek and Latin, mathematics, modern history, English language and literature and French and German language and literature. The Modern Division was intended for those wishing to pursue a military or naval commission or some form of applied science. Latin remained compulsory to an elementary level, religious instruction, languages, mathematics and modern history were retained but the classical options were largely replaced by natural philosophy, chemistry and drawing. History remained of minor importance in both divisions; in 1855, its weekly provision was increased from two to four hours a week. At neither of the two London colleges did the arguments favouring universities as research institutions have any real impact. It was 1921 before a doctorate in history was introduced at University College.

In consequence, the earliest teachers and tutors in the subject were seldom specialists but men whose livelihood often depended upon their adaptability to the wider teaching requirements of the universities. Whilst many of the Oxford history examiners were well known and well established historians – Kitchin, Boase, Gardiner, Green, Stanhope, Owen and various of the professors – the employment of others with more dubious qualifications was frequent. C. L. Shadwell, one of the examiners for 1869, was best known as a translator of Dante; Charles Neate who examined from 1853 to 1855 and lectured in the School in 1856 went on to become Drummond Professor of Political Economy the following year; the Rev. E. H. Hansell combined his examining for Law and Modern History with similar duties in *Literae Humaniores* and mathematics. He also tutored in both mathematics and divinity.

The same lack of specialist qualifications was evident amongst the history tutors at Oxford. W. W. Shirley, appointed to the Regius Chair of Ecclesiastical History in 1863, had taught mathematics at Wadham before his promotion. C. W. Boase lectured in both history and in Hebrew. Outside the two major

[44] *University College London Annual Reports.*
[45] F. J. C. Hearnshaw, *The Centenary History of King's College London, 1828–1928* (London, 1929) p. 112.

universities the same conditions prevailed. R. C. Christie taught history, political economy, jurisprudence and law in his professorial capacity at Manchester. Both Seeley and E. S. Beesly lectured in Latin as well as in history at London, Beesly holding the chair of Latin at Bedford College jointly with his history professorship at University College. J. S. Brewer covered English language and literature as well as classics and history in his teaching at King's College London. Nor was this lack of qualification or training a feature of the tutorial stratum alone. It was inevitable that the first generation of university historians would lack the training they were thereafter to provide for future generations.

The history professoriate were for the most part no more institutionally qualified in these years than the less fêted tutors. In the first instance, chairs were frequently governed by factors unconnected with academic merit. The bulk of these professorships had been established at a time when history had been outside the standard curriculum offered in the universities. Prior to the late 1860s certainly, few men were appointed for their specifically historical abilities. Charles Kingsley, Regius Professor at Cambridge from 1860 to 1869 was a churchman and popular novelist and Edward Creasy, professor at University College from 1840 to 1860, a practising lawyer. Inevitably such appointments encouraged a tradition – although not just in history – of dilettante professors.[46] In the earlier years of the century particularly, the lack of training available to the prospective historical student made the assumption of less institutional criteria a necessity. The importance attached to political and moral considerations over and above proof of historical ability explains in part why so wide a range of candidates felt confident in putting themselves forward despite their lack of historical attainment. Montagu Burrows was the first of the Oxford historical professoriate to possess a history degree, taking a first class in the Law and Modern History school there in the Easter term of 1857. His experience is not untypical. He secured a first in 'Greats' and having a few months to spare in the Second Honours school took up the Law and Modern History option for want of a better occupation. This casual approach to the subject was to determine his subsequent and successful career in history.[47] Professors of the pre-Stubbs and Seeley era – and even some thereafter – were necessarily untrained in their subject.

I am so well aware, that of late years my attention has been almost exclusively devoted to the cultivation of Ancient Literature and the study of Theology, that I must necessarily solicit the indulgence of the University on appearing before it as the director of a branch of knowledge which, though a favourite pursuit in earlier life, I had subsequently laid aside for other studies.[48]

---

[46] R. S. Porter in his 'Gentlemen and Geology', *Historical Journal* 21 (1978) 4 makes the point that geology professors were little more than visiting lecturers.
[47] S. M. Burrows (ed.), *Autobiography of Montagu Burrows, Captain R.N.* (London, 1908) pp. 203–4.
[48] J. A. Cramer, *An Inaugural Lecture on the Study of Modern History* (Oxford, 1843) p. 5.

The Rev Dr Cramer however, was not exceptional. Henry Vaughan's sole contribution to historical literature was a four page paper delivered to the British Archaeological Association in 1884 on an effigy in his own home at Upton Castle, Pembrokeshire.[49] Goldwin Smith's biographer maintained that Smith's 'defects as an historian were obvious [. . .] He had no taste for painstaking researches into primary sources and little capacity for objectivity'.[50] Goldwin Smith's taste for polemic might have made him an unusual choice for Oxford but the politician-professor was common enough. Sir James Stephen, Regius Professor at Cambridge from 1849, was translated directly from the courts of politics to the courts of Cambridge; he had been a colonial under-secretary in the Whig administration of 1836 and a Privy Councillor immediately prior to his election to the professorship. His successor, Charles Kingsley, is best known for his successful career as a fiction writer.

At University College London in 1840 there were three candidates for the professorship in history: a Dr Taylor, author of two volumes on universal history, a Mr Flintoff, barrister and the successful Edward Creasy, also a lawyer. In 1841, W. S. Farquharson, having unsuccessfully contested the Professorship of Natural History, wrote to the College authorities.

I am given to understand that the Professorship of History is vacant [. . .] Should the Council have any desire that the vacancy should be filled up, I beg leave to [. . .] offer myself as a Candidate for that office.[51]

In 1848 rumour once again prompted hopeful candidates to forward references. Thomas Hankey wrote on behalf of the Rev Mr Soutaine that his 'first-rate talents as a Preacher' and his 'literary pursuits' were indications that the candidate was 'fully up to the fulfilment of the duties' of the professorship of history.[52]

It thus comes as a surprise that C. H. Pearson declined an invitation to apply for a Praelectorship in Ancient History in 1870 on the grounds that, 'I thought I could not with propriety offer myself for a lectureship in a subject which I had never made my special study.'[53] Three out of the five electors were apparently prepared to vote for Pearson on that occasion. They clearly anticipated skills other than specifically academic ones.

The statutes governing the two Regius Professorships of Modern History required no more than that 'the person appointed [. . .] shall have taken a degree of Master of Arts, or Bachelor of Laws, or some higher degree in the University'.[54] 'In 1860, anyone who had obtained a first class in classics, and professed himself willing to devote himself to modern history, was regarded by the university as at least qualified.'[55] Publications were frequently held up as an

[49] Bill, *op. cit.* p. 175.   [50] E. Wallace, *Goldwin Smith, Victorian Liberal* (Toronto, 1957) p. 17.
[51] UCL MS. AM/21, 13 October 1841.   [52] *ibid.* 12 October 1848.
[53] C. H. Pearson, *Memorials by himself, his wife and his friends,* ed. W. Stebbing (London, 1900) p. 140.   [54] Oxford Royal Commission, *op. cit.* Part II, p. 268.
[55] O. Chadwick, 'Charles Kingsley at Cambridge', *Historical Journal* XVIII (1975) 2, 303–25 (p. 304).

illustration of the candidate's real historical potential. When Freeman heard that Goldwin Smith planned to resign from the Oxford chair, he wrote to his publisher. 'About my History of the Norman Conquest [. . .] I should like to get out Vol I and II this year [. . .] And as an advertisement for the Professorship, it would be a gain to get out Vol I the first possible moment.'[56] Four years earlier Freeman had rested his candidature for the Chichele Professorship primarily on his historical publications, and Froude's application for that position rested entirely on his published works. 'I do not send testimonials because I have been so long before the Public and my writings, such as they are, furnish sufficient evidence of my fitness or unfitness to be a Teacher of Modern History.'[57] However, these would appear to have weighed less heavily with the appointment boards than other factors. It was his faultless testimonials that earned Edward Beesly his succession to the chair at University College in 1860. Of the seven candidates considered by the committee, some offered their books and other testimonials as proof of their fitness for the post. Beesly offered testimonials from some of the most eminent Englishmen of the day – Benjamin Jowett, Richard Congreve, Frederic Harrison. The committee concluded their report with a strong recommendation. 'With such testimonials as Mr Beesly brings, the Committee without hesitation and with perfect unanimity recommend him to the Chair.'[58]

Competition for professorial posts was often fierce. Robert Peel informed the Duke of Wellington that the death of Thomas Arnold had resulted in 'a great number of applications for the appointment' of a new Regius Professor at Oxford.[59] Ten candidates, including Stubbs, Freeman and Froude, were disappointed in the elections for the first Chichele appointment in 1862. The Oxford Regius chair in 1866 attracted at least six nominations, many of them as reputable as that of the successful William Stubbs. When Beesly retired from his chair at University College in 1893, fourteen applications were received from those eager to fill the post. And yet that chair had remained vacant from 1830 to 1834 and no great attempt to fill it had been made.

These were problems which afflicted the newer institutions of learning as much as the established ones. The lawyer John Richardson offered himself as a candidate at University College London requesting that he be considered for any of the three chairs of 'History Ancient and Modern, Moral and Political Philosophy, Logic and Philosophy of the Human Mind'.[60] J. H. Merivale who had been an unsuccessful candidate for the Oxford Regius Professorship was, at the time of his candidature, the Professor of Political Economy. Charles Henry

---

[56] B. L. Add. MS. 55049, ff. 45–6. E. A. Freeman to A. Macmillan, 10 May 1866.
[57] Quoted in D. M. Owen, 'The Chichele Professorship of Modern History, 1862', *BIHR* xxxiv (1961) 217–20 (p. 220).   [58] UCL MS. AM/86, June 1860. p. 12.
[59] B. L. Add. MS. 40459, f. 251. Peel to Duke of Wellington, 19 July 1842.
[60] UCL MS. AM/21. Testimonial of John Richardson, October 1827.

Pearson who held the history chair at King's College London in the 1850s had turned to medical studies after taking his degree at Oxford. Whilst thus engaged, he applied for a lectureship in English Language and Literature at King's and in a short space of time had replaced G. W. Dasent as professor of history as well. His light duties – eight hours teaching a week over thirty weeks of the year – allowed him, like so many nineteenth-century academics, ample time for other pursuits. During his tenure of the chair, Pearson was an active journalist editing the *National Review* for a short while in 1862 and 1863.[61] At Manchester, the first chair in Ancient and Modern History established in 1853 brought forth many applications from candidates 'with whom history has not been a special study'.[62] The Trustees appointed R. C. Christie, a young Chancery barrister who combined his incumbency of the history chair with those of Political Economy and Law as well.

Seeley acknowledged that his appointment at Cambridge had little to do with historical prowess. Author of the anonymous *Ecce Homo* and professor of Latin for six years at King's College London, his appointment to the professorship in 1869 had the support of the incumbent Charles Kingsley and of F. D. Maurice. Seeley had no illusions: 'However highly Gladstone may think of me, he can have no reason to think that I have given any special attention to Modern History.'[63] His appointment, unlike that of Stubbs at Oxford three years earlier, hardly broke with tradition. His qualifications in history were no greater than those of many of his predecessors. William Smyth's appointment to that chair – a position he held for forty-two years from 1807 – had evinced the sarcasm of Harriet Martineau who had remarked that the appointment was 'an act of kindness to the individual, but scarcely so to the public'.[64] His contemporary at Oxford was no better qualified. Edward Nares, professor from 1813–41, had delivered the Bampton Lectures in 1805 and was the author of a successful satirical work *Thinks-I-to-myself* which appeared in 1811. His biographer Cecil White describes his studies as 'somewhat promiscuous and desultory', ranging over mineralogy, botany and other scientific subjects and suggests that Nares accepted the Regius Professorship 'chiefly in the hope that he might later exchange it for [. . .] a Deaconry or Canonry'.[65]

The appointment of such men tended inevitably to diminish the intellectual stature of the professoriate. An amateur air pervaded and electors frequently based their choice on considerations far removed from even general academic aptitude. When Montagu Burrows applied for the Chichele Professorship at

---

[61] C. H. Pearson, *op. cit.* pp. 77; 87–8.   [62] T. F. Tout, *op. cit.* p. 64.

[63] B. L. Add. MS. 41299, ff. 142–5, quoted in D. Wormell, *Sir John Seeley and the Uses of History* (Cambridge, 1980) p. 41.

[64] Quoted in K. T. B. Butler, 'A "Petty" Professor of Modern History: William Smyth, 1765–1841', *Cambridge Historical Journal* ix (1948) 2, 217–38 (p. 218).

[65] G. C. White (ed.), *A Versatile Professor: Reminiscences of the Rev Edward Nares, DD* (London, 1903) pp. 75; 244.

Oxford in 1862, 'there were many competitors, several of whom had attained considerable reputation [. . .] such as Stubbs, Freeman, Froude and Pearson'. Burrows' case for the chair rested largely on the success of his *Pass and Class* published in 1860, a copy of which he had sent to each of the five electors. 'This apparently more than compensated for the absence of historical reputation [. . .] The electors preferred the promise which my book conveyed as an earnest of my success in teaching the subject.'[66]

Political considerations were also paramount in the choice of a professor, more particularly in the case of the Regius Professors whose posts owed their origin to the attempt of George I to win the universities over to the Hanoverian succession and to encourage them to train diplomats for his court. The retention of Crown patronage in the appointment of these chairs rendered them peculiarly liable to political manoeuvre. All professorships were, however, inclined to be judged on these grounds. Burrows discounted the possibility of his being elected to the Chichele chair not simply because of his inexperience but because 'some of the five electors were liberals'.[67] 'The statesmen of the day [. . .] could as yet apparently see no reason why a Professor should have a particular knowledge of his subject or some special aptitude for the science he professed.'[68]

After the death of Arnold, the Regius Professorship at Oxford had passed to John Anthony Cramer, principal of New Inn Hall, who held the post for six years during which time he also became Dean of Carlisle. There had been many candidates for the post including more prominent historical figures such as A. P. Stanley, John Ormerod, son of the Cheshire historian George Ormerod, as well as Henry Halford Vaughan. Ormerod's hopes were dashed by reason of his political sympathies; writing to the Duke of Wellington, J. P. Wynter of St John's College dubbed Ormerod 'a person of great natural powers and extensive attainments [. . .] but [. . .] I think it right to state that his Political opinions are understood to be Whig [. . .] I should always look with some apprehension to the appointment of a Whig to so an important an office as that of Professor of Modern History.'[69] The two strongest contenders for the post were both men who had not sought the appointment: the Camden Professor of Ancient History, Dr Cardwell and the successfully mooted Dr Cramer. He was seen as 'a man of taste, of talent and industry [. . .] a safe [appointment]'.[70] Cramer's tenure of the chair, needless to say, effected no great changes in the status or study of history at Oxford.

His successor Henry Halford Vaughan was a man of very different political complexion however, whose election to the Professorship owed more to his friendship with a Prime Minister committed to university reform than to any

---

[66] S. M. Burrows, *op. cit.* pp. 215–16.   [67] *ibid.* p. 215.   [68] Mallet, *op. cit.* p. 225.
[69] B.L. Add. MS. 40459, f. 257, J. P. Wynter to Duke of Wellington, 20 July 1842, headed 'Private'.
[70] *ibid.*, and see Bill, *op. cit.* pp. 61–2 for full details of Cramer's appointment.

solid historical reputation. Vaughan resigned the chair in 1858 after the introduction of the Jurisprudence and Modern History School. Although he had little impact on the teaching of history at Oxford and was consistently excluded from examining in the school, his appointment was nonetheless a milestone for he was the first lay person to be appointed to the chair and his championship of a secular university system identified him as a reformer in a period of change.

His successor was also associated with the cause of university reform. Goldwin Smith whom Disraeli had dubbed the 'wild man of the Cloister'[71] held the chair for eight years. Like Vaughan, he had scant qualifications for a post in history but he had served as assistant secretary to Stanley on the Royal Commission of Inquiry in Oxford from 1850 to 1852 and his appointment was directly and openly political.

With the appointment of Stubbs to succeed Smith, the Professorship gained an incumbent of both intellectual and, more importantly, historical distinction. Stubbs was one of the foremost historians of his day and his works enjoyed an unchallenged supremacy. However, his removal from a living in Navestock to the Oxford Regius Professorship owed as much to the political currents at work in 1866 as to his growing and deserved historical reputation. Many politicians were anxious to avoid another appointment akin to those of Vaughan and Smith and the choice was entrusted to the Colonial Secretary Carnarvon, high steward of the university.[72] The competition was stiff for both Froude and Freeman had been nominated. Froude was cast aside on religious grounds whilst Freeman's reputation as a radical made him an inappropriate choice. Charles Pearson's liberalism counted against him and Church's associations with the reformer Stanley were sufficient to ruin his chances.[73]

Later in the century, Froude's appointment to the chair in 1892 also demonstrated the political considerations which played so important a part in deciding these professorships. Both Samuel Gardiner and James Bryce – two very strong contenders in terms of historical reputation – were passed over because of their attachment to the Home Rule Liberal faction.[74] Similar considerations dogged the development of other professorships too: the Ecclesiastical History chair vacated by the death of Walter Shirley in 1866 was awarded to H. L. Mansel, reader in moral and metaphysical philosophy. 'The Prime Minister took occasion to reward political service as well as conspicuous intellectual power, rather than special qualifications.'[75]

Oxford seemed more prone to such political sensitivities than other universities, perhaps because so many of England's political masters had

[71] John Sparrow, *Mark Pattison and the Idea of a University* (Cambridge, 1967) p. 81.
[72] N. J. Williams, 'Stubbs' Appointment as Regius Professor, 1866', *BIHR* xxxiii (1960) 121–5 (p. 122). [73] PRO 3.6.135, Carnavorn Papers.
[74] D. E. Strick, 'English Historiography, 1859–90, A Study of Froude, Freeman, Stubbs and Green', (unpublished PhD. dissertation, University of California, 1951), p. 90.
[75] W. H. Hutton, *Letters of William Stubbs, Bishop of Oxford, 1825–1901* (London, 1904) p. 113.

themselves passed through its portals. The appointment of the outspokenly radical Edward Beesly to the chair at London – a post he held for thirty-three years – would never have been contemplated at Oxford. Despite his positivist stance and trades union associations, Beesly was chosen in preference to George Harris on moral grounds.[76] The electors considering the seven candidates feared that 'the *moral* side of History [. . .] might be neglected [. . .] for mere *archaeology* by Harris'.[77]

All these factors added up to a general degradation of professorial history. Neither the universities nor the political establishment saw the subject as one of central importance, and though there was a prestige to be derived from a professorial appointment, often little real control attached to such positions. Tout has described Freeman's 'anomalous position of apparent dignity and real powerlessness in relation to historical teaching' during his tenure of the Regius Professorship at Oxford.[78] The point is expanded further by Rosemary Jann. 'The professors might have gained the apex of the pyramid of academic prestige, but the Oxbridge tutors continued to exercise effective control over the educational process. Thus from the beginning confusion existed about who controlled historical knowledge and for what ends.'[79] The appointment of men like Edward Nares and Charles Kingsley posed problems for the historical community struggling for academic recognition of their labours. They greeted such choices with derision but at the same time they were anxious themselves to fill the posts. Stubbs wrote to Freeman in 1860 on hearing of Kingsley's success.

What a horrid appointment of Kingsley – I suppose that it is on the principle of putting the worst man in the best place so that you have all the good ones trying to show how much better they are and so benefitting the world.[80]

Green in his *Saturday Review* article on the inaugural lecture of his friend Stubbs took a less sanguine view of the damage inflicted by such appointments. He dwelt at some length on the importance of the professorships with regard to historical scholarship.

The earlier Professors were either dependants [sic] of the Court or men of note in other fields of literature [. . .] It may be, indeed, that in the face of the singular conception which the powers that be seem to entertain as to what history is [. . .] efforts [. . .] are ineffective in removing the impression made [. . .] by the promotion of a popular novelist to the chair at Cambridge, or the elevation of a leading metaphysician to the chair of Ecclesiastical History at Oxford. The ground of such appointments is, no doubt, some vague notion in the minds of those to whom we owe them, that history is no special or definite study [. . .] It is the first merit in the appointment of an historian to the chair of

[76] See Chapter 5 for George Harris's connection with the founding of the Historical Manuscripts Commission.   [77] UCL MS. AM/86, June 1860, p. 8.   [78] T. F. Tout, *op. cit.* p. 130.
[79] Rosemary Jann, 'From Amateur to Professional: The Case of the Oxbridge Historians', *Journal of British Studies* XXII (1983) 2, 122–47 (p. 139).
[80] Bodl. Lib. Eng. misc. e. 148. Stubbs to Freeman, 31 May 1860.

History, in the case of Mr Stubbs, that it is at any rate a confession that such a study as that of history exists.[81]

There was little incentive for the professor to fill more than the bare bones of his statutory obligations. During his tenure of the Cambridge chair, Charles Kingsley was also in possession of a living in Hampshire. The financial, and indeed physical strain, of maintaining residence in both led Kingsley to withdraw from Cambridge. Thereafter he attended twice a year for the purpose of examining, delivered his mandatory lectures but had scant contact besides with the University.[82] Edward Creasy continued to practice at the bar throughout his twenty-year tenure of the University College chair. Required to lecture at the start of the academic year, Creasy found his academic and professional obligations in conflict. 'I fear that the opening day of the Session occurs in the week [when] I must be in Sussex at Quarter Sessions.'[83]

At Oxford, successive incumbents of the Regius Chair found the terms of their appointment trying. Edward Nares was called to task in the early 1830s for failing to deliver his statutory lectures. His reasons were sensible enough; attendance at his lectures was of no practical use to the student preparing for Schools. His attitude to his subject was, however, revealing. 'The young men are constantly engaged in higher pursuits to be able to afford time [. . .] for attendance on [. . .] a subject comparatively so light and unacademical as Mod[ern] History.'[84] Nares, like his successor Thomas Arnold, divided his time between the professorship and other pursuits. Arnold was headmaster of Rugby School simultaneously and his biographer thought it unlikely that his duties there permitted him more than three weeks a year in Oxford,[85] although the Regius Professor was officially required to be in residence for ninety days in each academic year, and liable to a fine of £1 for every day not thus spent. Nares and Arnold both fell foul of this rule as others were to do during the course of the century. Arnold's protests to the Hebdomadal Board on this issue resulted in the professor's lecturing requirements being reduced from twenty to sixteen annual lectures.

Vaughan also found the residence requirements of the chair irksome. It was this and his antipathy to lecturing as a duty which were the catalysts for his resignation in 1858. He wrote of his objections to Stanley a year or so before he resigned. 'I could pledge myself to any amount of study [. . .] but to lecturing under the legal and moral necessity of doing so, constantly felt, I have a dislike.'[86] The professors were naturally reluctant to invest energy in the preparation of lectures that would find but a meagre audience. In his second

[81] J. R. Green, 'Professor Stubbs's Inaugural Lecture', *Saturday Review* 2 March 1867, pp. 278–80.
[82] Sheldon Rothblatt, *The Revolution of the Dons: Cambridge and Society in Victorian England* (London, 1968) p. 152.   [83] UCL MS. AM/21, 2 August 1850.
[84] Bodl. Lib. Univ. Arch. W.P. β 11.3. Nares to Vice-Chancellor, 26 March 1832.
[85] A. P. Stanley, *The Life and Correspondence of Thomas Arnold, D.D.* II (London, 1844) 288.
[86] Bodl. Lib. Vaughan. Colln. MS. Top. Oxon. e. 526, ff. 2–3. Vaughan to Stanley, 19 May 1857.

year as professor, Nares' class numbered seven students.[87] 'For some time I complied with all ye rules [. . .] certainly without any material benefit to any member of ye University, being sometimes unable to procure any class.'[88]

With the introduction of examinations in history, it was assumed that the professoriate would have a captive audience for their lecture series, particularly since few colleges at Oxford and Cambridge established lectureships in the subject at this early date. At London, the professor was one of an even smaller staff consisting of at most two persons engaged specifically to teach history; in the department at University College 'the professors were little more than visiting lecturers'.[89] Even with the incentive provided by examination, however, professorial lectures did not always attract a large audience. Montagu Burrows maintained – not without a hint of satisfaction – that 'it was notorious that neither Stubbs nor Freeman [. . .] could ever keep a class together'.[90]

Inaugural lectures tended to attract a larger audience than a professor was ever likely to experience thereafter, particularly after 1861 when the compulsory lecture at Oxford, at least, was abandoned. Thomas Arnold's inaugural in December 1841 drew a crowd of four or five hundred listeners who packed the galleries and auditorium of the Sheldonian Theatre.[91] Some lecturers were even more successful. Even Kingsley's most vocal critics were aware of his success in attracting and maintaining large audiences with his 'eloquent sermonising'.[92] Seeley, in his own inaugural lecture, paid tribute to his predecessor's powers of oratory, his ability 'to command an audience worthy of his eloquence and earnestness'.[93] Dr Blake Odgers was a Cambridge undergraduate during Kingsley's tenure of the professorship and remembered his performances.

I shall never forget Kingsley standing up there lecturing to us in the Old Law Schools [. . .] He was constantly seized with a stutter but he crushed it down with a jerk of his right foot [. . .] There were some who thought Canon Kingsley carried his romancing into history! I remember his lecture on Vesalius [. . .] Kingsley saying with his stutter, "And so he d-d-died in harness, going about his work, gentlemen. He d-d-died doing his duty, and that is the best way a man can die, and t-t-that is all I have to say to you to-day, gentlemen.'[94]

Reputable historians did, however, on occasion decline invitations to these professorships. S. R. Gardiner refused an offer to succeed Beesly at University College; Macaulay had been asked to take the chair at Cambridge before Sir James Stephen was finally appointed in 1849 and Kingsley was the government's third choice as Stephen's successor. Seeley too was only offered the chair

[87] White, *op. cit.* p. 238.   [88] Bodl. Lib. Univ. Arch. W.P. β 11.3. 26 March 1832.
[89] Hale Bellot, *op. cit.* p. 331.   [90] S. M. Burrows, *op. cit.* p. 216.   [91] Stanley, *op. cit.* p. 282.
[92] McLachlan, *loc. cit.* p. 79.   [93] Seeley, *loc. cit.* p. 291.
[94] B. Odgers, 'Founder's Day Speech', *Journal of the Working Men's College* XIII (1913–14) pp. 435–9 (p. 437).

after both James Spedding, editor of Bacon's works, and Charles Merivale had both been unsuccessfully approached.[95] William Lecky was invited to the chair at Oxford in 1892. It was only when he declined it that Froude's dream was finally, if briefly, realised. Their reluctance was, in part, financial. Professorial salaries were poor both at Oxbridge and elsewhere. The intention of the London colleges to pay their professors solely through their fee income was not a success. At King's, Pearson maintained that he 'barely averaged £200 a year'.[96] When Robert Vaughan resigned his professorship at University College in 1839, he had six students whose fees, reduced by him from three guineas to £2 as an incentive for them to remain, hardly earned him the equivalent of an academic salary.[97] Beesly 'stated quite frankly that he could never see any reason to over-exert himself with his professorial duties which were both ill-paid and imposed upon him without adequate discussion or consultation'.[98] At Oxford Henry Vaughan's lecture course in his first year was given *gratis* to an audience of around one hundred and sixty. The following year when a fee of one guinea was levied, his listeners were quickly reduced to a third of the size of the previous year.[99]

Despite both the rejection of the research ideal implicit in the restructuring of the universities in the mid-century and the indignities which often attached to the choice and the functioning of these posts the professor remained the most significant and influential position in university history departments. Halsey and Trow have pointed out that the non-professorial academic class was as good as non-existent right through the nineteenth century,[100] excepting the largely transient tutors at Oxford and Cambridge fulfilling college duties in the hope of ecclesiastical preferment. Even the professorial class was, however, minute; there were only twenty-five professors at Oxford in 1850 whereas the University of Leipzig, less than half the size of Oxford, supported over a hundred professors.[101]

The Regius Professorships of Modern History at Oxford and Cambridge were the most prestigious of the professorial history posts throughout this period, if only by virtue of their long standing. Established in 1724 for political rather than academic reasons, the terms of the professorships had never been generous. Out of the original stipend of £40, the incumbents were expected to pay the salaries of 'two Persons at least well qualified to teach and instruct in writing and speaking [. . .] [Modern] languages'.[102] Before long this was raised

[95] Chadwick, *loc. cit.* p. 303; Wormwell, *op. cit.* p. 42.
[96] Pearson, *op. cit.* p. 86.   [97] H. Hale Bellot, *op. cit.* p. 116.
[98] R. Harrison, 'E. S. Beesly and Karl Marx', *International Review of Social History* IV (1959) 1, pp. 1–58 (p. 39).   [99] Oxford Royal Commission, *op. cit.* Appendix F.
[100] A. H. Halsey & M. A. Trow, *The British Academics* (London, 1971) p. 150.
[101] J. Sparrow, *op. cit.* pp. 111–12.
[102] Bodl. Lib. Univ. Arch. Hyp/LB/XXVIII. Letters Patent, 1724. With thanks to Dr Constant Mews for invaluable help with the translation.

to £400 at Oxford. Until 1855, payment came direct from the Exchequer, but in that year responsibility passed to the Universities' Chest although the appointments remained in the gift of the Crown.

By the time the Dixie Professorship of Ecclesiastical History had been founded at Cambridge, Oxford could already boast two professorships in modern history and sufficient funding for a third, a further chair in ecclesiastical history and a readership in Indian history. The Regius Professorship of Ecclesiastical History 'and the Study of the Ancient Fathers' had been constituted in 1840 at a yearly stipend of £300. Oxford's second chair in history, the Chichele Professorship of Modern History, was first elected in 1862 to be principally concerned with British and British colonial history.

At King's College London the relevant professorial post was one which combined English literature and history. When the College first opened, the chair was left unfilled as at University College, and its duties shared between the professors of mathematics and of classics – a telling comment on the status awarded both history and English. In 1853 the chair was expanded into two separate professorships, Charles Pearson filling the chair of history and J. S. Brewer – the more reputable of the two in historical circles – the literature post. They were reunited in 1865 when Pearson emigrated to Australia. An attempt to found a second chair of history in 1854 when a benefactor offered £100 to endow a new professorship of British History and Archaeology was apparently dropped when the College council found the donor's choice of incumbent unacceptable.[103]

Although the professoriate remained the most significant and certainly the most prestigious acknowledgement of academic prowess within the subject, the inclusion of history as an examinable subject created a parallel demand for a tutorial pool of experts which the champions of the new schools of history regarded as severely underfunded and understaffed. The Board of Studies for the Honours School of Modern History at Oxford regarded both the professoriate and the tutorial staff as inadequate for the efficient execution of their duties. Collegiate teaching was equally limited; 'by 1856, only four or five colleges had established lectureships in law and history', and in the 1870s there were only ten Law and Modern History tutors.[104] Without the establishment of intercollegiate teaching the provision of adequate undergraduate teaching would have proved impossible. The Board of Studies, soon after the establishment of the single Honours school, were pressing for expansion. In a submission to the university's Committee on Requirements in 1876, they proposed that the professoriate should number an ambitious total of nine; in addition to the

---

[103] F. J. C. Hearnshaw, *op. cit.* p. 242.
[104] E. G. W. Bill, *op. cit.* p. 177; A. J. Engel, 'From Clergyman to Don: The Rise of the Academic Profession in Nineteenth Century Oxford', (unpublished PhD dissertation, Princeton University, 1975), pp. 138–9.

established Regius and Chichele Professorships, they suggested that the proposed Ford Professor should concentrate on English History, preferably 1066–1547, and that professorships in Anglo-Saxon and early English Languages, in Foreign History and in Indian History, in English Literature 'in its historical aspect from 1271', in Modern Church History 'who may be a layman', and in Northern Antiquities should be set up. In addition, the 'proper development of the School' required readers in English Constitutional History and Political Economy, an occasional reader 'for instance in Historical Method and Criticism, in Archaeology, Numismatics and Palaeography' and 'from time to time, one or more University Lectureships in some special branch of the subject, such as for instance, the History of British Dependencies'.[105]

They also broached at the same time the difficult and central question of the rôle of research within the university community. Much of the nineteenth-century debate on education had concentrated on arguments over the relative importance of teaching and of research. In Oxford and Cambridge, that debate was articulated specifically in terms of the balance between tutorial and professorial staffing. Both Rosemary Jann and Doris Goldstein have stressed Stubbs' attachment to the research ideal, and yet it was he who voiced the commonly held view that:

I confess I do not like the idea of giving a man an income which would by itself be sufficient to make work unnecessary and telling himself to devote himself to research as he pleases [. . .] If we would provide for research it must [. . .] be done by paying for results.[106]

Undergraduate teaching certainly formed the bulk of university work. Research degrees were a late development; the first B.Litt by thesis in Oxford was not established until 1895 and it was 1917 before the doctorate came into existence.[107] Various reforms at Oxford served to emphasise the dominance of the teaching element. The introduction of written examinations in 1807, although not dispensing entirely with the oral *viva voce*, changed the nature of Oxford teaching substantially. Written competition led to the replacement of the more traditional catechetical style of tutoring by lecturing. In moving away from rote learning in this way, the value of the tutor was greatly increased and teaching became by far the most prominent activity of university dons. Nevertheless, the Oxford historians were anxious to maintain for themselves a learned profile. The Board's submission of 1876 stated their desire that

there should be established at Oxford a Professoriate not only strong enough to teach History with a view to the Examinations, but capable of taking a conspicuous part in the labours of historical investigation and discovery.[108]

---

[105] Bodl. Lib. Univ. Arch. W.P. γ 7.1, f. 19.
[106] Stubbs, *Two Lectures* p. 18; R. Jann, *loc. cit.* p. 127; D.S. Goldstein, *loc. cit.* p. 11.
[107] L. Woodward, 'The Rise of the Professorial Historian in England', ed. K. Bourne & D.C. Watt, *Studies in International History: Essays presented to W. Norton Medlicott* (London, 1967) p. 29.
[108] Bodl. Lib. Univ. Arch. W.P. γ 7.1.

In keeping with its mathematical traditions, Cambridge had far fewer historical preferments than Oxford to offer historians before the establishment of the Tripos. It had been the recipient, alongside Oxford, of a Regius Professorship of Modern History under the Hanoverians, but its poor showing in comparison with the sister university provoked comment thereafter. 'At Oxford [. . .] far more liberal provisions have been made for the teaching of History and for the encouragement of Historical Study than at Cambridge.'[109] Just as at Oxford too, complaints over the inadequacy of the staffing were voiced by the Board of History and Archaeology. Reporting in the early 1880s, the Board recommended that the single professorship and four lectureships should be raised to a teaching staff of at least eight or nine.[110] Lecturing timetables show the work shared between six or seven Fellows, most of them lecturing three mornings a week over two terms. Thus it was that throughout these early years, the new historians' professionalism was constantly undermined both by inadequate facilities and by arguments over the function of education.

II

It has been asserted that 'the prerequisite for the rise of historical studies in the nineteenth century was the reorganisation of the educational system' in which history began to be taught not as 'an auxiliary science' but as an independent subject.[111] When the subject became examinable in a university context, criteria by which to judge quality and competence were gradually standardised and from that time on the successful historian was increasingly one with proven ability through examination in these fields. Prior to the introduction of this competitive yardstick, no single standard of historical achievement or interest had been able to assert itself but by the end of the century criteria for the title of historian had been effectively established. However, at an institutional level many of the most influential developments of the century were well established before single honours history was first initiated. It was only with the relatively late appointment of reputable and scholarly figures to historical posts in the universities that academic history began to rival the serious activities of amateurs or of professional records experts.

In large part, history derived its new-found academic respectability from its concentration on contingent truth – the collection, in short, of factual material. The distinguishing feature of this aggressively empirical approach which marked its departure from the image of the polymath was that this faith in

---

[109] Ward, *op. cit.* p. 10.
[110] University of Cambridge, Seeley Library. Minutes of Board of History and Archaeology, n.d. – 1883 or 1884.
[111] Quoted in Engel, *op. cit.* p. 106.

factual knowledge was newly grounded in specialisation; the establishment of history courses rapidly became part of that move towards the fragmentation of knowledge. Until the foundation of the new universities during the course of the nineteenth century, Oxford and Cambridge had not only enjoyed an ill-used monopoly of the education of the well-to-do Anglican community but had determined that *Literae Humaniores* and Mathematics were their arbiters of absolute truth. The introduction of alternative or even supplementary subjects – history, law, non-classical philosophy, natural sciences – ushered in a greater potential for concentration on a single subject. The impact of such specialisation although only gradually felt, was the acquisition in university circles of a career ideal. The mushrooming of both subjects and students prompted by university reform and expansion led to a concomitant expansion in the size of the academic community; as opportunities for successful graduates offered themselves, a professional class of university teachers who regarded their academic work as a long-term prospect began to emerge.

The new professionals were unanimous in resisting the taint of material consideration. The unease current in intellectual circles about the spirit of commercialism made academics lay heavy stress on their attachment to a gentlemanly ideal of service just as their counterparts in the Record Office had done earlier in the century. The consolidation of social status was of primary importance. Charles Neate, fellow of Oriel College Oxford and Drummond Professor of Political Economy from 1857, articulated the ideal image of the Oxford don.

Teaching [. . .] is less with him a necessity, less a trade [. . .] he might live if he liked as an idle gentleman, taking his ease in his College, and borrowing from the shadow of its ancient walls, which are his property, something of dignity in his ease.[112]

Punctilious in their concern to retain an aura of gentility and breeding, the academics were anxious at the same time to see their work take on the semblance of a career. For most of the century, it was their clerical rather than their academic position which won them approbation. Thomas Arnold's comments on school teaching certainly apply to the nineteenth-century academic as well.

[The rank of schoolmaster] has not yet obtained that respect in England, as to be able to stand by itself in public opinion; [. . .] it owes the rank which it holds to its connexion with the profession of a clergyman for that is acknowledged universally in England to be the profession of a gentleman. Mere teaching, like mere literature, places a man, I think, in rather an equivocal position.

The problems of status led academics to stress their moral rôle as the teachers and guardians of young minds, and in particular the minds of the privileged

112 A. P. Stanley, *op. cit.* II. 149.

jeunesse dorée. Goldwin Smith's inaugural lecture as Regius Professor at Oxford dwelt at length on the class duties of the university teacher.

> Our care for the education of the middle classes [. . .] will ill compensate the country for our failure to perform thoroughly the task of educating of our peculiar charge, the upper classes, and teaching them how to do their duty to the people.[113]

Although the conditions for a meritocracy were gradually being brought into existence, it was to be a long time before considerations of sex, class and religion were laid aside. As long as they remained significant, no subject could entirely free itself from strong ideological overtones.

> To be really beneficial [education] must inculcate principle, polish taste, regulate temper, cultivate reason, subdue the passions, direct the feelings, create reflection, and refer all actions, sentiments and affections, to the love and fear of the Supreme Being.[114]

During J. R. Seeley's tenure of the Regius Professorship at Cambridge single honours status for history had been won and it was under his direction that the faculty board had begun to build the distinctive features of the new Tripos.[115] Seeley's view of history favoured teaching above research through his stress on the political lessons to be derived and applied from historical study. 'Our University is, and must be, a great seminary of politicians.'[116] His view of the function and direction of a historical education closely allied to political science clashed with that of Adolphus Ward, Professor of History at Owen's College Manchester from 1866 but active in the Cambridge faculty by virtue of his fellowship at Peterhouse. Ward's view of history was far closer to the research ideal in its advocacy of a pure history course uncluttered by allied disciplines. In the event it was the inclinations of the Regius Professor that triumphed: Cambridge undergraduates in history were required to sit papers in political economy, political science and economic history as befitted a study which Seeley himself had dubbed the 'school of statesmanship'.[117] Creasy had stated a similar view of history as a political tool quite clearly in his inaugural lecture at London. 'Conscious of how much Dignity and Duty are attached to the name of Englishmen we shall feel ourselves peculiarly and solemnly called on to turn for wisdom to the experience of former days, and qualify ourselves by the study of the Past for our high prerogative of controlling the Present and moulding the destinies of the Future.[118]

---

[113] G. Smith, *An Inaugural Lecture* (Oxford & London, 1864) p. 13.

[114] B. Malkin, *An Introductory Lecture on History* (London, 1830) p. 22.

[115] D. Wormell, *op. cit.*; S. Rothblatt, *op. cit.* pp. 168–80.   [116] Seeley, *loc. cit.* p. 299.

[117] *ibid.* p. 296. For a fuller discussion of the disagreement between the two factions, see Wormell *op. cit.*, Kitson Clark *loc. cit.* and McLachlan *loc. cit.* Deborah Wormell has analysed the post-university careers of those who took first and second class honours in the Historical Tripos during Seeley's time. 17.1% of them went on to more advanced historical scholarship or teaching, 18.1% entered public administration (colonial or civil service, local government) or Parliament and the remainder found work largely in the church, the legal profession, teaching and social work. (p. 119).

[118] E. S. Creasy, *The Spirit of Historical Study* (London, 1840) p. 31.

The educational assumptions that lay behind his thinking exercised a powerful effect on the development of academic history. Sheldon Rothblatt's distinction between notions of imitative and of innovative originality is important. In the historical context it is the imitative which was more influential, creating amongst the educated classes 'a vast community of common discourse' which 'provided them with the shared familiarity of a select, but not confined range of materials'.[119] This method took as its principle the idea of an authoritative and respected model designed more to inculcate a chosen set of standards than to encourage individual discovery or revaluation. Prebendary Gaisford's smugness upholds Rothblatt's point. 'The advantages of a classical education are twofold:– it enables us to look down with contempt on those who have not shared its advantages, and also fits us for places of emolument not only in this world, but the next.'[120]

Seeley's views on the relationship of history to contemporary affairs were shared by many of his fellow historians. In his inaugural lecture Stubbs had outlined the rôle that history was to play in citizenship. '[It is the] process of acquisition of a stock of facts, an ignorance of which unfits a man from playing the very humblest part as a citizen, or even watching the politics of his own age with an intelligent apprehension.[121]

Cramer, like Goldwin Smith, yoked this appreciation of latter day politics to the training of 'that class which naturally exercises [. . .] influence over [. . .] government [. . .] For it is more especially to the politician and statesman that the pages of history offers lessons and examples of the highest interest and value.[122]

These views were consonant also with the strident nationalism that characterised so much of nineteenth-century politics. Seeley had dubbed history 'the school of public feeling and patriotism'.[123] Patriotism in Victorian terms meant more than simple affection for one's country; it was an assumption as to the unchallengeable supremacy of Britain which motivated the Victorian patriot. 'It is our duty [. . .] to prepare ourselves for the right use of the vast power that England sways, a power over the fortunes of mankind such as no people or potentate ever before possessed.'[124] The inclusion of such a statement in the inaugural lecture of a professor of history was in no sense judged as misplaced in its enthusiasm. Montagu Burrows had advised candidates in the Jurisprudence and Modern History School at Oxford that 'English History is the basis of the whole course.'[125] That in itself says little, but the assertion of English pride and progress implicit in it was strong.

---

[119] S. Rothblatt, *Tradition and Change in English Liberal Education: An Essay in History and Culture* (London, 1976) p. 164.
[120] W. H. G. Armytage, *Civic Universities: Aspects of a British Tradition* (London, 1955) p. 175.
[121] W. Stubbs, *An Address delivered by way of inaugural lecture* (Oxford, 1867) p. 4.
[122] Cramer, *op. cit.* pp. 12; 19.   [123] Seeley, *loc. cit.* p. 298.
[124] Creasy, *op. cit.* p. 30.   [125] Burrows, *Pass and Class* p. 212.

Alongside this assertion of English virtue was to be found the common interpretation of progress in teleological terms. The transformation from barbarism to reason which was so dominant a Victorian theme was traced to the coming of Christianity. The slow process of secularisation initiated by the foundation of non-denominational institutions and by the Royal Commissions on Oxford and Cambridge of 1850 and 1877 was a necessary corollary to the acquisition of a professional career structure, but one of history's ideological 'tasks' was to combat that movement. Arnold enunciated the principle in 1841 that 'the perfection of moral and spiritual truth has been given by Christianity' and Stubbs echoed it sixteen years on; 'it is Christianity that gives to the modern world its living unity'.[126] Thus could Robert Vaughan at the start of his historical career at University College pronounce that Europe was 'the centre of everything of importance in the future history of the world'.[127] John Cramer took a similar view in lauding 'the meridian lustre of the present age' which had brought so many colonies 'into social relations with civilised Europe'.[128] Thomas Arnold took the argument a further teleological step in regarding modern history as bearing the 'marks of the fulness of time, as if there would be no future history beyond it'.[129]

History fulfilled a specific ideological rôle which comprised all the most important elements sustaining the *status quo*. As Rosemary Jann has commented, 'in the culturally dominant ancient universities, professionalisation of history meant first and foremost professionalisation of liberal educators in history'.[130] Those who, whatever their party affiliation, did not conform were liable to exclusion from the community. Henry Halford Vaughan's quasi-determinist view of history and outspoken criticism of Oxford's clerical domination made him one such outsider. For the most part, however, the university historians identified themselves with the Victorian establishment and saw their educative rôle as a fundamental prop of that society's order.

History was, from its first acceptance in academic circles, thus embroiled in the most important educational and political debates of the century. As a new discipline in university terms, its fight for recognition and status identified it with the move towards long term academic careers, and a structure compatible with a professional class of dons. At the same time, its rôle as guardian of the national consciousness inclined it towards the preservation of a disintegrating social and intellectual network. The paradoxes at work in Victorian society were mirrored in those of the newly emergent university history. The embracing of the subject within such confines cannot, however, be construed

---

[126] T. Arnold, *An Inaugural Lecture on the Study of Modern History* (Oxford, 1841) p. 39; Stubbs, *An Address* p. 24.

[127] R. Vaughan, *On the Study of General History, an Introductory Lecture* (London, 1834) p. 37.

[128] Cramer, *op. cit.* p. 30.   [129] Arnold, *op. cit.* p. 38.   [130] R. Jann, *loc. cit.* p. 145.

as pioneering a professional history. Its passage had been eased by government's willingness to allot funding, however cautiously, to historical archives, publications and catalogues and by the patent success of many of the privately organised institutions. Success in challenging the existing academic monopolies was not the first but one of the final steps which mark the recognition of history as a mainstream discipline in the universities of nineteenth-century England.

7

~~~~~~

Consolidation and division

> The conviction is already not far from being universal, that the times are
> pregnant with change; and that the nineteenth century will be known to posterity
> as the era of one of the greatest revolutions of which history has preserved the
> remembrance, in the human mind, and in the whole constitution of human
> society [. . .] It is felt that men are henceforth to be held together by new ties, and
> separated by new barriers; for the ancient bonds will now no longer unite, nor the
> ancient boundaries confine.
>
> (J. S. Mill, *The Spirit of the Age*)

The foundation of the *English Historical Review* in 1886 marked the academic
arrival of the professional historian. The provision of a journal affecting to
represent serious academic opinion and involving many of the nation's most
reputable university historians was of considerable importance both in
determining the ascendancy of professional university history and in strength-
ening a sense of community within its precincts. The *Review* was the
culmination of a series of related developments central to the asserting of the
primacy of the professional historian. In 1884 a highly distinguished trio of
men had all been rewarded with academic preferment: Mandell Creighton
became the first Dixie Professor of Ecclesiastical History at the University of
Cambridge, E. A. Freeman succeeded his friend Stubbs in the Regius Professorship of Modern History at Oxford and the legal historian Frederick Maitland
became reader in English Law at Cambridge. The following year the reform of
the Historical Tripos at Cambridge and the division of Oxford's arts faculty into
the three areas of *literae humaniores*, oriental languages and modern history
declared that history had finally won academic respect as an autonomous area
of study.

The idea for a journal devoted exclusively to historical matters and academic
book reviews was one which had been in currency for some twenty years prior
to the appearance of the *English Historical Review*. England from the 1830s and
earlier had supported a respectable circulation for many genealogical and
heraldic, numismatic and antiquarian journals and many archaeological
societies expended the greater part of their efforts and funds in turning out an
annual volume of transactions. Private publishing ventures such as Llewellyn
Jewitt's *The Reliquary* (1860) and Dunkin's *The Archaeological Mine* (1853)

were initiated though few survived the rigours of the marketplace longer than a year or two. The new *English Historical Review* however sought a more specialised readership and even the earliest attempts of the 1860s at founding such a periodical had come from the specifically historical community. It was to become, in a sense, the house journal of the new university-based and professional historians, a declaration of their institutional status.

In 1867 J. R. Green, James Bryce and William Hunt had discussed the 'starting of a purely Historical Review [. . .] avoid[ing] the rock of mere archaeology and the making it too much "First Period"'.[1] Even at that early stage, there were anxieties lest considerations of popular appeal should conflict with its intellectual standing. 'I fancy one of the difficulties would be, what to do with the Stanleys and Kingsleys. If they were shut out, the thing would fail. And yet would you let them in?'[2] A decade later Green made explicit the project's aims – which were not entirely coincident with his own – in a letter to his friend and publisher Macmillan.

The original notion of such a review was [. . .] a purely scientific organ of historical criticism [. . .] which would undoubtedly raise sympathy and secure even unpaid support among a certain section of historic scholars. But its character was to be scientific and not popular, and the literary tone of articles was to be entirely subordinate to their critical value.[3]

It was after Green's early death, however, that the *Review* finally came to fruition, following in the wake of similar ventures on the continent. The *Historische Zeitschrift* founded in Germany in 1859 had been the first European journal of academic history. It was followed by the French *Revue Historique* in 1876, and in 1884 Italy's *Rivista storica italiana* made its début. In England, James Bryce brought together a nucleus of contributors and planners in 1885 to consider reviving the enterprise which he had planned with Green and Hunt in the 1860s. The academic bias proposed for this new venture was reflected in Bryce's choice of colleagues. He approached Lord Acton, Mandell Creighton, Frederick York Powell, Adolphus Ward and Dean Church – an impressive collection of present and future professors of high historical repute.[4] In the 1860s William Stubbs had seemed the obvious choice for editor but his elevation to the bishopric in 1884 now removed any such possibility. It was to the ecclesiastical historian Mandell Creighton that the task fell. He took the post without remuneration; 'I will edit for nothing, to start the concern, for a year.'[5]

The *Review* represented, without doubt, a new departure both in periodical publishing and in the presentation of contemporary scholarship. Historical

[1] J. Coll. Oxon. MS. 199, ff. 303–5. J. R. Green to E. A. Freeman, 28 January 1867. See Chapter 2.
[2] *ibid.*
[3] J. Coll Oxon. Unnumbered MS., J.R. Green Colln., Miscellaneous Corresp. Green to Macmillan, 15 June 1876.
[4] L. Creighton, *Life and Letters of Mandell Creighton by his wife* (London, 1904) p. 333.
[5] *ibid.* p. 333.

journals prior to its inception were of an entirely different nature. The *Transactions of the Royal Historical Society* were only gradually recovering from their moribund years under the dilettante editorship of Charles Rogers whilst the short-lived popular historical magazines of the 1850s – *The Historian* and *The Historical Educator*, both far broader in range than their titles suggest – were long forgotten and little mourned. A number of antiquarian journals, other than those tied to particular societies appeared, more particularly in the 1870s and 1880s. They were cheap and popular journals – *The Antiquary: a fortnightly medium of intercommunication for archaeologists, antiquarians, numismatists, the virtuosi, and collectors of articles of virtù and curiosities* founded in 1871 was 4d; *Long Ago: A Monthly Journal of Popular Antiquities* was 6d. The two merged in 1873.

The most successful of these journals was *The Reliquary: A Deposit for Precious Relics – Legendary, Biographical and Historical; illustrative of the habits and customs and pursuits of our forefathers*. Begun in 1860, *The Reliquary* ran to twenty-six annual volumes, the last appearing appropriately enough in 1886 when the *English Historical Review* began publication. It claimed to be of 'real value and service [. . .] to men of science and of letters in every walk of life' and had a clear idea of the nature of its readership, calling for the assistance of 'literary men, of the clergy, of country gentlemen'.[6] A number of notable antiquaries contributed on a regular basis including Eliza Meteyard – Wedgwood's biographer – and the barrow-digger Thomas Bateman. It was typical of such publications in interleaving full-length articles – on genealogy, topology, botany, archaeology – with 'notes and queries' sections, a format modelled on the earlier enterprise, *The Gentleman's Magazine*.

The *English Historical Review* was, from the outset, of a deliberately different ilk. Its champions were practising full-time academics, concerned to enhance the prestige of their discipline by providing a forum for research and debate. Many of the foremost university historians of the day – Lord Acton, Edward Freeman, J. R. Seeley, Sidney Owen, A. W. Ward, Hastings Rashdall, S. R. Gardiner – contributed to its volumes. From the first, it was dogged by financial difficulties and an anticipated low circulation. Creighton had remarked of it, not long before the publication of the first volume, 'They are indeed misguided who fear lest the Review be too popular. My fear is lest it die of dullness.'[7] Its appeal was not, and was never to be, to the lay public. In consequence its position in the 1890s was highly precarious, dictating a decrease in the print-run and the introduction of a policy of not paying contributors.[8] It was, nonetheless, a successful enterprise in that as well as surviving the battlefield of

[6] 'Introduction', *The Reliquary* (1860) pp. iii–iv.
[7] L. Creighton, *op. cit.* p. 337; letter to R. L. Poole, 8 September 1885.
[8] Doris S. Goldstein, 'The Organisation and Development of the British Historical Profession, 1884–1921', *BIHR* LV (1982) 132, 180–93 (p. 182); Creighton, *op. cit.* p. 343., Letter to C. J. Longman, 28 October 1889.

the free market, it clearly did provide a basis for the dissemination and discussion of historical research. Acton was delighted with the first issue.

I congratulate you very sincerely. The Review is solid, various and comprehensive, very instructive and sufficiently entertaining [. . .] I discern the makings of a sacred band of university workers.[9]

He was concerned not with the wider appeal of his subject, but with the needs and desires of the new academic community of historians; he saw the *Review* as their collective voice.

Conceptions of the subject still differed widely, but few academic historians would have dissented in asserting the growing need for a specialist journal of this sort. 'An attempt to issue an editorial programme would be a mistake. We have not sufficient agreement about the method and scope of history. Freeman and Seeley may appear side by side, but I could not draw up a detailed prospectus in which they could both agree.'[10] The reluctance to commit the *Review* to a specific school of thinking reflected both the diversity of historical method in this period and the fact that the dividing line between professional and amateur was as yet not wholly distinct. Creighton when he agreed to edit the proposed *Review* confessed to Acton, 'I have lived long in the country away from books, and only able to pick up such as I actually needed. I have no thorough knowledge of history as a whole.'[11] It was to Acton that he voiced his early doubts. 'We must confess that we are not strong in historical method in England. Our work has all the advantages and all the disadvantages of amateur work. Most of the well-known persons have already said all that they have to say.'[12] Creighton did not, perhaps, foresee at this stage that the existence of the *Review* would be an important step in developing the professional consensus he sensed they lacked. The anonymous prefatory note that introduced the first volume, penned by James Bryce, admitted that the *Review*'s main function was the provision of a journal for the professional historian.[13] He declared that 'states and politics will [. . .] be the chief part of its subject'.[14] These were the subjects, of course, which had brought the subject to academic and hence professional respectability.

In general, the early years of the *Review* saw a close adherence to that definition of the historical discipline. It dealt mostly with British and European topics, and in particular with political history. In the first volume, Seeley wrote on the 'House of Bourbon' and Ward on the Hanoverian succession. S. R. Gardiner wrote in Volume II on 'Charles I and the Earl of Glamorgan' and in 1890, in Volume V, Kate Norgate (one of the few women admitted to this

---

[9] Creighton, *ibid.* p. 339. Letter from Lord Acton, n.d.
[10] *ibid.* pp. 335–6. Letter to Acton, 6 August 1885.   [11] *ibid.*
[12] *ibid.* p. 334. Letter to Acton, 28 July 1885.
[13] 'Preface', *English Historical Review* I (1886) (p. 5). See Rosemary Jann's comments in her article 'From Amateur to Professional: The Case of the Oxbridge Historians', *Journal of British Studies* XXII (1983) 2, 122–47 (p. 134).   [14] *English Historical Review loc. cit.* p. 3.

charmed circle) discussed 'Odo of Champagne, Count of Blois and "Tyrant of Burgundy"'. A substantial proportion of its articles concentrated on ancient history – J. B. Bury contributed articles on Roman history in Volumes IV and V. Historiographic material too was awarded considerable attention, under the influence of Acton who himself wrote a number of pieces on German academic history. Conspicuously absent, however, was the intrusion of those dilettante items of more general interest – archaeological, antiquarian or even scientific – which were so common a feature of the more popularly directed journals. The *Review* was unique in providing an exclusively historical forum outside the confines of a learned society. In doing so, it was necessarily limiting itself to the then-expanding but nonetheless exclusive and tiny community of professional historians for whom it certainly created a well-defined institutional location.

It differed from the journals of the British Archaeological Association and Royal Archaeological Institute, and even the Royal Historical Society, in directing its observations primarily to a class of experts for whom reviews of the works of German and French historians writing for an academic readership were of value and interest. Whereas the journals of the societies were available to those sufficiently motivated to take up membership, the limitations on access imposed by the *English Historical Review* were in one sense less striking but far more significant. It was a costly item at five shillings a volume, but more importantly it made few concessions to the reader unfamiliar with the style and interests of the élite represented by Creighton, Acton and Bryce. They were in the process of successfully colonising whole areas of study such that at the close of the century Sir Henry Howorth noted that 'the processes of writing history have become more difficult, more precise and more methodical, and [. . .] there is less and less room for the untrained, untaught, and unscholarly amateur.'[15] The imposition of particular techniques and skills characteristic of historical analysis and research certainly contributed towards crowding out the enthusiastic amateur from those branches of the discipline deemed appropriate for academic consumption. Both in the professional and the popular field, however, the realisation of potential new areas of study served to open up opportunities in the historical arena. Thorold Rogers, albeit critical of what he regarded as an overly diplomatic and political bias in the writing of history, recognised the importance of the developments which later nineteenth-century scholars were implementing.

I [. . .] gladly acknowledge that the solid study of history has made considerable progress. The narrative is no longer merely one of war and peace, of royal genealogies, of unrelated dates [. . .] History has begun to include the study of constitutional antiquities [. . .] has begun to recognise the progress of jurisprudence [. . .] It has touched lightly,

[15] Henry H. Howorth, 'Old and New Methods in Writing History, being the Opening Address of the Historical Section at the Dorchester Meeting', *Archaeological Journal* LV (1892) 122–44 (p. 143).

very lightly, on social history, on the condition of the people, on the varying fortunes of land and labour.[16]

It was not only in the well-trodden fields of constitutional and political history that such advances were made, however. Thorold Rogers, in his tireless promotion of economic and social history, pursued 'documents which have probably never been read after the immediate object for which they were compiled was satisfied [. . .] farming accounts, elaborate accounts of buildings', and castigated his colleagues for their narrow and unimaginative use of even such widely prized material as Domesday, manorial court rolls and pipe rolls.[17] Henry Howorth, addressing the Historical Section of the Archaeological Institute at Dorchester in 1897, celebrated the work of Rogers and others who 'searched through the songs, the travellers' tales, the bestiaries, the crude scientific manuals, and let us peep into kitchen and hall and parlour, into cottage and castle, and not merely escorted us from one battlefield to another'.[18] The wheel, in a sense, had come full circle for Howorth was lavishing his enthusiasm on precisely those areas in which the antiquarian community had for so long been delving. The printing clubs of the 1840s had found much of their material in political ballads, early scientific texts and the like. Less than half a century on, their customary materials were quarried by the new professionals.

It is not the old-fashioned evidence with which modern historians have revolutionised both our methods and results, but by going far afield – Archaeology, Philology, Comparative Mythology, Folk Lore, the survival of old creeds and of old institutions. These, and such as these, furnish the best of the modern historians with their most effective bricks and mortar.[19]

C. H. George has spoken of the 'tragic bifurcation of analysis and scholarship' in the new history of the nineteenth century. He contrasts the theoretical framework provided by Marx with the empirical and evidential emphasis represented by historians such as Ranke and Gardiner.[20] The split is an artificial one, for the empiricism of nineteenth-century English historical work, with its stress on detailed reconstruction, was in itself a theoretical stance. In rejecting – or more accurately, not considering – the materialist interpretation proposed by Marx, historians were asserting their adherence to a historical universe presided over ultimately by Providence. The hostility with which all systems of thought were received in English historical circles reflects precisely the foundations on which their work was erected.[21] Historians of repute were

[16] J. E. Thorold Rogers, 'The Economical Side of History', *The Economic Interpretation of History – lectures delivered in Worcester College Hall Oxford 1887–8* (London, 1888) pp. 1–22 (p. 4).
[17] *ibid.* pp. 2–4.   [18] Howorth, *loc. cit.* p. 135.   [19] *ibid.* p. 37.
[20] C. H. George, 'Puritanism as History and Historiography', *Past and Present* 41 (1968) 77–104 (p. 95).
[21] See Chapter 4.

frequently ignorant of major intellectual developments occurring in their own lifetime; Stubbs' refusal to countenance the ideas of his contemporary Thomas Buckle cannot be regarded merely as an eccentric quirk.[22] Dale Strick has pointed out that his lack of interest extended to 'Darwin, J. S. Mill, Marx or any other new line of thought introduced during the last half-century of his life'.[23] At the same time, however, Stubbs boasted a knowledge of and a respect for German academic developments in history, although he embraced the methodology of the Rankean school without its consonant philosophy.[24]

In archaeology, though the acquisition of full university status continued to elude its cultivators, the community found a far more secure intellectual footing with the inception in the 1880s of two new projects which were to have a significant impact both in extending archaeology's influence and in determining its future both methodologically and institutionally. Petrie's excavations on the Nile were to form the backbone of modern Egyptology whilst the work of Pitt Rivers on the substantial estate he inherited at Cranborne Chase enshrined many of the techniques which were to become the standard apparatus of the modern archaeologist. Glyn Daniel maintains that at the start of the twentieth century technical difficulties continued to dog the discipline;[25] nonetheless by, if not before the 1870s, archaeology had established its fundamental and controversial importance. The Newnham classicist Jane Ellen Harrison spoke of the influence of archaeological method and discovery in her own field. 'We Hellenists were in truth at that time [the 1870s] a people that sat in darkness but we were soon to see a great light, two great lights: archaeology and anthropology. The classics were turning in their long sleep.'[26]

It was not only in classical studies, however, that the shockwaves of archaeological discovery reverberated. Archaeology had asserted – and not for the first time – the antiquity of the human race almost simultaneously with the publication of Darwin's *Origin of the Species* and together they represented a direct challenge to the authenticity of Biblical teaching and to long-standing assumptions about the nature of humankind and its superiority over its fellow inhabitants on earth. The Darwinian revelations of the 1860s had derived much of their public impact from the theological implications of the theory of natural selection.[27] Darwin's work was a commercial success, but the excitement it generated was primarily ideological in substance rather than

---

[22] See Chapter 4.
[23] D. E. Strick, 'English Historiography 1859–1890, A Study of Froude, Freeman, Stubbs and Green' (unpublished PhD dissertation, University of California, 1951) p. 241.
[24] See Chapter 4.   [25] G. Daniel, *A Short History of Archaeology* (London, 1981) pp. 145–7.
[26] Quoted in J. G. Stewart, *Jane Ellen Harrison* (London, 1959) p. 2.
[27] A. Ellegard, 'Darwin and the General Reader: The Reception of Darwin's Theory of Evolution in the British Periodical Press, 1859–1872', *Göteborgs Universitets Arsskrift* LXIV (1958) pp. 1–394 (p. 331).

technical or scientific. Once implicated, archaeology could not escape its rôle in a debate immeasurably wider than the immediate Darwinian controversy.

It was within this context that archaeology struggled to win academic recognition and a place in the university curriculum. Nearly thirty years after the initial uproar over these disturbing assertions, although the debate was by no means settled, the leading archaeologist Pitt Rivers could contrast what he saw as the enlightenment offered by archaeological discovery and yet still yoked to a hint of humanity's more advanced condition.

No one now requires to be reminded of the great advance of knowledge that has been brought about by the study of the drift gravels, which at the lowest computation has quadrupled the time in which we are enabled to investigate the works of man [. . .] No individual among those who assembled here [Salisbury] in 1849 had the least idea that beneath his very feet were to be found the relics of man's workmanship at a time when he was contemporaneous with the elephant and other extinct animals.[28]

A further implication of Pitt Rivers' speech was its emphasis on the growing maturity of the discipline in contrast with its earlier methods. The divide between amateur and professional was growing more marked in this period with an increasingly vocal anxiety about the damage wrought by amateurs. In 1881, the *Edinburgh Review* deplored the well-meaning spades and pick-axes of 'the free-lances of archaeology'.[29] At the close of the century archaeological investigation had not wholly shed its amateur ethos nor succeeded in limiting access in the way that the professional historians had done, for Henry Howorth was still alarmed by the extent of such activities.

May I again express the hope [. . .] that those who have the custody of what remain will refuse to allow amateurs and people without the requisite training, knowledge or resources to tamper with [. . .] the very title deeds of our earliest history.[30]

Inevitably the persistence of that amateur association was an impediment to claims for professional and institutional recognition. Oxford inaugurated a chair of Classical Archaeology in 1884 but prehistoric archaeology was not similarly recognised until after the Second World War. At Cambridge the Archaeology and Anthropology Tripos replaced the Anthropology Tripos in 1928 but the Laurence Chair of Classical Archaeology was not founded until 1930 and it was 1946 before Egyptology was deemed worthy of a professorial post at Cambridge.[31]

Archaeology is the latest born of the sciences. It has but scarcely struggled into freedom, out of the swaddling clothes of dilettante speculations. It is still attracted by pretty

[28] A. H. L. F. Pitt Rivers, 'Inaugural Address to the Annual Meeting of the Institute held at Salisbury. Delivered 2 August 1887', *Archaeological Journal* XLIV (1887) 261–77 (pp. 272–3).
[29] Quoted in Joan Evans, *A History of the Society of Antiquaries* (Oxford, 1956) p. 345.
[30] Howorth, *loc. cit.* p. 141.
[31] G. Daniel, *Cambridge and the Back-Looking Curiosity* (Cambridge, 1976) pp. 11–12.

things, rather than by real knowledge. It has to find shelter with the Fine Arts or with History, and not a single home has yet been provided for its real growth.[32]

The criticism was a pert one for Petrie knew well that alongside the clues offered by such disciplines as philology, ethnology and anthropology, technical sophistication was crucial in the determination of the future direction of the subject; geology and palaeontology in particular substantiated many of the findings of archaeologists in this period. Its continued association with an arts-based learning was a hindrance. The growing confidence of the archaeological community was apparent in the introduction and increased use of a specifically technical terminology. Certainly by the 1890s, the use of the terms palaeolithic, neolithic and the like to denote specific periods of antiquity had become a commonplace, at least among the nascent professionals. And yet simultaneously, in the institutional context, it could not easily shake off its old associations.

The significant advance of professional identity in this period whilst successful in pushing antiquarian pursuits to the periphery certainly did not destroy the impetus or enthusiasm of these subjects. The many related amateur societies showed no real sign of deterioration in this period.[33] The Society of Antiquaries of London increased its membership quite substantially towards the end of the century, sometimes attracting upwards of fifty new members a year.[34] A spate of new societies also began to appear. In the 1880s, new provincial historical societies were formed in Birmingham and Oxford, often more urban in composition than the earlier archaeological societies. At county level, record societies pledged to publication began to take shape towards the end of the 1880s: the North Riding Record Society (1884) publishing quarter session records was followed by the Middlesex County Record Society and the Somerset Record Society in 1886 and the Hampshire Record Society two years later. Other local societies, such as the Worcestershire Historical Society publishing similar material of local interest, were founded in the 1890s and later.

Printing clubs at a national level also enjoyed something of a renaissance. The Navy Records Society and the Thoresby Society both began work in the 1890s and the Selden Society, in which F. W. Maitland played a leading rôle, commenced publishing its historico-legal material in 1888. Ecclesiastical societies also found an audience; the Church Historical Society, with Mandell Creighton as its first President, was founded in 1894. Other new ecclesiastical societies of the period included the Henry Bradshaw Society (1890) publishing a miscellany of missals, martyrologies, breviaries and the like, and the Alcuin Club (1897) whose first year's publications consisted of a book of English altars

[32] Quoted in G. Daniel, *The Origins and Growth of Archaeology* (Harmondsworth, 1967) p. 233.
[33] See Chapter 3.   [34] Joan Evans, *op. cit.* p. 323.

from illuminated manuscripts and a reproduction of a fifteenth-century French manuscript about the mass.

The vitality of such organisations is proof not merely of the tenacity of a particular communal structure in nineteenth-century English intellectual circles but of the strength and vigour of the antiquarian tradition. Alongside the more specialised societies which began to emerge, often under the tutelage of historians of repute, those societies embracing a more general interest in the past were maintaining their position in the face of the growing divide between professional and amateur. The sense that the gap was widening in itself served to secure the loyalties of the motivated amateur. Within the boundaries of informed amateurism, those social and intellectual considerations which had throughout the century governed the societies continued to operate.

The commemoration of Domesday in 1886 prompted the Royal Historical Society into co-ordinating a *Domesday Studies* volume to mark the occasion. It loftily declared that 'some benefit might accrue to the encouragement of historical studies without unduly promoting popular manifestations'. They claimed to have courted only 'technical contributions rather than those belonging to the domain of general history',[35] and yet the contributors to the volume were largely culled from local societies and not from those guardians of technical expertise, the professional historians. The Royal Historical Society was at this juncture caught uncomfortably between the amateur tradition and a desire to emulate the rigour of the new professionals. The damage wrought by Charles Rogers had clouded the society's reputation such that it was some time before they could claim the *cachet* attached to attracting historians to their ranks. Their problem symbolises a dilemma rather wider in application than the institutional boundaries of this now august organisation.

The successful introduction of historical studies into the universities and the professionalisation associated with that were instrumental in bringing about stricter criteria to the definition of history, archaeology and antiquarianism although it would be erroneous to trace a direct line of 'progress', of growth from early antiquarianism to professional history or archaeology.[36] The triumph of the new professionals was in confining antiquarianism to the fringes of historical enterprise where their efforts posed no threat to the monopoly of expertise necessary to the standing of the new professions. The antiquarians, rarely salaried to their historical interests and lacking access to the university community, found themselves marginalised. Local history,

---

[35] 'Preface', *Domesday Studies, being the papers read at the meetings of the Domesday Commemoration 1886* (London, 1888).

[36] William Keylor has pointed out that amongst French historians at this juncture, there was an increasing tendency to associate professional history with concentrated monographic scholarship. W. R. Keylor, *Academy and Community: The Foundations of the French Historical Profession* (Cambridge, Massachusetts, 1975) p. 103.

increasingly spurned by cosmopolitan academics, was reinforced as their particular concern; amateurism and antiquarianism were becoming synonymous. Curricular control further helped the new professionals to define with authority the components of the subject.

It was, in essence, an attack on individual provincial cultures. The growing strength of a metropolitan élite capable of relegating less articulate and powerful movements to a historical backseat was central to this process. The middle-class local pride which had given Victorian England its characteristic civic halls and universities, its municipal structures, its strong interest in the past, was waning in the face of this metropolitan colonialism.[37] The imposition of the standards, preoccupations and concerns of an élite dominated by the intellectual triangle of Oxford, Cambridge and London was apparent in the sharp separation of the three historical disciplines in the late nineteenth century. The growth of the intellectual professions served the needs of an expanding non-industrial middle-class and allowed at the same time a convenient distancing from the taint of commercial interest. The decision of the *English Historical Review* not to pay its contributors stemmed from a need to conserve fast-diminishing finances but the practice became a standard one as academic journals were established, reflecting the common cry of the professionals that their motives were purer than those of the cash-conscious trader. Culturally the spotlight had shifted from a provincial to a metropolitan bourgeoisie who succeeded in creating and containing a separate class of intellectuals tied to the university system, distinct on the one hand from the amateur dabblers and dilettantes and on the other from the materialist concerns of commercial occupations.

Intellectual and class mechanisms thus combined to confine access to specialised knowledge to a privileged minority. The *English Historical Review* is one example of this urge to define boundaries through restriction. In both form and content it was off-putting to the casual reader, a fact which its promoters accepted. 'We must recognise [. . .] that at present the Review is chiefly the organ of historical students and has little attraction for the general public.'[38] Professor Creighton did not, however, suggest that the format be changed to embrace a wider readership. Professional status, after all, remains to this day dependent upon the power implied by a specialised and inaccessible body of knowledge; specialised expertise invokes authority.

With the growing confidence and stature of the university professionals, government-employed archivists and historians were increasingly seen as auxiliary. Their staffing of the libraries and consultative services in which academic historians found their principal materials lent them a servicing function. The professions in general were, of course, enhanced in this period by

[37] Goldstein, *loc. cit.* p. 192 talks of the demise of localism as the strength of the professions grew.
[38] Creighton, *op. cit.* p. 343. Letter to C. J. Longman, 28 October 1889.

the necessary and near-simultaneous growth of auxiliary services such as nursing, legal clerking or university administration. In the case of the historical profession, the fact that most Public Record Office and museum employees were trained within the Civil Service rather than in the new schools of history only confirmed their growing alienation from the new professionals. Prior to the introduction of both a specifically historical university education and a competitive career-structured Civil Service, such employees had frequently been numbered amongst the most respected historical minds of their day – Henry Ellis, Joseph Hunter, A. W. Franks and Samuel Birch are good examples. The disjunction of the two occupations which arose as stricter definitions were imposed led inevitably to a down-grading in the academic hierarchy of those not part of the university fraternity.

Such institutional changes are, of course, secondary to and consonant with deeper changes of a social and cultural delineation. They are consequent upon cumulative changes, particularly in the structure of privilege and its concomitant power. New outlets for middle-class talent, essentially reproducing itself whether through undergraduate instruction or its encroachment on the means of communication, were a major factor in determining the cultural boundaries of Victorian England. History became the powerful mouthpiece of a class which had embedded itself not just in the economic and political institutions of industry and government but which successfully defined cultural expression and expectation. The irony of the separation of the three historical disciplines was that their values and beliefs remained largely consistent. The ideological armoury of religion and nationalism was not the exclusive province of either amateur or professional, but one shared alike by them all.

The intrusion of religious views into historical studies was commonplace in this period. Its intention was to stress the Christian principles of conservatism and gratitude.[39] The relation of religion to the nationalism common to historical texts was particularly important. Imperial aggrandisement was frequently interpreted as the peculiar gift of the English; it encouraged a genteel xenophobia as well as lending glory to the colonial ventures of the day. History was the tangible manifestation of loyalty and of pride. 'The grandiose development of historical studies in nineteenth century Europe became related to the alliance of history with the dominant and victorious forces of nationalism and liberalism.'[40] Behind the trumpeting of English glories – past, present and indeed future – lay the close relationship subsisting between historians and the political establishment. Antiquarianism, too, with its middle-class image of

[39] B. S. Pulgram, 'The Myth of the Anglo-Saxon in Nineteenth Century England' (unpublished PhD thesis, Radcliffe College, M. I. T., 1953) p. 415; see too Chapter 4.
[40] F. Gilbert, 'The Professionalisation of History in the Nineteenth Century', in J. Higham, L. Krieger and F. Gilbert, *History* (Princeton, 1965) pp. 320–39 (pp. 322–3).

pious respectability was ideologically at one with the power structures operating in Victorian Britain. Even the rebel archaeology, tarred with the brush of unbelief, was essentially in harmony with Victorian perceptions of moral and political government. Radical interpretations of history were in circulation but their currency was far more restricted than the middle-class preoccupations of mainstream historical thinking which successfully stormed the worlds of literature, poetry, visual art and architecture.

History offered the Victorians not merely the chance to revel in images of their own past but to interpret their own age in terms of that past, to regard themselves as the natural and rightful heirs to long and fine traditions which they sought to uphold and sustain. History was not the servant but the master of a powerful ideology, based on exploiting the reconstruction of tradition and change.

No history is worth preserving which does not at once illustrate the progress of a race, or a permanent influence [. . .] History which does not [. . .] inquire how any contemporaneous set of facts can be pressed into the interpretation is a mere disordered and imperfect discovery.[41]

As political considerations shifted, so too did historical analysis and preoccupations.[42]

History is a continuous process of reconsideration and reconstruction. Contemporary historiographical works which assert that modern scholarship can be said to have started with Tout, Round *et al.*, or with any other group of historians, or with the coming of the subject to the universities, are built on a false assumption. The separation of the three historical disciplines, the introduction of the *English Historical Review*, the methodological revolution of Pitt Rivers – all these can be interpreted severally, either as the end or the beginning of an era. They represent both, in being a culmination of the changes to which this study has been devoted and also a stepping stone to the subsequent phenomena we now deem 'historical'.

[41] Rogers, *loc. cit.* p. 2.
[42] A good example is the changing attitude of British historians to the French Revolution over the course of the nineteenth century. A survey of their attitudes is provided by Hedva Ben Israel in *English Historians on the French Revolution* (Cambridge, 1968).

Appendix I

Collective biography used as a means of determining the social location or locations of the sample is a technique which owes much to the methods of the history of science. Its use poses a series of important methodological questions concerned with the implicit problem of how to define those included within the sample, and the criteria which are thus employed to determine inclusion, and following on from that the question of how one ensures that the resulting data set is in any sense effectively representative.

This instance of prosopographical research is, however, not intended to stand trial as a piece of statistical evidence. It would be impossible to compile a complete list of every published antiquarian or collector in nineteenth-century England, or indeed to find relevant biographical information on all such individuals. Any form of statistical sampling would thus be open to massive, if unintentional, bias and error. And as Macfarlane has noted for groups of under 800, it is 'difficult to assemble meaningful statistics.' *op. cit.* p. 35. This sample covers 201 persons, all of whom fulfil at least two of the six criteria listed below to earn inclusion.

A. Teacher, lecturer, professor or examiner in modern history or archaeology.
B. Employed in record or archive work (for instance, at the Public Record Office, by the Historical Manuscripts Commission or the earlier Record Commissions).
C. Employed in work on antiquities (for instance, museum work, excavation etc.,)
D. Publishing in the fields of modern history, antiquarianism or archaeology.
E. Active membership of archaeological, historical and antiquarian societies.
F. Significant collector of manuscripts, antiquities and the like.

This seemed a wide enough range of activities to embrace the majority of those who made a contemporary impact. There is, of course, a danger that some will have escaped attention but the breadth of activities thus included does minimise that problem. And as authoritative a voice as Roderick Floud has in any case suggested that 'in particular cases it may be possible to produce approximate answers by methods that violate statistical theory' as long as the assumptions necessary in such a procedure are made explicit. (*Quantitative Methods for Historians*, (2nd edition, London, 1979) p. 189.) These assumptions are categorised in the delineation of the six areas considered relevant within the historical disciplines.

It is instructive, perhaps, to compare the criteria which thus structured the characteristics of these three historical communities with those which Shapin and Thackray suggested as tentatively definitive for the British scientific community in the period 1700–1900. They devised three categories for inclusion: (i) those with publications in science, (ii) those active in scientific societies and institutions or who taught and disseminated scientific knowledge and (iii) 'a large mixed bag of cultivators of science who patronized, applied or disseminated scientific knowledge and principles, but who themselves neither published science, taught science, nor actively associated themselves with scientifically-oriented institutions'. (S. Shapin & A. Thackray, 'Prosopography as a Research Tool in History of Science: The British Scientific Community 1700–1900', *History of Science* 12 (1974) 1–28 (pp. 12–13).

Table 1: *Percentage totals showing social and intellectual commitments of active archaeologists, historians and antiquarians, 1838–86.*

	Archaeologists	Historians	Antiquarians	Museum Employees	Total
Anglican	50%	85.4%	55.8%	54.8%	61.5%
Oxford/ Cambridge	31%	83.3%	30.5%	31%	44%
F.S.A.	31%	16.7%	54.8%	40.5%	35.8%
Active in archaeol./hist. socs.	56%	23%	49.5%	50%	44.7%
Clerics or ordained	18.8%	23%	21%	14.3%	19.3%

Appendix II: English printing clubs of the 1830s and 1840s

listed alphabetically

(1) Successful clubs

Aelfric Society 1842–8. Publication of Anglo-Saxon and other literary monuments, civil and ecclesiastical. Named after the author of *The Homilies of Aelfric*, their first publication.

Anglia Christiana Society, 1846–8. Lives, letters and documents of early ecclesiastical history.

Arundel Society, 1849. For promoting the knowledge of art by copying and publishing important works of ancient masters. Named after Thomas Howard, earl of Arundel in the reigns of James and Charles I – the father of 'vertu' in England.

Berkshire Ashmolean Society, 1840–2. Regional publications. Named after the antiquary Elias Ashmole.

Camden Society, 1838. Amalgamated with the Royal Historical Society, 1897. Named after William Camden, author of *Britannia*.

Caxton Society, 1845–54. Memoirs and Chronicles of the Middle Ages. Named after William Caxton.

Chetham Society, 1843. Remains Historical and Literary connected with the Palatine Counties of Lancaster and Chester. Named after the philanthropist Humphrey Chetham.

Ecclesiastical History Society, 1846–54.

English Historical Society, 1836–56. Medieval chronicles.

Granger Society, 1841. For the publication of ancient portraits and family pictures.

Hakluyt Society, 1846. Discovery, voyages, travels. Named after Richard Hakluyt.

Hanserd Knollys Society, 1845–51. Works of early English and other Baptist writers.

Historical Society of Science, 1840–1.

Lincolnshire Topographical Society, 1841. Regional publications.

Motett Society, 1840. Merged with Ecclesiological Society, 1852. Plan for reprinting early Church music.

Musical Antiquarian Society, 1840. To print scarce and valuable musical works which at present exist only in manuscript.

Parker Society, 1840–53. Works connected with early English Reformed Church. Named after Archbishop Matthew Parker.

Percy Society, 1840–52. Early English ballads and popular literature. Named after Thomas Percy, author of *Reliques of Ancient English Poetry*.

Ray Society, 1844. Early works of natural history.

Society for the Publication of Oriental Texts, 1840.

Surtees Society, 1834. Regional publications – North East England and the Border Country. Named after local historian Robert Surtees.

Sydenham Society, 1843. Early medical literature. Refounded 1858 as New Sydenham Society. Named after Thomas Sydenham, M.D. (1624–89) – the 'English Hippocrates'.

Wycliffe Society, 1843. For the publication of a series of writings of early Puritan and Non-Conformist writers. Named after the English martyr, John Wyclif.

(2) Unsuccessful clubs

Cabot Society, 1845. Maritime history. Named after Sebastian Cabot.

Columbus Society, 1845. Taken over by the Hakluyt Society. Named after Christopher Columbus.

Essex Morant Society, 1841. Regional publications. Named after Essex historian, Morant.

Leland Society, 1840. For the promotion of British topography, genealogy and biography.

Society for the Publication of Collections from the Public Records, 1840.

Wiltshire Topographical Society, 1839. Regional publications.

Appendix III: Architectural societies

listed alphabetically

(1) Exclusively architectural societies

Bristol and West of England Heraldic and Architectural Society, 1841.
Cambridge Camden Society, 1839 (from 1846, Ecclesiological Society).
Durham Architectural Society, 1841.
Exeter Architectural Society, 1841.
Lichfield Society for the Encouragement of Ecclesiastical Architecture, 1841.
Northampton, Architectural Society of the Archdeaconry of, 1844.
Oxford Society for Promoting the Study of Gothic Architecture, 1839.
St Paul's Ecclesiological Society, 1879.
West Norfolk Architectural Society (date of foundation unknown).
Wykeham Brotherhood, 1846. (N.B. A Roman Catholic body.)
Yorkshire Architectural Society, 1842.

(2) Architectural and archaeological societies

Bedford Architectural and Archaeological Society, 1847.
Berkshire Archaeological and Architectural Society, 1871.
Buckinghamshire Architectural and Archaeological Society, 1847.
Chester Architectural, Archaeological and Historical Society for the County, City and Neighbourhood of, 1849.
Durham and Northumberland, Architectural and Archaeological Society of, 1861.
Leicestershire Architectural and Archaeological Society, 1855.
Lincoln and Lincolnshire Architectural Society, 1844. (title as above until 1848; then Lincolnshire Architectural Society until 1852; then Lincoln Diocesan Architectural Society until 1882; then Lincolnshire and Nottinghamshire Architectural and Archaeological Society until 1903.)
Liverpool Architectural and Archaeological Society, 1848 (became exclusively architectural, 1876.)
St Albans Architectural and Archaeological Society, 1845.
Sheffield Architectural and Archaeological Society, 1868.
Worcestershire Diocesan Architectural Society, 1854 (added in archaeology, 1876).

Appendix IV: Complete list of county and local societies to 1886

listed alphabetically

Bath Natural History and Antiquarian Field Club, 1868
Bedfordshire Architectural and Archaeological Society, 1847
Berkshire Archaeological and Architectural Society, 1871
Birmingham Archaeological Society, 1870
Birmingham Historical Society, 1881
Birmingham and Midland Institute, 1867
Bradford Historical and Antiquarian Society, 1876
Bristol and Gloucestershire Archaeological Society, 1876
Buckinghamshire Architectural and Archaeological Society, 1847
Burton-on-Trent Natural History and Archaeological Society, 1876
Cambridge Antiquarian Society, 1841
Chester, Architectural, Archaeological and Historic Society of, 1849
Clifton Antiquarian Club, 1884
Cumberland and Westmorland Antiquarian and Archaeological Society, 1866
Derbyshire Archaeological and Natural History Society, 1878
Dorset Natural History and Antiquarian Field Club, 1875
Durham and Northumberland, Architectural and Archaeological Society of, 1861
Eastbourne Natural History and Archaeological Society, 1867
Essex Archaeological Society, 1852
Glastonbury Antiquarian Society, 1886
Hampshire Field Club and Archaeological Society, 1885
Historic Society of Lancashire and Cheshire, 1848
Huddersfield Naturalist, Photographic and Antiquarian Society, 1850
Kent Archaeological Society, 1858
Lancashire and Cheshire Antiquarian Society, 1883
Leicestershire Architectural and Archaeological Society, 1855
Lewisham Antiquarian Society, 1886
Lincoln and Lincolnshire Antiquarian Society, 1844
Liverpool Architectural and Archaeological Society, 1848
London and Middlesex Archaeological Society, 1855
Louth Naturalists' Antiquarian and Literary Society, 1884
Maidstone Scientific and Antiquarian Society, 1834
Manx Society, 1859
Norfolk and Norwich Archaeological Society, 1846
Oxford Society for Promoting the Study of Gothic Architecture: merged in 1839 with
    University of Oxford Genealogical and Heraldic Society, becoming Oxford Architec-
    tural Society in 1848 and Oxford Architectural and Historic Society in 1860

Oxfordshire Archaeological Society, 1853 (first founded as North Oxfordshire Archaeological Society)

Oxford Historical Society, 1884

Penzance Natural History and Antiquarian Society, 1839

Peterborough Museum Society, 1871

St Albans Architectural and Archaeological Society, 1845

Scarborough Philosophical and Archaeological Society, 1861

Sheffield Architectural and Archaeological Society, 1868

Shropshire and North Wales Natural History and Antiquarian Society, 1835

Shropshire Archaeological and Natural History Society, 1877
  (The above two societies merged in 1877)

Somersetshire Archaeological and Natural History Society, 1849

Suffolk Archaeological Association, 1846

Suffolk Institute of Natural History and Archaeology, 1848 (1848–53: Bury and West Suffolk Archaeological Institute; 1854–63: Suffolk Institute of Archaeology, Statistics and Natural History; 1864, as above)

Surrey Archaeological Society, 1854

Sussex Archaeological Society, 1846

Warwickshire Naturalists and Archaeologists' Field Club, 1864

Warwickshire Natural History and Archaeological Society, 1836

Wells Natural History and Archaeology Society, 1885

William Salt Archaeological Society, 1879 (from 1936, Staffordshire Record Society)

Wiltshire Archaeological and Natural History Society, 1853

Worcestershire Archaeological Society, 1854

Yorkshire Archaeological Society, 1863 (1863–70: Huddersfield Archaeological and Topographical Association; 1870–93: Yorkshire Archaeological and Topographical Association; 1893, as above)

Appendix V: Clerical membership of local societies expressed as percentages of total membership for the year given

Date in brackets is date of earliest membership list available.

Over 50% (of total membership)
Northamptonshire	1844	77%
Buckinghamshire	1854	65%
Lincolnshire	1850	64%
Oxfordshire	1855	52.5%

40–49%
Worcestershire	1854	47%
Durham/Northumberland	1868	42%
Suffolk	1849	42%

30–39%
St Albans	1845	37%
Bedfordshire	1849	36%
Essex	1852	33%
Chester	1849	32.5%
Wiltshire	1853	31.5%
Norfolk	1849	31%
Bath	1868	30.5%

20–29%
Sussex	1846	29%
Somerset	1849	26.5%
Dorset	1885	26%
Berkshire	1888	25%
Shropshire	1878	25%
Lancashire/Cheshire	1848	24%
Kent	1858	23%
Leicestershire	1857	23%
Derbyshire	1879	22%

10–19%
Hampshire	1887	18%
Bristol/Gloucestershire	1878	16%
Cumberland/Westmorland	1869	14.5%
Shropshire	1835	14.5%

Staffordshire	1880	14%
Yorkshire	1871	14%
Wiltshire	1839	11%
Surrey	1854	10.5%

Under 10%

London/Middlesex	1855	7%

Bibliography

A. MANUSCRIPT SOURCES

Birmingham Central Library, Local Studies Department: Birmingham Archaeological Society, Minute Book Volume I

Bristol Record Office: Bristol and Gloucestershire Archaeological Society, Minutes of Council meetings, 1876–81; 1881–4; 1884–8

Haddon Library, University of Cambridge: Cambridge Antiquarian Society, Minute Book I; Letter Book I

Seeley Library, Faculty of History, University of Cambridge: Minutes of the Historical Board of the University of Cambridge, 1875–90

Durham Cathedral, Dean and Chapter Library: Surtees Society Minutes 1834–86; correspondence files

Liverpool Record Office: Historic Society of Lancashire and Cheshire Minute Books from 1847

British Museum, London:
    Diaries of Henry Ellis, Add. MSS. 36653, 36658, 36659
    Correspondence of Thomas Hugo, Add. MSS. 30296–30298
    Correspondence of Joseph Hunter, Add. MSS. 24864–24875
    Diary of Joseph Hunter, Add. MS. 33601
    Papers of A. H. Layard, Add. MSS. 38942–3; 38946
    Macmillan Archives (E. A. Freeman) Add. MS. 55049
    Letters of Thomas Wright to Joseph Mayer, Add. MSS. 33346–7.

London Museum, Barbican Centre: London and Middlesex Archaeological Society Minutes of General, Council and monthly evening meetings; records of attendance

Public Record Office, Kew:
    Civil Service Commission, CSC 2; 6; 10
    Chronicles and Memorials, PRO 37
    Foreign Office, FO 82.234
    Historical Manuscripts Commission, HMC 1
    Public Record Office, PRO 1; 2; 4; 5; 6; 8; 9; 35; 36;
    Treasury, T1 5968A/19558

Royal Historical Society, University College London:
    Camden Society Minute Books, 1838–85; Secretary's Correspondence, C3/1; miscellanea, C4
    Royal Historical Society Minute Books 1868–86; Treasurer's Correspondence, H3/1 1–2
    Prothero Papers, Correspondence 1866–99, PP 2/1

Society of Antiquaries of London:
    Manuscript material relating to the society, unindexed
    Papers of Albert Way, MS. 700

Diary of Thomas Crofton Croker, 1852, MS 751
Papers of Charles Roach Smith, MS 875.1
Society of Jesus, Farm Street, London: Joseph Stevenson Collection – AAAL/5–6; CB/5; CB/7
University College London:
College Correspondence
Notebook of James Yates
Manchester Central Library: Crossley Papers
Chetham's Library, Manchester: Journal of W. H. Black, Mun. A.2.111.
John Ryland's Library, Manchester: Diaries of Edward Peacock
Bodleian Library, Oxford:
University Archives – W.P. α/55/2; W.P. β/11/1; W.P. β/11/3; W.P. β/11/8; W.P. β/11/15; W.P. γ/7/1; N.W. 4/1/7; N.W. 17/3; N.E.P. A/12; Hyp./LB/XXVIII
MS. Top. Oxon. d. 358, Notebook of Edward Nares
Dep. d. 510; 518; 538; 589; 590, Papers of Oxford Architectural Society
MSS. Phillipps-Robinson b.123; c.476; c.484; d.137; d.141; d.160
MS. Eng. misc. e. 148, Letters of William Stubbs to Edward Freeman
MS. Top. Oxon. d.717; e.526, Vaughan Collection
G.A. Oxon. c.74 (178), Regius Professorship of Modern History 1858
MS. Eng. lett. d.74, Letters of Edward Freeman
Griffith Institute, Oxford: Journals of W. M. F. Petrie
Jesus College Oxford: Papers of J. R. Green, MSS. 198–202; 216; 218; 222; 231; letters of Edward Freeman to W. B. Dawkins, MSS. 192–3
Brett Centre, St Albans: St Albans Architectural and Archaeological Society Minute Books
Somerset Record Office: Somerset Archaeological and Natural History Society Correspondence, DD/SAS. C/2646. 1; 3; 4
Taunton Castle, Somerset: Somerset Archaeological and Natural History Society Committee Minute Book, 1878–95
Guildford Castle, Surrey: Surrey Archaeological Society Minute Books, SAS 2/1, 2/2, 8/3/2–4; members and visitors book, SAS 8/1
Warrington Reference Library: Diaries of William Beamont, MSS. 284–7; 293–4; 296–300; 701–3

B. PRINTED SOURCES

(1) Primary sources

Government Papers
Parliamentary Papers, House of Commons
1867–8 LV 425, Durham Records
1872 xxxvi 441
1875 xxiii 1, First and Second Reports of Civil Service Inquiry Commission
1878–9 xlviii 1, Estimates for Civil Service and Revenue Departments, 1880
1884 xlvii 157, Civil Services (Expenditure)
1902 lxxxiii 61, Return showing the total number of persons in the Established Civil Service of the State
1912–13 First, Second and Third Reports of the Royal Commission on Public Records

Periodicals
Antiquarian Magazine and Bibliographer
Antiquary
Archaeologia Cantiana
Archaeological Journal
Associated Architectural Societies Reports
Bedfordshire Architectural and Archaeological Society Notes
Bradford Antiquary
English Historical Review
Journal of the British Archaeological Association
Journal of the Architectural, Archaeological and Historic Society for Chester
Journal of the Derbyshire Archaeological and Natural History Society
The Reliquary
Sussex Archaeological Collections
Transactions of the Bristol and Gloucestershire Archaeological Society
Transactions of the Essex Archaeological Society
Transactions of the London and Middlesex Archaeological Society
Transactions of the Royal Historical Society
Transactions of the Shropshire Archaeological and Natural History Society
Wiltshire Archaeological and Natural History Magazine
Aelfric Society Prospectus (1842)
Akerman, J. Y., *Directions for the Preservation of English Antiquities, especially those of the
    first three periods* (London, 1851)
Anglia Christiana Society Prospectus (1846)
Arnold, Thomas, *An Inaugural Lecture on the Study of Modern History* (Oxford, 1841)
Arundel Society Prospectus (1846)
Babington, Churchill, *An Introductory Lecture on Archaeology* (Cambridge, 1865)
Bateman, Thomas, *Ten Years' Digging in Celtic and Saxon Grave Hills, in the Counties of
    Derby, Stafford and York from 1848 to 1858* (London, 1861)
Beesly, E.S., 'Mr Kingsley on the Study of History', *Westminster and Foreign Quarterly
    Review* (1861) 305–336
Berkshire Ashmolean Society Prospectus (1840)
Birch, Samuel, *Inaugural Discourse delivered in the section of General Antiquities at the
    Annual Meeting of the Archaeological Institute* (London, 1866)
Brent, John, *Canterbury in the Olden Time. From the Municipal Archives and other Sources*
    (London, 1860)
British Museum Sales Catalogues:
  S-C.S. 477 (5) 3 February 1860, J. S. Brewer
  S-C.S. 507 (3) 19 December 1861, Joseph Hunter
  S-C.S. 513 (3) 12 May 1862, Francis Palgrave
  S-C.Sg. 116 (10) 30 March 1864, G. R. Corner
  S-C.S. 619 (3) 19 July 1869, Henry Ellis
  S-C. 960 (4) 27 April 1870, John Bruce
  S-C.S. 736 (1) 19 May 1876, Agnes Strickland
  S-C.S. 920 (8) 7 December 1886, H. H. Vaughan
  S-C.S. 1007 (4) 7 April 1891, C. R. Smith
Britton, John, *The Autobiography of John Britton, F.S.A.* (London, 1850)
Bruce, J. C., *The Roman Wall: A Historical, Topographical and Descriptive Account of the
    Barrier of the Lower Isthmus* (London/Newcastle, 1851)
Burrows, Montagu, *Is Educational Reform required in Oxford, And What?* (Oxford, 1859)

Pass and Class: An Oxford Guide Book through the courses of Literae Humaniores,
Mathematics, Natural Sciences and Law and Modern History (Oxford/London, 1860)
Inaugural Lecture of the Chichele Professor of Modern History (Oxford, 1862)
Antiquarianism and History. A Lecture delivered before the University of Oxford, 26 May
1884 (Oxford, 1885)

Burrows, S. M. (ed.)., *Autobiography of Montagu Burrows, Captain, R.N.* (London, 1908)

Cabot Society Prospectus (1845)

Cambridge Historical Register

Camden Society *Annual Reports, 1839–86*

Chetham Society Prospectus (1843)

Cramer, John A., *An Inaugural Lecture on the Study of Modern History* (Oxford, 1843)

Creasy, E. S., *The Spirit of Historical Study* (London, 1840)

Dales, Samuel, *An Essay on the Study of the History of England* (London, 1809)

Domesday Studies, being the papers read at the meeting of the Domesday Commemoration,
1886 (London, 1888)

Dunkin, A. J., *Prospectus for a New History of Kent* (n.d.)

Early English Text Society Prospectus (n.d.)

Essex Morant Society Prospectus (1841)

Evans, J., 'The Progress of Archaeology', *Archaeological Journal* xlviii (1891) 251–62

Ewald, A. C., *Our Public Records. A Brief Handbook to the National Archives* (London, 1873)

Ferguson, R. S., *A History of Cumberland* (London, 1890)

The Fourth School, unsigned broadsheet printed Oxford, n.d.

Freeman, E. A., *Thoughts on the Study of History, with reference to the proposed changes in the*
Public Examinations (Oxford/London, 1849)
'Historical Study at Oxford', *Bentley's Quarterly Review* i (1859) i, 282–300
History of Federal Government from the Foundation of the Achaian League to the disruption
of the United States (London, 1863)
The History of the Norman Conquest of England, its causes and results i (Oxford, 1867)
'Address to the Historical Section of the Annual Meeting of the Archaeological
Institute held at Cardiff, September 1871', *Archaeological Journal* xxviii (1871)
177–95
The Office of the Historical Professor (Oxford, 1884)

Granger Society Prospectus (1841)

Green, J. R., 'Professor Stubbs' Inaugural Lecture', *Saturday Review* (1867) 278–80
A Short History of the English People (London, 1874)

Hakluyt Society Prospectus (1845)

Hardwick, Charles, *History of the Borough of Preston and its Environs, in the County of*
Lancaster (Preston/London, 1857)

Hardy, Thomas Duffus, *Memoirs of the Rt. Hon. Henry Lord Langdale* (London, 1852)

Hartshorne, C. H., *An Endeavour to classify the Sepulchral Remains in Northamptonshire, or*
A Discourse on Funeral Monuments in that County (Cambridge, 1840)

Historical Register of the University of Oxford (Oxford, 1900)

Hodgkin, T., 'Opening Address of the Historical Section at the meeting of the
Archaeological Institute at Edinburgh, 12 August 1891', *Archaeological Journal*
xlviii (1891) 263–73

Hogarth, D. G. (ed.) *Authority and Archaeology. Sacred and Profane. Essays on the relation of*
monuments to biblical and classical literature (London, 1899)
Accidents of an Antiquary's Life (London, 1910)

Howorth, H., 'Old and New Methods in Writing History', *Archaeological Journal* lv
(1898) 122–44

Hugo, Thomas, 'Introductory Address', *Transactions of the London and Middlesex Archaeological Society* I (1856)

Hume, A., *The Learned Societies and Printing Clubs of the United Kingdom* (London, 1847)

[Humphreys, H. N.], *Stories by an Archaeologist and his Friends* (London, 1856)

Hunter, Joseph, *The History and Topography of Ketteringham in the County of Norfolk, the seat of Sir J. P. Boileau, Bart.*, (Norwich, 1851)

Kemble, J. M., 'The English Historical Society', *British and Foreign Review* VII (1838) xiii, 167–92

 The Saxons in England. A History of the English Commonwealth till the period of the Norman Conquest (London, 1849)

 Horae Ferales; or Studies in the Archaeology of the Northern Nations (London, 1863)

Kingsley, Charles, 'The Limits of Exact Science as applied to History', *The Roman and the Teuton: A Series of Lectures delivered before the University of Cambridge* (Cambridge/ London, 1864)

Kirwan, R., 'The Prehistoric Archaeology of East Devon', *Archaeological Journal* XXIX (1872) 34–44

Layard, A. H., *Nineveh and Its Remains: With an Account of a Visit to the Chaldaean Christians of Kurdistan, and Yezidis, or Devil Worshippers; and an Enquiry into the Manners and Acts of the Ancient Assyrians* (London, 1849)

Leland Society Prospectus (1840)

Lingard, John, *A History of England* I (6th edition, London, 1854)

Loftus, W. K., *Travels and Researches in Chaldaea and Susiana: with an account of the excavations at Warka, the 'Erech' of Nimrod and Shush, "Shushan the Palace" of Esther, in 1849–52* (London, 1857)

Luards, H. R., *Suggestions on the Establishment of a Historical Tripos* (Cambridge, 1866)

Lubbock, John, 'Address delivered to the section of Primeval Antiquities at the London meeting of the Archaeological Institute, July 1866', *Archaeological Journal* XXIII (1866) 190–211

Malkin, B. H., *An Introductory Lecture on History* (London, 1830)

Marsden, J. H., *Two Introductory Lectures Upon Archaeology* (Cambridge, 1852)

 Inaugural Lecture delivered to the members of the Essex Archaeological Society on its formation, 14 December 1852 (Colchester, 1852)

Musical Antiquarian Society Prospectus (1840)

Nares, Edward, *Syllabus of a course of lectures in Modern History* (London, 1816)

Newton, Charles, 'On the Study of Archaeology', *Archaeological Journal* VIII (1851) 1–26

Nicolas, N. H., *Notitia Historica* (London, 1824)

 Observations on the State of Historical Literature (London, 1830)

Oxford University Commission: *Report of Commissioners appointed to inquire into the State, Discipline, Studies and Revenues of the University and Colleges of Oxford* (1852)

Palgrave, Francis, *Truths and Fictions of the Middle Ages: The Merchant and the Friar* (London, 1837)

Peacock, Edward, *English Church Furniture, Ornaments and Decorations at the period of the Reformation. As Exhibited in a List of Goods destroyed in certain Lincolnshire churches, A.D. 1566* (London, 1866)

Petrie, W. M. F., *Inductive Metrology: or the recovery of ancient measures from the monuments* (London, 1877)

 The Pyramids and Temples of Gizeh (London, 1883)

 Seventy Years in Archaeology (London, 1931)

Pettigrew, T. J., 'On the Study of Archaeology, and the Objects of the British Archaeological Association', *Journal of the British Archaeological Association* VI

(1851) 163–77

Planché, J. R., *The Recollections and Reflections of J. R. Planché: A Professional Autobiography* (London, 1872)

Public Record Office, *Reports of Deputy Keepers* (1840 on)

Quaritch, Bernard, *Account of the Great Learned Societies and Associations of the Chief Printing Clubs of Great Britain and Ireland* (London, 1886)

Record Commission, *Annual Reports* (1800–36):
  Report of Select Committee appointed to inquire into the management and Affairs of the Record Commission and the Present State of the Records of the United Kingdom, 11 July 1836

Rhind, A. H., *British Archaeology: Its Progress and Demands* (London, 1858)

Rivers, A. H. L. F. Pitt, *Excavations in Cranborne Chase* I–IV (London, 1887–98)
  'Address', *Archaeological Journal* XLI (1884) 58–78; XLIV (1887) 261–77

Rogers, Charles, *The Serpent's Track: A Narrative of Twenty-Two Years Persecution* (London, 1880)
  Parting Words to the Members of the Royal Historical Society, in a letter to the President, the Rt. Hon. Lord Aberdare (London, 1881)

Rogers, J. E. Thorold, *The Economic Interpretation of History* (London, 1888)

Rye, Walter, *Records and Record Searching: A Guide to the Genealogist and Topographer* (London, 1888)

Seeley, J. R., 'The Teaching of Politics: an inaugural lecture delivered at Cambridge', *Lectures and Essays* (London, 1870)
  'Inaugural Address', *Transactions of Birmingham Historical Society* I (London, 1880–1)
  'The Teaching of History', *Health Exhibition Literature XV: Conference on Education Section C: Organisation of University Education* (London, 1884) 34–43

Smart, W., 'The Cerne Giant', *Journal of the British Archaeological Association* XXVIII (1872) 65–70

Smith, C. R., *The Antiquities of Richborough, Reculver and Lymne in Kent* (London, 1850)
  Illustrations of Roman London (London, 1859)
  Retrospections I–III (London, 1883–91)

Smith, Goldwin, *An Inaugural Lecture* (2nd edition, Oxford/London, 1864)
  The Study of History. Two Lectures (Oxford/London, 1861)
  The Reorganisation of the University of Oxford (Oxford, 1868)

Society for the Publication of Collections from the Public Records Prospectus (1840)

Stubbs, William, *An Address delivered by way of inaugural lecture* (Oxford, 1867)
  Two Lectures on the Present State and Prospects of Historical Study (not published, 1876)
  Last Statutory Public Lecture (London, 1884)

Thompson, James, 'The Objects and Advantages of Architectural and Archaeological Societies', *Associated Architectural Societies Reports* X (1869–70) 153–9

Thorpe, Benjamin, *Northern Mythology, comprising the principal popular traditions and superstitions of Scandinavia, North Germany and the Netherlands. Compiled from original and other sources* I (London, 1851)

University College London, examination papers in history 1853–4; 1880–1

Vaughan, H. H., *Two General Lectures on Modern History* (Oxford/London, 1849)

Vaughan, Robert, *On the Study of General History, an Introductory Lecture* (London, 1834)

Ward, A. W., *Suggestions towards the establishment of a History Tripos* (Cambridge, 1872)

Warne, Charles, *Ancient Dorset. The Celtic, Roman, Saxon and Danish Antiquities of the County including the early coinage* (Bournemouth, 1872)

Willson, E. J., 'Opening Address', *Lincolnshire Topographical Society* (1843)

Wood, J. T., *Discoveries at Ephesus including the Site and Remains of the Great Temple of*

Diana (London, 1877)

Wright, Thomas, *Popular Treatises on Science written during the Middle Ages in Anglo-Saxon, Anglo-Norman and English* (London, 1841)

   The Archaeological Album; or Museum of National Antiquities (London, 1845)

   'Antiquarianism in England', *Edinburgh Review* LXXXVI (1847) CXXIV, 307–28

   Wanderings of an Antiquary, chiefly upon the traces of the Romans in Britain (London, 1854)

   On the Early History of Leeds in Yorkshire, and on some questions of prehistoric archaeology agitated at the present time (Leeds, 1864)

   The Celt, the Roman and the Saxon. A History of the Early Inhabitants of Britain, down to the conversion of the Anglo-Saxons to Christianity (3rd edition, London, 1875)

Wycliffe Society Prospectus (1843)

Wykeham Brotherhood Prospectus (1846)

(2) Secondary sources

Aarsleff, Hans, *The Study of Language in England, 1780–1860* (Princeton, 1967)

Allen, D. E., *The Naturalist in Britain: A Social History* (Harmondsworth, 1978)

Altick, Richard D., 'The Social Origins, Education and Occupations of 1100 British Writers, 1800–1935', *Bulletin of the New York Public Library* 66 (1962) 6, 389–404

Anderson, Olive, 'The Political Uses of History in mid-Nineteenth Century England', *Past and Present* 36 (1967) 87–105

Annan, Noel, 'The Intellectual Aristocracy', in ed., J. H. Plumb, *Studies in Social History. A Tribute to G. M. Trevelyan* (London, 1955) 243–87

Armytage, W. H. G., *Civic Universities: Aspects of a British Tradition* (London, 1955)

Ash, Marinell, *The Strange Death of Scottish History* (Edinburgh, 1980)

Auchmuty, J. J., *Lecky, A Biographical and Critical Essay* (Dublin, 1945)

Ausubel, H. H., J. B. Brebner & E. M. Hunt (eds.), *Some Modern Historians of Britain: Essays in Honour of R. L. Schuyler* (New York, 1951)

Bann, S., *The Clothing of Clio. A Study of the representation of history in nineteenth century Britain and France* (Cambridge, 1984)

Benas, B. B. B., 'A Centenary Retrospect of the Historic Society of Lancashire and Cheshire', *Transactions of the Historic Society of Lancashire and Cheshire*, supplement to vol. 100 (1948)

Benton, G. M., 'The Early History of the Society and of the Colchester and Essex Museum', *Transactions of the Essex Archaeological Society* n.s. XVIII (1928) 276–89

Berman, M., '"Hegemony" and the Amateur Tradition in British Science', *Journal of Social History* 8 (1975) 30–50

Bill, E. G. W., *University Reform in Nineteenth Century Oxford: A Study of Henry Halford Vaughan, 1811–85* (Oxford, 1973)

Blaas, P. B. M., *Continuity and Anachronism: Parliamentary and Constitutional Development in Whig historiography and in the Anti-Whig reaction between 1890 and 1930* (The Hague, 1978)

Blatchly, J., *The Topographers of Suffolk. Brief Biographies and Specimens of the Hands of Selected Suffolk Antiquaries* (Suffolk, 1976)

Bowen, John, *A Brief Memoir of the life and character of William Baker, F.G.S.* (Taunton, 1854)

Brady, G., 'Naturalists' Field Clubs: their Objects and Organisation', *Natural History Transactions of Northumberland and Durham* (1867) 107–14

Bratchel, M. E., *Edward Augustus Freeman and the Victorian Interpretation of the Norman Conquest* (Ilfracombe, 1969)

Brentano, R., 'The Sound of Stubbs', *Journal of British Studies* vi (1967) 2, 1–14

Briggs, Asa, *Saxons, Normans and Victorians* (Sussex, 1966)

Burrow, J. W., *Evolution and Society. A Study in Victorian Social Theory* (Cambridge, 1966)
  A Liberal Descent: Victorian Historians and the English Past (Cambridge, 1981)

Butler, K. T. B., 'A "Petty" Professor of Modern History: William Smyth, 1765–1841', *Cambridge Historical Journal* ix (1948) 2, 217–38

Butterfield, Herbert, 'Delays and Paradoxes in the Development of Historiography', in K. Bourne and D. C. Watt (eds.), *Studies in International History: Essays presented to W. Norton Medlicott* (London, 1967) 1–15
  'Some Trends in Scholarship 1868–1968, in the Field of Modern History', *Transactions of the Royal Historical Society* 5th series xix (1969) 159–84

Bynum, W. F., Time's Noblest Offspring: The Problem of Man in the British Natural Historical Sciences, 1800–63 (unpublished PhD thesis, University of Cambridge, 1974)

Cam, Helen, 'Stubbs Seventy Years After', *Cambridge Historical Journal* ix (1948) 129–47

Campbell, G. A., *The Civil Service in Britain* (2nd edition, London, 1965)

Cantwell, John, 'The 1838 Public Record Office Act and its aftermath: a new perspective', *Journal of the Society of Archivists* 7 (1984) 5

Carbonell, C. O., *Histoire et historiens: une mutation idéologique des historiens français, 1865–85* (Toulouse, 1976)

Chadwick, Owen, 'Charles Kingsley at Cambridge', *Historical Journal* xviii (1975) 2, 303–25
  Catholicism and History: The Opening of the Vatican Archives (Oxford, 1976)

Chandler, Alice, *A Dream of Order. The Medieval Ideal in Nineteenth Century English Literature* (London, 1971)

Chapman, R. A., *The Higher Civil Service in Britain* (London, 1970)

Chapman R. A. & J. R. Greenaway, *The Dynamics of Administrative Reform* (London, 1980)

Charlton, H. B., *Portrait of a University, 1851–1951* (Manchester, 1951)

Chatwin, P. B., *Incidents in the life of Matthew Holbeche Bloxam* (Oxford, 1959)

Clark, E. K., *The History of One Hundred Years of the Life of the Leeds Philosophical and Literary Society* (Leeds, 1924)

Clark, G. K., 'The Romantic Element – 1830 to 1850', in J. H. Plumb (ed.), *Studies in Social History. A Tribute to G. M. Trevelyan* (London, 1955) 211–39
  'A Hundred Years of the Teaching of History at Cambridge, 1873–1973', *Historical Journal* xvi (1973) 3, 535–53

Clark, Grahame, 'Archaeology and the State', *Antiquity* viii (1934) 32, 414–28
  Archaeology and Society. Reconstructing the Prehistoric Past (London, 1968)

Cockshut, A. O. J., *Truth to Life: The Art of Biography in the Nineteenth Century* (London, 1974)

Creighton, L., *Life and Letters of Mandell Creighton by his wife* (London, 1904)

Cronne, H. A., 'Edward Augustus Freeman, 1823–92', *History* xxviii (1943) 78–92

Cunnington, B. H., 'The Origin and History of the Wiltshire Archaeology and Natural History Society', *Wiltshire Archaeological and Natural History Magazine* xlv (1930) clii, 1–9

Daniel, G. E., *A Hundred Years of Archaeology* (London, 1950)
  The Idea of Prehistory (London, 1962)

The Origins and Growth of Archaeology (Harmondsworth, 1967)

'From Worsaae to Child: The Models of Prehistory', *Proceedings of the Prehistoric Society* xxxvii (1971) ii, 140–53

Cambridge and the Back-Looking Curiosity (Cambridge, 1976)

A Short History of Archaeology (London, 1981)

David, Joseph Ben-, *The Scientist's Rôle in Society. A Comparative Study* (New Jersey, 1971)

Dawson, W. R., *Memoir of Thomas Joseph Pettigrew, F.R.C.S., F.R.S., F.S.A., 1791–1865* (New York, 1931)

Delheim, C. J., Medievalism in Modernity: the Victorians' Encounter with their own Inheritance (unpublished PhD thesis, Yale University, 1979)

Dickins, Bruce, *J. M. Kemble and Old English Scholarship* (London, 1938)

Dorson, R. M., *The British Folklorists. A History* (London, 1968)

Douglas, D., *The Norman Conquest and British Historians* (Glasgow, 1946)

Dow, L., 'A Short History of the Suffolk Institute of Archaeology and Natural History', *Proceedings of the Suffolk Institute of Archaeology* xxiv (1949) 129–43

Dunlop, W. R. Buchanan-, 'A Hundred Years 1854–1954. The Story of the Worcestershire Archaeological Society', *Transactions of the Worcestershire Archaeological Society* n.s. xxx (1953) 2–15

Dunn, John, 'The Identity of the History of Ideas', *Philosophy* 43 (1968) 164, 85–104

Dunn, W. H., *James Anthony Froude: A Biography* i: *1818–56* (Oxford, 1961), ii: *1857–94* (Oxford, 1963)

Dymond, D. P., *Archaeology and History. A Plea for Reconciliation* (London, 1974)

Ellegard, A., 'Darwin and the General Reader: The Reception of Darwin's Theory of Evolution in the British Periodical Press, 1859–72', *Göteborgs Universitets Arsskrift* lxiv (1958)

Ellis, R. H., 'The Historical Manuscripts Commission', *Journal of the Society of Archivists* ii (1962) 6, 233–42

'The Building of the Public Record Office', in A. E. J. Hollaender (ed.), *Essays in Memory of Sir Hilary Jenkinson* (London, 1962)

'The Royal Commission on Historical Manuscripts: a short history and explanation', in *Manuscripts and Men* (catalogue of the centenary exhibition of the Royal Commission on Historical Manuscripts, London, 1969)

Engel, A. J., From Clergyman to Don: The Rise of the Academic Profession in Nineteenth Century Oxford (unpublished PhD thesis, Princeton University, 1975)

Evans, Joan, *Time and Chance. The Story of Arthur Evans and his forebears* (London, 1943)

'The Royal Archaeological Institute: A Retrospect', *Archaeological Journal* cvi (1949) 1–11

A History of the Society of Antiquaries (Oxford, 1956)

Fawcett, J. (ed.), *The Future of the Past. Attitudes to Conservation 1174–1974* (London, 1976)

Finley, M. I., 'Myth, Memory and History', *History and Theory* iv (1964–5) 3, 281–302

Firth, C. H., 'Modern History in Oxford, 1724–1841', *English Historical Review* 32 (1917) 1–21

Modern History in Oxford, 1841–1918 (London, 1920)

Fleishman, A., *The English Historical Novel. Walter Scott to Virginia Woolf* (Baltimore, 1971)

Forbes, D., *The Liberal Anglican Idea of History* (Cambridge, 1952)

Foucault, M., *The Archaeology of Knowledge* (London, 1978)

Fowler, J. T., *Durham University: Earlier Foundations and Present Colleges* (London, 1904)

Fredericq, P., 'The Study of History in England and Scotland', *Johns Hopkins University Studies in Historical and Political Science* 5th series x (1887)

Galbraith, V. H., *An Introduction to the Use of the Public Records* (Oxford, 1934)
'Historical Research and the Preservation of the Past', *History* n.s. 22 (1937–8) 303–14

Galton, F., *English Men of Science: their nature and nurture* (London, 1874)

George, C. H., 'Puritanism as History and Historiography', *Past and Present* 41 (1968) 77–104

Gladden, E. N., *Civil Services of the United Kingdom, 1855–1970* (London, 1967)

Goddard, T. R., *History of the Natural History Society of Northumberland, Durham and Newcastle-upon-Tyne 1829–1919* (Newcastle, 1929)

Goldstein, Doris S., 'The Organisational Development of the British Historical Profession, 1884–1921', *Bulletin of the Institute of Historical Research* LV (1982) 132, 180–93
'The Professionalisation of History in the Late Nineteenth and Early Twentieth Centuries', *Storia della Storiografia* 1 (1983) 3–26

Gooch, G. P., *History and Historians in the Nineteenth Century* (London, 1919)

Goss, C. W. F., 'An Account of the London and Middlesex Archaeological Society 1855–1930', *Transactions of the London and Middlesex Archaeological Society* n.s. VI (1933) 405–35

Gras, N. S. B., 'The Rise and Development of Economic History', *Economic History Review* I (1927–8) 12–34

Gray, I., *Antiquaries of Gloucestershire and Bristol* (Bristol/Gloucester, 1981)

Haile, M. & Bonney, E., *Life and Letters of John Lingard* (London, n.d.)

Hale, H. B., *University College London, 1826–1926* (London, 1929)

Halsey, A. H. & Trow, M. A., *The British Academics* (London, 1971)

Hardy, B. Cozens-, 'The Early Days of the Society', *Norfolk Archaeology* XXIX (1946) 1–7

Hardy, Thomas, 'A Tryst at an Ancient Earthwork', in *Collected Short Stories* (London, 1928)

Harrison, R., 'E. S. Beesly and Karl Marx', *International Review of Social History* IV (1959) 1 & 2, 1–58; 208–38

Haverfield, F., 'The Study of Roman Britain: A Retrospect', in *The Roman Occupation of Britain* (Oxford, 1924)

Hearnshaw, F. J. C., *The Centenary History of King's College London, 1828–1928* (London, 1929)

Henderson, Heather, 'Carlyle and the Book Clubs: A New Approach to Publishing', *Publishing History* VI (1979) 37–62

Heyck, T. W., *The Transformation of Intellectual Life in Victorian England* (London, 1982)

Higham, J., Krieger, L., & Gilbert, F., *History* (Princeton, 1965)

Hill, Christopher, 'The Norman Yoke', in *Puritanism and Revolution: Studies in the Interpretation of the English Revolution of the Seventeenth Century* (London, 1958)

Hobley, B., 'Charles Roach Smith (1807–90); Pioneer Rescue Archaeologist', *The London Archaeologist* 2 (1975) 13, 328–33

Hudson, K., *A Social History of Archaeology. The British Experience* (London, 1981)

Hughes, Thomas, *The Scouring of the White Horse; or the Long Vacation Ramble of a London Clerk* (Cambridge, 1859)

Humphries, R. A., *The Royal Historical Society 1868–1968* (London, 1968)

Hutton, W. H., *Letters of William Stubbs, Bishop of Oxford 1825–1901* (London, 1904)

Iggers, G. G., *New Directions in European Historiography* (Connecticut, 1975)

Inkster, I. & Morrell, J., *Metropolis and Province. Science in British Culture, 1780–1850* (London, 1983)

Jackson, J. A. (ed.), *Professions and Professionalisation* (Cambridge, 1970)

Jackson, J. W., 'The Genesis and Progress of the Lancashire and Cheshire Antiquarian Society', *Transactions of the Lancashire and Cheshire Antiquarian Society* XLIX (1933) 104–12

James, T. G. H., *Excavating in Egypt. The Egypt Exploration Society 1882–1982* (London, 1982)

Jann, Rosemary, The Art of History in Nineteenth Century England: Studies in Victorian Historiography (unpublished PhD thesis, Northwestern University, 1975)
    'From Amateur to Professional: The Case of the Oxbridge Historians', *Journal of British Studies* XXII (1983) 2, 122–47

Jeaffreson, J. C., *A Book of Recollections* (London, 1894)

Jenkyns, R., *The Victorians and Ancient Greece* (Oxford, 1980)

Jessup, F. W., 'The Origin and First Hundred Years of the Society', *Archaeologia Cantiana* LXX (1956) 1–43

Johnson, C., *The Public Record Office* (London, 1918)
    'The Public Record Office', in J. C. Davies (ed.) *Studies presented to Sir Hilary Jenkinson* (London, 1957)

Jones, Gareth Stedman, 'History: the Poverty of Empiricism', in R. Blackburn (ed.), *Ideology in Social Science* (Glasgow, 1972) 96–115

Kargon, R. H., *Science in Victorian Manchester: Enterprise and Expertise* (Baltimore, 1977)

Kendrick, T., 'The British Museum and British Antiquities', *Antiquity* III (1954) 132–43

Keylor, W. R., *Academy and Community. The Foundation of the French Historical Profession* (Massachusetts, 1975)

Knowles, D. M., *Great Historical Enterprises* (London, 1963)

Kubie, Nora, *The Road to Nineveh: The Adventures and Excavations of Sir Austen Henry Layard* (London, 1965)

Larson, M.S., *The Rise of Professionalism: A Sociological Analysis* (California, 1977)

Lester, G. A., 'Thomas Bateman, Barrow Opener', *Derbyshire Archaeological Journal* 93 (1973) 10–22

Levy, F. J., 'The Founding of the Camden Society', *Victorian Studies* VII (1964) 3

Lloyd, S., *Foundations in the Dust. A Story of Mesopotamian Exploration* (London, 1947)

'Local Scientific Societies', anon. article in *Nature* IX (1873–4)

Lowther, A. W. G., 'A Brief History of the Society', *Transactions of the Surrey Archaeological Society* LIII (1954) 1–34

Lynch, B. D. & T. F., 'The Beginnings of a Scientific Approach to Prehistoric Archaeology in Seventeenth Century and Eighteenth Century Britain', *Southwestern Journal of Anthropology* 24 (1968) 1, 33–65

McCrimmon, B., *Power, Politics and Print. The Publication of the British Museum Catalogue 1881–1900* (Hamden, Connecticut/London, 1981)

Macfarlane, Alan, *Reconstructing Historical Communities* (Cambridge, 1977)

Maclachlan, J. O., 'The Origin and Early Development of the Cambridge Historical Tripos', *Cambridge Historical Journal* IX (1947) 1, 78–105

Mallett, C. E., *A History of the University of Oxford* III (London, 1927)

Mandelbaum, M., *History, Man and Reason: A Study in Nineteenth Century Thought* (Johns Hopkins, 1971)

Marsden, B. M., *The Early Barrow Diggers* (Aylesbury, 1974)

Mason, T. W., 'Nineteenth Century Cromwell', *Past and Present* 40 (1968)

Meyerhoff, H., *Time in Literature* (Berkeley, 1955)

Millerson, G., *The Qualifying Associations. A Study in Professionalisation* (London, 1964)

Milne, A. T., 'History at the Universities: Then and Now', *History* 59 (1974) 33–46

Mitford, R. Bruce-, *The Society of Antiquaries of London* (London, 1951)

Momigliano, A. D., *Studies in Historiography* (London, 1966)

Morgan, P., 'George Harris of Rugby and the Prehistory of the Historical Manuscripts Commission', *Transactions of the Birmingham Archaeological Society* 82 (1967) 28–37

Morrell, J. & A. Thackray, *Gentlemen of Science: Early Years of the British Association for the Advancement of Science* (Oxford, 1981)

Munby, A. N. L., *Phillipps Studies* i–v (Cambridge, 1951–60)

Myres, J. L., *Learned Societies* (London, 1922)

Odgers, B., 'Speech of Charles Kingsley', *Journal of the Working Men's College* xiii (1913–14) 435–9

Ollard, S. L., 'The Oxford Architectural and Historical Society and the Oxford Movement', *Oxoniensa* v (1940)

Oman, C., *Memoirs of Victorian Oxford* (London, 1941)

Owen, D. M., 'The Chichele Professorship of Modern History, 1862', *Bulletin of the Institute of Historical Research* xxxiv (1961) 217–20

Pantin, W. A., 'The Oxford Architectural and Historical Society 1839–1939', *Oxoniensa* iv (1939)

Parsons, Talcott, 'Professions', in D. L. Sills (ed.), *International Encyclopaedia of the Social Sciences* xii (1968) 536–47

Payne, B. & D., 'An Eye-Witness Account of the Meeting of the Royal Archaeological Institute at Ripon, July 1874', *Archaeological Journal* cxxviii (1971) 186–90

Pearson, C. H., *Memorials by himself, his wife and his friends* (London, 1900)

Pearson, H. S., 'The Birmingham Archaeological Society, 1870–1920', *Transactions and Proceedings of the Birmingham and Midland Institute* xlvii (1921) 2–7

Pettigrew, T. J., *Memoir of Beriah Botfield* (London, 1863)

Piggott, S., 'Prehistory and the Romantic Movement', *Antiquity* xi (1937) 41, 31–8
  'The Ancestors of Jonathan Oldbuck', *Antiquity* 115 (1955) 1506
  'The Origins of the English County Archaeological Societies', in *Ruins in a Landscape: Essays in Antiquarianism* (Edinburgh, 1976) 171–95

Plarr, V. G., *Men and Women of the Time: A Dictionary of Contemporaries* (5th edition, London, 1899)

Plumb, J. H., *The Death of the Past* (London, 1969)

Pocock, J. G. A., 'The Origins of the Study of the Past: A Comparative Approach', *Comparative Studies in Society and History* iv (1961–2) 209–46

Pollard, J. G., 'The History of the Society', *Cambridge Antiquarian Society Proceedings* lxviii (1978) 105–16

Porter, R., 'Gentlemen and Geology: the emergence of a scientific career, 1660–1920', *Historical Journal* 21 (1978) 4, 809–36

Price D. de J. S., *Little Science, Big Science* (Columbia, 1963)
  with Beaver D. de B., 'Collaboration in an Invisible College', *American Psychologist* 21 (1966) 1011–18

Prothero, G. W., 'Historical Science in Great Britain', *American Historical Association Report* (1909) 231–42

Public Record Office Guide to the Public Records Part I (London, 1949)

Pulgram B. S., *The Myth of the Anglo-Saxon in Nineteenth Century England* (unpublished PhD thesis, Radcliffe College, M. I. T., 1953)

Pyenson, L. S., '"Who the Guys Were": Prosopography in the History of Science',
    History of Science xv (1977) 155–88
Raine, J., *A Memoir of the Rev. John Hodgson* I & II (London, 1857)
Ralph, E., 'The Society 1876–1976', in P. McGrath and J. Cannon (eds.), *Essays in
    Bristol and Gloucestershire History: Centenary Volume of the Bristol and Gloucester-
    shire Archaeological Society* (London, 1976)
Rawlinson, G., *A Memoir of Major-General Sir Henry Creswicke Rawlinson* (London,
    1898)
Reader, K. M., *The Civil Service Commission, 1855–1975* (London, 1981)
Reader, W. J., *Professional Men: The Rise of the Professional Classes in Nineteenth Century
    England* (London, 1966)
Richardson, H. G. & Sayles, G. O., *The Governance of Medieval England from the Conquest to
    Magna Carta* (Edinburgh, 1963)
Ringer, F. K. *The Decline of the German Mandarins. The German Academic Community,
    1890–1933* (Massachusetts, 1969)
Roach, J. P. C., 'Victorian Universities and the National Intelligentsia', *Victorian Studies*
    III (1959) 2
Rodden, J., 'The Development of the Three Age System: Archaeology's First Paradigm',
    in Daniel, G. (ed.), *Towards a History of Archaeology* (London, 1981)
Ronchetti, B. J., Antiquarian and Archaeological Scholarship in Warwickshire, 1800–
    1860 (unpublished M.A. thesis, University of Birmingham, 1952)
Rothblatt, Sheldon, *The Revolution of the Dons: Cambridge and Society in Victorian England*
    (London, 1968)
    Tradition and Change in English Liberal Education: An Essay in History and Culture
    (London, 1976)
Salzman, L. F., 'A History of the Sussex Archaeological Society', *Sussex Archaeological
    Collections*, LXXXV (1946) 3–76
Saunders, A. M. Carr- & Wilson, P. A., *The Professions* (Oxford, 1933)
Shapin, S. & Thackray, A., 'Prosopography as a Research Tool in History of Science: The
    British Scientific Community 1700–1900', *History of Science* xlii (1974) 1–28
Silverberg, R., *The Man Who Found Nineveh. The Story of Austen Henry Layard* (Surrey,
    1968)
Simmons, J., 'The English County Historians', *Transactions of the Hunter Archaeological
    Society* VIII (1963) 5, 272–87
Simmons, J. C., *The Novelist as Historian. Essays on the Victorian Historical Novel* (The
    Hague, 1973)
Smetham, H., *Charles Roach Smith and his Friends* (London, 1929)
Sparrow, J., *Mark Pattison and the Idea of a University* (Cambridge, 1967)
Stanley, A. P., *The Life and Correspondence of Thomas Arnold, D.D.* (London, 1844)
Steeves, H. R., *Learned Societies and English Literary Scholarship in Great Britain and the
    United States* (Columbia, 1913)
Stenton, D., 'The Pipe Rolls and the Historians, 1600–1883', *Cambridge Historical
    Journal* x (1952) iii, 271–92
Stephens, W. R. W., *The Life and Letters of Edward A. Freeman* (London, 1895)
Strick, D. E., English Historiography 1859–90, A Study of Froude, Freeman, Stubbs and
    Green (unpublished PhD thesis, University of California, 1951)
Strong, R., *And When Did You Last See Your Father? The Victorian Painter and British
    History* (London, 1978)
Tait, J., 'The Chetham Society: A Retrospect', *Chetham Miscellanies* n.s. VII (1939)

Taylor, A. J., 'History at Leeds, 1877–1974: The Evolution of a Discipline', *Northern History* x (1975) 141–64

Templeman, G., 'Edward I and the Historians', *Cambridge Historical Journal* x (1950) i, 16–35

Thompson, M. W., *General Pitt-Rivers: Evolution and Archaeology in the Nineteenth Century* (Wiltshire, 1977)

Vollmer, H. & Mills, D. L., *Professionalisation* (New Jersey, 1966)

Walker, J. W., *The History of the Yorkshire Archaeological Society* (n.d.)

Wallace, E., *Goldwin Smith. Victorian Liberal* (Toronto, 1957)

Ward, W. R., *Victorian Oxford* (London, 1965)

Waterfield, G., *Layard of Nineveh* (London, 1963)

Wernham, R. B., 'The Public Record Office', *History* 23 (1968) 222–35

Whipp, D. & Blackmore, L., 'Thomas Layton, F.S.A. (1819–1911): "A Misguided Antiquary"', *The London Archaeologist* 3 (1977) 4, 90–6

White, G. C. (ed.), *A Versatile Professor. Reminiscences of the Rev Edward Nares, D.D.* (London, 1903)

White, J. F., *The Cambridge Movement: The Ecclesiologists and the Gothic Revival* (London, 1962)

Williams, N. J., 'Stubbs' Appointment as Regius Professor, 1866', *Bulletin of the Institute of Historical Research* xxxiii (1960) 121–5

Winstanley, D. A., *Early Victorian Cambridge* (Cambridge, 1940)
Later Victorian Cambridge (Cambridge, 1947)

Wood, L. S., *Selected Epigraphs. The Inaugural Lectures of the Regius Professors of Modern History at Oxford and Cambridge since 1841* (London, 1930)

Woodward, L., 'The Rise of the Professorial Historian in England', in Bourne K., and Watt, D. C. (eds.), *Studies in International History. Essays presented to W. Norton Medlicott* (London, 1967) 16–34

Wormell, Deborah, *Sir John Seeley and the Uses of History* (Cambridge, 1980)

Wright, M., *Treasury Control of the Civil Service, 1854–1874* (Oxford, 1969)

Index

Index